To Roy, 14ᵗʰ June 1990
on the
an auspicous occasion
love Mary
xxxp

Footloose in the Himalaya

Footloose in the Himalaya

Mike Harding

Michael Joseph
London

MICHAEL JOSEPH
Published by the Penguin Group
27 Wrights Lane, London W8 5TZ, England
Viking Penguin Inc., 40 West 23rd Street, New York, New York 10010, USA
Penguin Books Australia Ltd, Ringwood, Victoria, Australia
Penguin Books Canada Ltd, 2801 John Street, Markham, Ontario, Canada L3R 1B4
Penguin Books (NZ) Ltd, 182-190 Wairau Road, Auckland 10, New Zealand
Penguin Books Ltd, Registered Offices: Harmondsworth, Middlesex, England

First published 1989

Copyright © Mike Harding 1989

Typeset in 10/12pt Bembo by Goodfellow & Egan, Cambridge
Colour reproduction by Anglia Graphics, Bedford
Printed and bound in Spain by Cayfosa Industria Grafica, Barcelona

A CIP catalogue record for this book is available
from the British Library

ISBN 0 7181 3137 1

You ask me why I dwell in the green mountain
I smile and make no reply.
As the peach blossom goes downstream
And is gone into the unknown,
I have a world apart that is not amongst men.

– Li Po

Moonrise near Kargia

Contents

Prologue ix

BOOK ONE

Over the Shingo La

I

BOOK TWO

To the Roof of the World

113

Appendix 237
Acknowledgements 238
Index 240

Prologue

'The hills, to me, was somethin' God put here in the beginin' and they been here, I imagine, for four million years. The streams were clear, the timber was green, there was all sorts of wildlife. They weren't put here to be torn all to hell by bulldozers, by greedy people.'
   – Joe Begley. Quoted in *American Dreams Lost and Found* by Studs Terkel

WHEN I WAS A small boy I was taken with all the other children in my school to the local cinema to see two films. The first showed the coronation of the new Queen Elizabeth, a pageant of costume, ceremony and tradition, all gold coaches, nodding horses, blaring trumpets and waving crowds. It was raining on Coronation Day and I have a vague memory of wet beefeaters trudging glumly through the shiny streets of London. Unlike the other films that I saw at this cinema on a Saturday morning at the 'Tuppenny Rush'*, there was no wagon train being shot up by Indians and no cartoon cat falling out of the sky leaving a spreadeagled, cat-shaped hole in the pavement. I was not greatly impressed with a film of wet beefeaters and a lady waving out of a pantomime coach, particularly when it seemed to go on for ever.

The second film, however, had me open-mouthed and motionless with awe and excitement. It showed two men climbing through a world of white angular planes, struggling upwards, the sun flashing and sparking off their snow goggles, ice rimed round their oxygen masks, to stand at last on the roof of the world. For, as though to add another jewel in the crown that was placed on the young Queen's head that day, Sir Edmund Hillary, a beekeeper from New Zealand, and Sherpa Tensing Norgay from the Khumbu Valley of Nepal, had become the first men to climb the summit of the world's highest mountain, Mount Everest.

I still remember, in that musty Manchester cinema, being electrified by the achievement, the drama and the mystery of it all and I still retain an image in my mind's eye of two tiny figures, hopelessly small specks moving slowly upwards on that fearsome white wall. More importantly, I remember being just as moved and fascinated by the beauty of the high mountain world they had climbed in. It had all seemed so pure and clear and so immense. For days afterwards images of white peaks and savage crevasses replaced Dan Dare and Hopalong Cassidy in my daydreams.

But they were only daydreams. As time went on I saw all the films of course: the failed attempt by Don Whillans and Dougal Haston to reach the summit with an expedition riven by jealousy and bickering:

*The children's matinée held every week. It was cheap to get in and there was always a rush.

[ix]

the disastrous attempt by Rheinhold Meisner on K2 the Savage Mountain and his ascent of Everest without oxygen.

I read Joe Tasker's *Savage Arena* and Peter Boardman's *Sacred Summits*, two of the best books on climbing ever written. But for years the Himalaya seemed just too far, another world, somewhere gods and superheroes like Whillans, Bonington and Boardman went, not at all the sort of place where a non-climbing, non-hero type from a northern English town might one day go.

But, over the years, things changed. I began to travel and although my wanderings never took me into the remote areas of the Himalaya, they did take me into some fairly strange places. Gan Island, for example, a tiny coral atoll on the southern tip of the Maldive Islands and virtually on the Equator, where the small, slight, gentle Maldivians rowed to work at the RAF camp each morning in their outriggers refusing the outboard motors offered by the British Government in case the men grew lazy and forgot how to row, thus losing their knowledge of the tides and currents.

Another, starker and more forbidding place was the Empty Quarter in the Sultanate of Oman where I had stood looking out across hundreds of miles of lifeless barrens, an ocean of sand where few men have been and which fewer still have crossed. In Egypt I had climbed up from the banks of the Nile through clouds of shouting and begging children to wade through the heat to the temple at Abydos. There in the cool dark I had experienced a sort of mild electric shock that swelled up in me and almost became a choking panic. I hated the place and couldn't wait to get out. I learned later that Abydos was the door through which all the dead of Egypt passed into the underworld.

In Australia I had gazed at the Great Sandy Desert from the edge of a gold mine and in the frozen winter wilds of Newfoundland I had walked across permafrost under a shaking infinity of stars.

But for all that, the Himalaya still seemed a far off and unreachable dream.

Then, increasingly over the years, I began to meet people who had been out there, either on climbing expeditions or simply trekking through the lower foothills and, reading as many books as I could find on the subject, I began to see that it was now possible to trek in some of the more remote valleys of the Himalaya without the support of massive expeditions or tons of gear.

That was early in the nineteen eighties. But work took over and I found myself circling the British Isles on a seemingly never-ending spiral of one-night stands: book promotions, record promotions, chat shows, radio shows, television films and newspaper and magazine interviews that seemed to fill almost every crack and corner of my life.

It wasn't until 1987 that I was able to set the time aside for a long trip to the mountains that was more or less open-ended. I planned to leave sometime in early autumn and, providing I was back for Christmas, time was not greatly rationed.

I had been involved in an ecology series for Central Television called ECO, making programmes on the problems of mineral extraction in the national parks and on the destruction of public footpaths.

I mentioned to my producer, John Thornicroft, that, over the years, friends coming back from the Himalaya had hinted that this earthly paradise, this Shangri-La, was being destroyed by the very people who were seeking the freedom and beauty of its remoteness. The influx of tourists and trekkers had caused the destruction of much of the high Himalayan forests that were being cleared to fuel the fires that cooked the tourists' food and heated the water for the hot showers they demanded at the end of the day's trek, while the sides of the trail were littered with pink toilet paper and human excrement.

I suggested to John that we make a programme on the Himalaya called 'The Kleenex Trail – Everest the Soft Way'. For a while nothing happened and, thinking that the idea had been shelved, I went on with my own vague arrangements for my trek in the hills.

Then one rainy blustery April day in Newcastle, half-way through

Dying trees show the result of deforestation: Annapurna is unchangeable in the background

a concert tour of the UK, a day of sudden squalls and pelting rain broken with cold watery sunlight, John phoned me at my hotel.

A very small amount of money (in the event it was a laughably small amount) was available for us to make a programme on the deforestation, erosion and pollution caused by the commercialisation of the Himalaya. The money would just about get us there and back and pay for the film crew. Would I be on for the idea?

Of course I said yes, and since the main areas of concern in the Nepal Himalaya at the moment are the areas around the Annapurna Sanctuary and the Khumbu Valley leading to Everest, I suggested that we should perhaps concentrate our work in those two areas.

John said that seemed to make sense.

I put the phone down and stared out at the spring rain lashing the roofs of Newcastle, the Tyne Bridge shining in the shaking storm light, and wondered just what sort of adventure I'd let myself in for.

At a Ramblers Association conference two years before I had met a lady called Biddy Carr who talked with great excitement and fervour about a trip she had made to Zanskar and Ladakh, still relatively unknown and unspoilt mountain kingdoms near the Indo-Pakistan and Indo-Tibetan borders.

Biddy later wrote me a long and fascinating letter describing the high mountain passes, the isolated villages where life was lived as it

Moonrise over Ama Dablam

had been for thousands of years and where the people, open and friendly, were largely untainted by the greed and violence of the West.

Inspired by her obvious love of the place I set about collecting and reading every book I could get my hands and eyes on that dealt with the two kingdoms. It wasn't easy because most of the expeditions in that area had been made by French and German explorers and their books were only gradually being translated into English. Over a period of time, however, I managed to put together a small library of books on Zanskar and Ladakh. Trekkers had begun to go there but as yet only in small numbers; the area was said to be still fairly unspoilt.

I thought that a trek in Zanskar and Ladakh would provide a good contrast with the heavily trekked Nepal Himalaya, help me to get fit for the climb to Everest Base Camp and give me a chance to see what seemed to be a vanishing Shangri-La.

On Biddy's advice I phoned Bill Norman at Roama Travel in Dorset. Bill has travelled widely in Zanskar and Ladakh as well as in the Nepal Himalaya and is an expert at organising small treks. Through Bill I arranged that my wife Pat and I would fly out to India early in September, and spend a month trekking in Zanskar, Ladakh and Kashmir. The plan was that Pat would then return home while I continued on to Nepal where I would meet up with John for our trips to the Annapurna and Everest areas.

For months I studied maps and photographs and hauled anybody I could find who had been to the Himalaya off into corners where, like an Ancient Mariner in reverse, I dragged their stories out of them, one by one, until I built up a picture, cloudy and fuzzy as it was, of the place I was going to.

At the head of the Khumbu Valley in the Mount Everest National Park there is a spur valley leading westward and northwards to a pass called the Changri La. On some maps it is shown as the Shangri-La. I was going to be finishing my journey at the head of the Khumbu Valley under Mount Everest where it would be possible, as it says in Chapter Seven, Book Two, to turn left for Shangri-La.

I looked at the maps over and over again and tried to visualise that white world at the end of the trail, daydreaming of its icy wastes and towering peaks. But nothing could have ever prepared me for what was going to happen.

What we did was neither heroic nor even venturesome. It was hard work at times, pretty uncomfortable at others and more than a little hairy on one or two occasions. But in the end it was not the mountains alone that moved and changed me but the people of the Himalaya. Their warmth and intelligence, their openness and hospitality, and their sense of peace and acceptance impressed me as much as the 'Abode of Snows'* in which they live. It is a rare, fragile and beautiful place.

*'Abode of Snows' is the literal translation of the word Himalaya. It is Himalaya, by the way, and never Himalayas.

A note on the spelling of place names in this book:
Before you old Himalaya hands start reaching for your pens and paper, let me say that while we've done everything we can to standardise spelling, it has been incredibly difficult. Cartographers of various nationalities have produced anything up to four different spellings of some villages and peaks. We've tried to be consistent and where possible have kept the spellings that seem to make most sense.
If we've slipped up occasionally, please forgive us.

BOOK ONE

Over the Shingo La

1 The Seventh Best Curry in the World
2 To the Hill Station
3 The 'Terrible' Shingo La
4 The Desert at the Top of the World
5 The Dancing Monk
6 Tea Soup and a Baby Horse
7 The Jalabi Bends to Leh
8 Land of the Broken Moon
9 By the Zoji La to Dal Lake

I

The Seventh Best Curry in the World

'Let the civilised world go to the devil!! Long live nature, forests and ancient poetry!'
– Théodore Rousseau

I'VE ALWAYS FELT that the hardest part of any journey is taking the first few steps over the threshold. Leaving home. Closing the door behind you. Because you always close it on something – on the ones you love, on your family or friends, sometimes on your whole life – and you are always going to be changed by that journey. It will be a different you that comes back. The preparations that you can make for the spiritual side of your journey are limited – an open mind and a sense of survival are the two most important things you should leave home with. After that come the nuts and bolts: the visas and maps, the toothpaste and pile ointment.

Pat and I spent weeks reading up on equipment and talking to people. The tents and cooking gear would be hired in the mountains and would travel by pony in India and with Sherpa and yak in Nepal. All we had to decide was what to take for ourselves. After all the advice and reading we had a list of supplies three pages long. We went through it again, got rid of most of it and in the end we found that the most vital pieces of equipment were our boots, our sleeping bags and our down duvet jackets.

Medically, we had been advised to take all sorts of stuff for everything from dysentery to blisters. In truth, we needed very little in the way of medicine although the tablets against altitude sickness and the iodine for the treatment of drinking water were to prove essential.

Water in the Himalaya is suspect. Though the mountain water of Zanskar and Ladakh is probably pure enough, in Nepal it is almost certain that the water you are drinking contains human excrement and amoebic dysentery; giardia and other enteric disorders are endemic.

If you drink untreated water the very least you will get is acute diarrhoea. If you are really unlucky you could fall seriously ill and being ill at eighteen thousand feet, ninety miles from the nearest airstrip and two hundred miles from a proper hospital is not something you'll do twice.

We spent the days before we left going through the list of things we were taking, having our final injections and saying goodbye to friends and relations. On the first Thursday in September we got up before dawn, finished the last pieces of packing, did a hurried 'idiot check' and loaded the car. A friend drove us to the airport through lashing rain, the English summer going out in a vicious sulk. An Indian summer, if it did come, would come too late for us; we'd be in India in time for their autumn. On the way along the dual carriageway out of town, the dim light of dawn just seeping through the night, the car's headlights picked out first the burning eyes and then the rust-red coat

Deforestation in the Kulu Valley in the Himachal Pradesh

and brush of a big dog-fox frozen motionless on the island in the centre of the carriageway. Now that the developers have swallowed up most of the open country around our cities the foxes are making their way into the urban centres, adapting to a scavenging way of life.

We checked in on the KLM flight without any problems; we would have to change planes at Amsterdam but luckily we could check the baggage through to Delhi. We sat in the lounge trying to read the books we had brought with us but I suppose most of the time we were both thinking about the trek to come. The route we had planned would take us from Amsterdam to Delhi and from Delhi on by light aircraft to Kulu, which is in the valley of the same name, in the Himachal Pradesh. From there we would travel by jeep over the Rohtang Pass to Darsha where our ponyman guide would be waiting with the packhorses and the trek proper would begin.

From Darsha we were to trek into the mountains, up over a pass called the Shingo La*, at over seventeen thousand feet the highest either of us had been. The Shingo La would take us down into the Zanskar Valley which we would follow to Padum where we would try and pick up a lorry to Kargil via the Rangdum Gompa, one of the most forsaken places on earth. From Kargil we would go by jeep to Leh, a hidden Himalayan town and the heart of Ladakh, or Little Tibet as it is often called for, since the Chinese invasion of Tibet, Ladakh alone has retained most of the old Tibetan customs that its oppressed neighbour has lost. The invasion of Tibet and the swamping of its culture by the Han Chinese is a depressing and sordid tale.

We were to spend a few days in Leh looking at the 'gompas', or monasteries, and the surrounding country before travelling by air to Srinagar where we would spend a few days lounging on a house boat on Dal Lake before returning to Delhi from where Pat would fly back

*'La' means 'pass' hence Zoji La and Fotu La. Zoji La pass is like saying Zoji Pass pass.

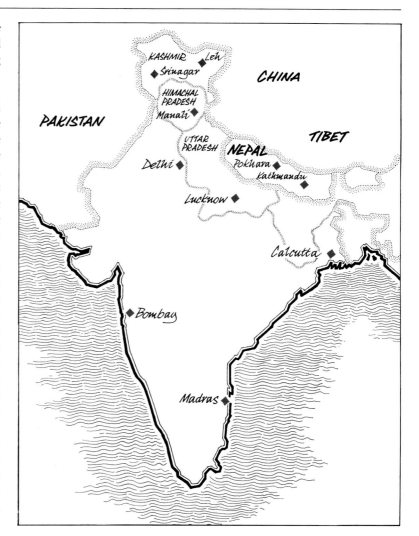

[5]

to the UK and I would travel on to Kathmandu to meet up with John. At least, that was the theory.

I should have really taken it as a sign of things to come when we landed at Amsterdam Airport later that day and had to transship from the Manchester flight to the Delhi flight, running the length of the airport with all our hand baggage, cameras and film, arriving at the departure gate soaked in sweat, hearts banging, just as the flight was about to close.

We were the last passengers to board the plane. Ahead of us was a bustling, shouting, whooping bunch of Indian humanity carrying all its earthly goods and chattels in black plastic bin-liners.

In ten seconds I learnt two things.

Firstly, Indian travellers don't trust their belongings to anybody else including airlines – so they carry everything themselves, usually in cardboard boxes or bin-liners.

Secondly, though they don't mean to tread on you, elbow you in the eye, sit on you or emasculate you with the wrought-iron telephone table they're taking back to their cousin in Goa, the sort of queuing employed in India is less like a queue line than the Pontypool front row going for a loose ball.

We soon developed queuing elbows and learned to push without being rough or violent, because quite simply that is the only way to survive in India.

An Indian in a queue would be mortified if you pointed out that he'd jumped in front of you and trodden on your head into the bargain. He would probably apologise profusely but think it queer that you mentioned it in the first place. We finally got on the plane to find it crammed to the ceiling with hand-luggage and with what looked like live goats in bin-liners and three-piece suites in carrier bags. Travel makes strange bedfellows of us all and often you find yourself talking to and sharing the most intimate secrets with total strangers, largely because your thighs are jammed so tightly together that when you go to pull your handkerchief out of your pocket you end up pulling the shirt out of someone's trousers instead. Luckily I was sitting by the aisle and the Dutchman next to me went to sleep so I read and dozed and watched a bad Michael Caine movie in which he played a really bad artist really badly. At the most interesting part I nodded off and awoke as we were falling out of the clouds above India to land at Delhi in the early hours of the morning.

We landed safely but two items of luggage did not. The flight case with some of the camera equipment and my recording gear and the big Karrimor kit bag with most of our clothes and all the medical supplies had gone missing.

I went to see the people on the 'baggage lost and damaged' desk and came across my first example of that wonderful head-rolling gesture that expresses so much in this part of the world. It is impossible to describe in words fully but the head gimbals smoothly from side to side on a pliant neck expressing everything: wonder, sorrow, disbelief, sympathy, acceptance; any one of a myriad of emotions.

At the baggage desk I'm afraid I acted like a sahib.

A crowd of people were swarming round angrily waving their tickets, many of them obviously in the same boat as us. I pushed my way to the desk. A harassed little man was trying to placate them. I worked my way round to his side of the desk where a senior officer was standing alone surveying the chaos with the air of somebody who has seen it all before and is patiently waiting for it to go away.

'You have lost two items of my baggage!' I shouted imperiously standing under his nose.

He smiled and rolled his head, sympathetically. 'Maybe here Sunday morning.'

'That's no good,' I said. 'We fly out Saturday morning. That is tomorrow. Very early.'

There followed much rolling of his head from side to side.

I explained that film costing thousands of rupees was at stake and that I would sue KLM. 'Maybe tonight,' he said rolling his head in a hopeful way.

A young Sikh girl with a Rochdale accent, dressed in a sari and with three small children had lost everything. Her relatives had driven hundreds of miles from the Punjab to collect her and in the missing luggage were all the children's clothes and presents for all her relations.

There was much sympathetic nodding of heads but nothing could be done.

The only thing we could do was to leave the airport and book into the hotel. There, at least, were telex machines and telephones. Perhaps some Genie of the West could be summoned up to deal with the problems of the East. It was certain that nothing would be gained from watching understanding but ultimately powerless and guiltless Indian airport officials rolling their heads from side to side. If nothing else, we could get a shower and perhaps a few hours' sleep while somebody sorted out the mystery of the vanishing luggage.

By now dawn was breaking and Delhi was already up and going about its business.

The drive to the hotel alone was worth the trip and all the hassle. Even at this early hour in the morning the streets were thick with people. Buses snarled and hooted as they swung round corners belching smoke, people clinging to every step, pole and window-ledge. Motorised tricycle rickshaws puttered past, and everywhere there were bicycles: newly-made versions of the old-fashioned English bikes with calliper brakes, sit-up-and-beg handlebars and chain-cases. In India they are used to carry everything. One trundled along the road with a bed on it. A man pedalled past on another, threading his way suicidally through the traffic, hardly visible under a mountain of metal boxes that were strung all around him clanking and shining in the hazy morning sun.

Along the side of the road hawks swooped and soared and, before a statue of Mahatma Gandhi with the people of India following him in train, walked the people of Delhi at the beginning of another day.

We checked into our hotel – a sort of air lock between East and West where the neat and clean foyer with clocks showing the time in Tokyo and Berlin gave way to corridors in which the carpet, where it was not rolling away from the wall, was splashed in one or two places with last night's vomit. There was a shower in the bathroom but the curtains fell off when you got in it. But that was the least of our worries.

I went down to the foyer to see if I could telex England to try and trace the missing baggage. The musak machine in the lobby was playing a terrible version of a piece I never liked much anyway, 'I Got a Girl in Kalamazoo'. What this had to do with Delhi I didn't know. It was in any case hardly recognisable because the tape machine had developed so much wow and flutter that it sounded as though it were being played by an orchestra of Ravi Shankars on a bad day under water.

When I told the hotel manager our luggage had not arrived he rolled his head from side to side and said, 'You must jigger them up, sir, very quick.'

So I set about the traditional sahib's pastime of jiggering. I waited for half an hour but the hotel telex man never appeared.

'Today is Muslim holiday, sir,' said the manager. 'I will try and find somebody who knows how to work the telex machine.'

Another hour passed and nobody appeared.

Eventually Mr Mandip Singh Soin, our liaison man from Ibex Travel (who handles the Indian side of Roama's expeditions), arrived. Mr Singh is a handsome young man; a Sikh who speaks perfect English. He has been the liaison officer on a number of Himalayan expeditions and is also a mountaineer and rock climber who has spent some time in Britain. It appeared that Mr Singh's telex machine had broken down so we would have to use the public telex office in

Connaught Place; alternatively he thought we might be able to persuade KLM to send a telex.

Off we went to do some jiggering, bouncing through the steaming hot streets of Delhi, honking and swerving in Mr Singh's car, like a whooper swan on drugs.

At KLM we failed to jigger them up – miserably.

A man punching a computer keyboard listened to my story without pausing in his work then went through an incredible amount of head rolling.

'You must go to airport,' he said.

'I've just come from there and they couldn't do anything.'

'Nobody is here who can deal with you.'

'Why not?'

'Today is Muslim holiday.'

'It is very important.'

'I appreciate this, sir. Today to you this is very important and regrettable. Tomorrow it will not be so important. Also are many other things important to many other people. Life is always thus.'

I hadn't expected a debate on existentialism this early in the day.

'It is unavoidable what is happening.' There was more head rolling. He smiled gently and carried on punching the keyboard.

'At least let us send a telex at KLM's expense to Mr Bill Norman.'

'Who is Mr Bill Norman?'

'He is the organiser of our trek in England.'

'Does he have the baggage?'

'No, KLM has the baggage.'

'Then what for you want to telex this Mr Norman?'

'Because he may be able to jigger things up from the European end.'

'No, I send telex to KLM London and they phone Bill Norman.'

It seemed better than nothing so we left him at it and phoned the airport, and a lady there said they would see what they could do.

So we got back in the car and bumped through the Delhi traffic to the public telex office, a dingy brown- and green-painted relic of Empire days where Raj-type, ticker-tape-driven telexes and old steam-driven Bakelite telephones were the nerve centre of a mighty communications Empire.

A lizard ran up the wall. Men sat in derelict chairs eating bananas and staring into space.

'Why are they not working the other machines?' I asked impatiently from my position twenty-first in the queue.

'They are Muslims,' said the man behind the counter who was reading a form about forms, 'today is Muslim holiday.'

'Then why don't they stay at home instead of coming here and eating bananas?'

'They stay at home, they get no pay,' said the man.

And there, logic fulfilled, we let the matter rest.

Eventually we fought our way to the head of the queue and handed our telex over. A man punched it into the ether and we left.

By now it was three p.m. in Delhi but four a.m. somewhere in the murky alleyways of my brain, and cats were yowling on the dustbin lids of my desperate mind.

We made our way back through the noisy, busy streets. Everywhere the air was heavy with that thick black smoke that all Indian buses and lorries seem to pump out. We were to see so much of this before the journey was over.

Through it all, like tiny coracles in a harbour full of lunging supertankers, men pedalled rickshaws piled high with galvanised watering cans, drainpipes and turned chair legs.

The score thus far in the Delhi Jigger stakes was: KLM 10 – Harding Sahib 0.

'Don't worry,' said Mr Singh, 'I'm sure that your luggage will arrive on time. And tonight, to take your mind off your luggage, I'll take you to where they serve the seventh-best curry in the world.'

*

Later that day a message was left at the hotel telling us that the baggage would be coming in on the Thai airlines flight at three o'clock in the morning of the next day. Almost immediately after there came another message from Mandip Singh to say that Bill Norman had received the telex, had chased up KLM and that the two missing pieces would be arriving around midnight.

There was just one more problem: the KLM warehouse didn't open until nine o'clock – our plane to Kulu was leaving at nine-thirty from another terminal.

At eight-thirty that night Mandip Singh and his lovely wife Anita arrived to take us for a meal at the seventh-best Indian restaurant in the world and we set off yet again through the whirling streets of Delhi feeling as though our feet had never touched the ground.

Delhi by night is as fascinating as Delhi by day. Remnants of old Raj architecture with avenues of trees and Victorian porticoed buildings stand cheek by jowl with stalls where kerosene lamps throw their yellow light on mounds of pokhoras, purries, sweetmeats and salted nuts.

Not having tried the other six best Indian restaurants in the world I'm not really able to make comparisons, but the food was excellent. We had mutton tikka, naan bread and a wonderful fish curry. We pigged out that night knowing it was probably the last good meal we would have for some time and left the restaurant stuffed to the gills, waddling towards the taxi that took us to the airport. It was just past midnight. Indian airport security is incredibly tight and of course I didn't have the necessary bits of paper to get me on to the concourse so that by the time I'd fought my way through dozens of security men and customs officers, it was almost one o'clock in the morning.

Then luckily the gods did smile on us. I found the luggage under a mountain of lost sacks and parcels, got through customs and out to the taxi and back to the hotel where we had four hours' sleep before getting up again to return to the airport for our internal flight to Kulu.

Just as we were packing our toothbrushes away, the phone rang. It was Mandip wondering if the luggage had arrived.

'Everything came through fine,' I said. 'In fact we're now just about to order a taxi to the airport.'

'No don't order a taxi,' said Mandip. 'I'll send you a car because I have a special tent for you.'

'Good,' I said, 'because I have a special body I want to put in it.'

The car arrived and we piled our gear into it.

'Where is the tent?' I asked.

'No tent,' said the driver. 'Maybe ticket man at airport has it.'

When we arrived at the airport the man bringing the tickets from Mandip was not there.

'Maybe man at other airport,' said the driver and set off looking for him.

The man, thinking that we had arrived on an international flight that morning, was in fact at the other airport. The driver brought him back and he gave us our tickets for all the internal flights.

'Where is the tent from Mr Mandip Singh?' I asked him.

'No tent,' he said.

By now we were beginning to panic a bit. Pat in particular had visions of us sleeping out in the snows with nothing but our foam mats and sleeping bags. There was nothing that could be done until we got to Kulu so we shrugged and got on the plane.

It was full of harassed mothers and screaming children. Cloud came in and, in a relative humidity approaching ninety per cent, we rolled down the runway.

The children screamed. Once in the air they screamed even more.

Looking out of the window I watched the ochre of the city slip away to be replaced by the brown and green patchwork of the Indian plains. We turned and headed east towards the crinkled smudge on the horizon that was the far Himalaya, the landscape below becoming greener and more hilly as we moved into the foothills.

One of the causes of pollution: the village thunderbox poised over the stream

As yet we couldn't see the mountains we had travelled all this way to journey in but it was fascinating looking at the narrow valley beneath us and the dark green forests climbing above its lush quilt.

For the first time, and after all the hassle with the luggage, we finally felt that we were on our way.

After a couple of hours we landed at Kulu Airport where we were met by Mr Tickoo who was to see to the nuts and bolts of our trek.

Mr Tickoo is a neat, handsome, intelligent Kashmiri with a trim moustache and dark-brown eyes. We shook hands and, after collecting all of our baggage, made our way out of the airport.

As we left the tin hut that was the terminal building under tall trees, a band playing gongs, drums and wooden horns piled round us banging, blowing and dancing and leading the way for us through the hot dusty streets to where our jeep was waiting.

'Did you lay this on, Mr Tickoo?' I asked, well impressed by the jigging musicians.

A typical Punjabi lorry, highly painted and decorated

'It is for the man behind us, sir. He is an important government minister and I think maybe we should get out of his way.'

We drove out of Kulu along winding and narrow roads past low wooden houses and open-fronted shops selling Kashmiri shawls and brass pots and pans and past scores of people wearing the loose-fitting costume of the valley: the women with brightly coloured scarves

about their heads, the men bareheaded or wearing little knitted caps.

It was our first real experience of Indian driving on mountain roads, and it is only really bearable if you shut your eyes and pray devoutly and a little desperately to whatever god you worship. If you're an atheist, you soon change your mind. Our driver, a remarkably cool and capable man with high cheekbones and the slightly Tibetan looks of the Lahoul Valley people, drove straight at oncoming cars, his horn bleating furiously until one or the other gave way.

'Here everyone drives on their hooters,' said Mr Tickoo, smiling.

All along the Kulu-Manali road people were working, in the fields and in the forests, gathering in the harvest of rice, barley and millet. Men with crates of apples on their heads staggered along the road teetering under the crippling weight. From the road the great forests rose steeply way up above us to where the tree-line ended and the pale white tops of the mountains came and went through the wispy clouds that were hanging on the lips of the valley.

Everywhere on the road we saw colourfully painted Punjabi lorries with tinsel draped all over them, their cabs and sides decorated with scrolls and curlicues in gold, turquoise and yellow. Buses rocked and rolled past stuffed with people, the overflow either

Prayer-flags flapped everywhere, from lines, trees and poles

squatting on top or hanging on the sides so that the smoking vehicles looked like scorpions carrying their babies. Brightly clothed women walked along the road struggling under man-sized bundles of fodder that they had brought down from the verdant meadows for the animals. Close to Manali we passed the villages of Tibetan refugees where, above the houses and schools and playing children who danced and rolled in the dust, prayer flags flapped everywhere from lines and trees and poles.

2

To the Hill Station

'For me there is only one path and that is the path of the heart. And there I travel, and there I travel – looking, looking breathlessly.'

– Don Juan, Yaqui Indian

MANALI, ACCORDING TO THE guide book, is 'the Queen of the Mountains'. It stands at an altitude of almost five and a half thousand feet and has a population approaching three thousand. It is the last town at the head of the Kulu Valley, a random collection of small guest houses, tea stalls and shops flanking a busy main street. On three sides it is bound by snow-capped peaks ranging between fifteen thousand and eighteen thousand feet in height.

Manali seems quite a small place now but it was once an important part of the Kulu Rajahs' domain because it controlled the busy trade routes from the Indian plains to the lands of Zanskar and beyond. Something that struck me most forcibly as we trekked over the mountains was that the paths we were using had been in their heyday as important as the railways and motorways of Europe and America are now. All trade went this way and some of it still does. Pashmina wool still finds its way over the Shingo La on the backs of hill ponies and donkeys and to the people of the isolated villages of the Zanskar Valley the old trade route is their only way to market, to school and to the outside world. But the trade routes also served another function. They were, and still are, a means for travellers and pilgrims to cross the high Himalaya, spreading news and ideas and affirming their faith.

Until 1847 Kulu was under the rule of the Rajahs. After that it fell into the hands of the British, who administered it from Daramsala, where the Dalai Lama now has his palace. It became, with the coming of the British, a hill station where, at the height of the hot season, one could escape the raging heat and terrible humidity of the cities on the plain. It was never a hill station for the rich and noble of the Raj as Simla was, but it attracted the middle-class Indian and the more adventurous of the English. People speak of the Kulu Valley as having been one of the most tranquil and uncrowded of the hill stations.

When the road was driven up the valley in 1927 the British saw it as the beginning of the end for their peaceful sanctuary and began to leave. By 1947 and Independence most of them had gone.

Now the valley is a summer resort for middle-class Indians and a departure point for the few trekkers and climbers, the twentieth-century pilgrims, who are making their way towards Zanskar and Ladakh.

There is still a great deal of trade here because the valley is rightly famous for its apples. They are sweet and juicy. What's more they are plentiful. At the time of our arrival the harvest was just beginning and everybody, from little infants to old grannies, was busy picking the

Manali, 'the Queen of the Mountains', is the last town at the head of the Kulu Valley

fruit and packing it into wooden crates for transport south on the infamous, foul-smoking Punjabi lorries.

The area is also famous for its Kulu shawls which, though they may not be as well known as the Kashmir ones, are fine and costly, woven from the wool of the Angora, Pashmina and Manali sheep.

The town is the market place for all the surrounding valleys and is a mad honking whirl of people: a mixture of many different ethnic types ranging from the light-boned people of the Himachal Pradesh through to the round-faced, high-cheekboned tribes of the northern valleys who look more Tibetan than Indian.

Around the town are beautiful forests clinging to the hillsides and down the cheeks of the hill flow the numberless streams that help to make the Kulu Valley one of the most fertile areas of the Himachal Pradesh.

After checking in at the John Bannon Hotel, a pleasant, two-storeyed, Raj-style building set at the foot of hills amongst apple and pear trees heavy with fruit, we had a cup of tea with Mr Tickoo and discovered that he hadn't got the special tent either. In fact poor Mr Tickoo didn't have any tent at all.

'By the way, where is the tent?' he asked smiling politely as we sat on the veranda drinking tea in the warm afternoon sun, the valley glistening and crisp below us.

'What tent?' I asked. 'I haven't got a tent!'

'No tent?' he queried unbelievingly.

He put his hand to his forehead. 'Oh my God!!' he moaned softly. 'I left the tent in Srinagar. Mandip told me he was sending special four-men tent.'

'Yes,' I said, 'but I thought he'd changed his mind and that you had one.'

'No,' he replied, looking very sad and glum.

More visions of being eaten by snow leopards or Himalayan bears raced across my mind. Mr Tickoo departed, looking worried.

Later that day we walked up the hill through the woods to visit one of the Himalaya's most important shrines, a pagoda-roofed temple dedicated to a powerful Hindu female god, Hadimba, made entirely of wood and more than a thousand years old.

In the heart of the woods, halfway up the hills, there was a Tibetan children's holiday camp with groups of smiling broad-cheeked kids squealing and shouting and playing the same sort of games children play in England. Some were playing what we call 'Jacks' where you squat on the ground and throw a small stone into the air, trying to pick up as many others from the floor as you can; some were playing hopscotch while others were playing skipping, tig, and a game that we used to call 'Paper and Scissors' which you play in twos bringing your hands from behind your back in the shape of a pair of scissors, a stone, or a piece of paper. They were exactly the same games that I had played as a kid in the streets of Manchester and it made me wonder, had the refugee children learnt the games from the children of the valley, who in turn had learnt them from English children or was there perhaps some universal childhood which meant that children all over the world innately gravitated to the same games?

The temple was very beautiful, standing four-square in a grove of tall pines, covered from ground to eaves in ornately-carved wooden panels, a large bell hanging before a tiny door. The shrill cries of children at play drifted through the pines towards us mingling with the smell of woodsmoke from the fires of woodmen who were working somewhere in the thick forest. We stood before the door wondering if, as non-believers, we would be allowed in. As we were standing there a Hindu family climbed on to the forecourt and, slipping off their shoes, went inside ringing the bell as they did so. They motioned us to do the same.

Inside, a trodden earth floor sloped towards the back of the temple. A stone slab made a natural canopy at our feet where, in the space beneath, a light showed a small stone lion covered in a red paste,

Rice fields in the Kulu Valley, one of the most fertile areas of the Himachal Pradesh

rubbed on by thousands of pilgrims' hands. Bright orange and yellow marigolds lay before the lion and impressed deeply into the stone bed of the crypt were the footprints of the goddess Hadimba. With his thumb a young Hindu boy put the mark of the tikka on our foreheads from a bowl of red paste and we stood for a while watching the family praying and laying flowers in the lamplit shrine.

On our way back down the hill towards Manali men walked before us, carrying massive loads of apple boxes through the trees, toiling down the hundreds of old worn stone steps that threaded the thickly wooded hillside. The rich apple harvests of Kulu are, ironically, helping to destroy the forests. The crates used for transporting the fruit out of the valley are all made here and their manufacture is deforesting the slopes. They are made in a really ingenious way. A tree is selected which, when cut and squared into a beam, is exactly the width of one apple crate. It is then chopped into pieces the length of two apple crates and just the weight one man can carry on his own. With a 'tump line' slung round his forehead, the man takes the block down to a lower camp where it is cut into thin crate-sized planks. There is hardly any wastage at all. The problem is that the crates, once they go south, never return. It is a one-way traffic. Plastic crates are being developed but they are costly. Here the labour and wood are cheap, in the short term at least. But all around the valley the marks of deforestation and the landslides that inevitably come as a result of the loss of tree cover can easily be seen.

In town, lights were coming slowly on and all the noises of the hill station threaded through the air; the Punjabi lorries revving their engines on the outskirts of town, people calling and shouting down in the market, children playing on the bandstand in the park.

We sat and watched the children for a time. They were dressed in the loose smock and trousers traditional to the Kulu Valley. The girls were dancing while the little boys, typically, were fighting; chasing each other and rolling on the earth. The girls danced beautifully, their

Manali men bringing down apple crates through the forest

hands and eyes fluttering gracefully as they sang in high sweet voices imitating the music and dancing of their mothers and elder sisters.

In the dusk men gathered like moths round the lamplit stalls that sold betel paste. Wrapped in fresh green leaves the locals chew the betel like chewing gum. I found it very pungent and it made my teeth red. I don't think I'll try it again. Two small boys were kneeling on the ground trying to peer under the door of a ramshackle little cinema that was showing an Indian love film; like small boys everywhere they were trying to get a free show.

In the market meat lay open on the stalls; bags of pulses, bright-orange lentils and pale chickpeas, yellow dhal and green chillies, mounds of rice, blocks of salt and mountains of apples, heaps of shoes and bundles of cloth were piled high. In the street a Tibetan woman pushed around her drunken husband giving him a good clouting for being so drunk. Men were cobbling, sewing, cutting hair, smithying; a butcher was holding a knife upright between his toes and running the meat up and down it. It was all intensely alive, a busy jumble of colour, smells and noise and I loved it.

One thing that we both found disturbing were the beggars. There were plenty of them. A man, little more than an armless, legless trunk, was being pulled along flat on his back on a low wooden trolley by a small girl rattling a tin cup. A woman with both legs off below the knee lay up against a wall with a monkey dressed in dhoti and pants at her side. A man with one arm was smiling and gently begging, waving his stump at the passers-by; there were many more.

The following day the saga of the tent continued. We breakfasted on what I can only describe as sub-Raj snotty eggs. I don't believe that anybody should go into anybody else's country and teach them how to cook. God knows, British food isn't anything to write home about and when I'm abroad I usually try to avoid it like a dose of salmonella but here one of the worst traditions of the Raj remained, the belief that all sahibs like runny eggs for breakfast. As I looked at the slimy goo in the shell I wished I'd ordered a chapatti.

Mr Tickoo came, still looking glum. Still no tent.

'I must hire one for you. But they are hard to find. Today there is a

Stall selling betel paste in Manali

car that will take you along the valley sightseeing. I will in the meantime go and look for a tent for you. Do not worry.'

Strangely I wasn't particularly worried. For some reason I felt that something would turn up and that a tent would be found. Don't ask me why. I think it was a combination of stupid optimism, an odd sense that India in spite of all its muddles would manage to get things done, and my trust in Mr Tickoo.

The car came, a made in India car that looked like an old Rover Ninety, driven by a young man with the broad cheeks and smiling eyes of the Lahoul Valley. Mr Tickoo waved us goodbye and went in search of a tent.

The morning was cool and sunny. The air glass-clear and breathless. Men and women were working in every field and orchard and all along the road people were carrying the fruit of the harvest. Sun-burnished clouds rolled along the wall of the valley, hanging back on the rim of hills, leaving the paddy fields and terraces on fire with light.

On the way to Nagar by the back road we made a side trip to a temple that local legend said was built in the space of one night by the five brothers of Hadarum. A roadside barber was busy with a customer in front of the temple, shaving him closely with an old cut-throat razor. Made of stone, this temple was smaller than the temple at Manali and stood in an open courtyard surrounded by statues and carved stone pillars. The shrine itself was locked so we strolled across the stone

Two small boys in Manali market attempting to steal a free film show

The Hindu temple in Manali

flags in the morning sun, looking at the beautiful carvings. Here in the hills the Hindu religion appears to be of a particularly fervent kind. I think it might be something to do with the mountains. In the Yorkshire Dales the most fervent Methodists were always those further up the Dale in the bleaker, more inaccessible regions.

Mountain streams and rivers were ranting down in full flood, a milky green colour from the stone dust they were carrying from high up above, gabbling over boulders in the sun. Children, even tiny ones, humped baskets of apples on their backs.

The car wound its way up a rough track to Nagar, a cluster of dwellings, and came to a lurching halt outside a large square-built house. The driver got out and lit a cigarette.

'Very good pictures,' he said, pointing at the house. 'This man English. He live here many years ago and make good paintings. You want go look? I take you to meet this man.'

We looked round at the neat well-tended garden. Below us the valley lay green and shining in the sun. A sudden movement on a nearby tree caught my eye and turning I saw a lizard a foot or so long, staring calmly at me just inches from my head. It winked a couple of times, then turned and scuttered away.

We knocked on the house door. After a few minutes a shuffling sound preceded the drawing back of bolts and after some time the

The winking lizard

door opened and a little old man popped his head out.

He smiled a greeting at us and said something in the local dialect.

The driver said. 'He says you should go in and see paintings.'

The old man beckoned and we followed him in.

The two downstairs rooms were full of paintings and little else: abstract landscapes of the Himalaya, visionary devotional images of sunswept mountains, moonlit summits and shooting stars, painted in fierce primitive colours and achieving an almost symbolist, mystical effect.

A slip of paper stuck on the wall told us that the paintings had been made by a man called Nicholas Roerich who lived here in the nineteen thirties. The guidebook told us a little more: Roerich was a Russian painter of the post 1917 avant-garde whose reputation was enhanced by the work he did during his stay at Nagar during the nineteen thirties and forties when he made the house his home. He was also apparently a mystic and a visionary, which accounts for the style of the paintings. The only other time I had seen paintings like this was in London years ago when I marvelled at a pavement artist's work executed in bright chalks showing mythical and I suppose mystical landscapes on the flagstones of the Embankment in London. I remember wondering at the time what the artist had been smoking.

I suppose you could wonder the same about Roerich's work and not without a certain amount of justification because the Kulu Valley does have a number of marijuana plantations, particularly way back up in the hills in some of the spur valleys. There are said to be quite a few western hippies still left over from the days of flower power running their own little kingdoms up there. They are tolerated by the locals but not greatly liked. Hash smoking has long been a part of Himalayan life (in Nepal this is particularly true) but it was mainly indulged in by the older folks as a medicine and as a relaxant.

From the house we moved back down the valley on to the Kulu road, stopping at a tea house for a cup of 'tchai': sweet, milky tea served in glasses. I find it a little too sickly for my taste but it's often welcome at the end of a long hard day in the hills. By the tchai house were a number of hot baths, open pools where men were bathing in scalding water that poured

Children throughout the Himalaya made bubble gum balloons

out of natural springs. There are a number of hot springs in the area and since the water is loaded with minerals the baths are said to be very good for you. As we were watching the men bathing I noticed that one of them had a much paler skin than the others. He waved and I waved back and shouted hello. When we got talking it turned out that he was from Stoke-on-Trent in the heart of the Staffordshire Potteries although his accent was so strange he could have been from anywhere. He'd been living in the hills, way back in one of the hidden valleys in Kulu, and hadn't spoken English, he said, for nearly three

years. He was quite content living a life of extreme simplicity in one of the hill villages and wasn't sure that he would ever return to the West.

I can see how the Kulu Valley can have that effect on people. Months later, back home in the Yorkshire Dales, I met a couple from England who had spent a lot of time living and working in the valley, and who described their stay there as one of the happiest and most contented times of their life together. It is a place of great beauty and, looking around at the forested slopes and rushing river, particularly in that full but not blinding light that you get in these upper valleys, there was a sort of brightness and clarity that enhanced all the colours. It's easy to see how the hills give birth to mysticism.

At the tchai house a group of little boys gathered round us blowing bubble gum, bright pink bubbles growing in front of their faces until they all but obscured them. We were to find bubble gum all over the Himalaya and almost every village would have its small boys or girls waving at us, enormous pink balloons half hiding their faces. We talked to the boys in a mixture of broken English and sign language.

What I thought to be a young man holding a baby turned out to be a boy of about twelve and when I asked the best English speaker in the group if he was the baby's father all the boys fell on the floor kicking their legs in the air and laughed and shrieked in the dust for nearly five minutes. The man who ran the tchai shop came out to see what was the matter and he almost threw himself on the floor laughing as well, only of course this would have been beneath him. He just laughed until the tears ran down his face, then he wiped them away with a grubby cloth and went back inside to make more tchai, shaking his head at the Westerner's foolishness.

We waved goodbye to the giggling boys and made our way back to Manali.

'You like see gompa?' the driver asked.

I hadn't realised that there was a Buddhist gompa in Manali. It was an area I had thought of as being mainly Hindu although we had obviously seen a number of Tibetan refugees in the valley.

The driver told us that he was a Buddhist and came from Darsha where our trek would begin. He said that once over the Rohtang Pass we would be in an area that was totally Buddhist.

We turned off the main road and he parked the car.

Walking through a narrow street past market stalls and rough walled houses we came to a stream where facing us across a bridge there were the fluttering prayer flags of the gompa while to our left, downstream, a little wooden hut suspended on two planks was obviously one of the community's toilets. It would be recognised in the Appalachian Mountains of America as a 'thunderbox' and in the Yorkshire Dales as an 'Old Country Closet' but it did seem strange to see it suspended over a gushing stream; both dangerous and unsanitary: unsanitary in that everything dropped straight into what was the drinking water of the village downstream and dangerous because it looked a bit too precarious for anyone to feel comfortable while seated in it. Unfortunately the belief in these mountain areas that running water cleanses and purifies everything means that people spread all their diseases through the drinking water. Here, as in Nepal, you can never be absolutely sure that you aren't drinking somebody else's diluted stool.

Flaubert once wrote, 'Human language is a cracked kettle on which we beat our tunes for bears to dance to, when all the time we wish to move the stars to pity.' There are times when I cannot but agree with him. Any attempt I may make to try and describe Manali Gompa or any of the gompas we were to meet on our journey will of necessity fall short.

Physically the interior of the gompa was cool and dim. The rich red walls had been recently painted with 'thankas', the religious paintings that figure so much in Buddhism. There was a smell, not at all unpleasant, that was a mingling of smoke, incense, human bodies and butter oil from the burning brass lamps.

At the far end of the gompa stood several statues of the Buddha wreathed in white scarves, before which burned hundreds of small butter-oil lamps casting a golden light on dozens of small shining brass bowls of pure, clear water, which had been placed symbolically before the Buddha.

Caught in a shaft of sunlight, a group of squatting monks were moulding 'tsampa' (ground barley meal) and yak butter into hand-high cones for a ceremony that was to take place the next day. Their red robes and yellow garments harmonised with the red and gold of the gompa. They sang as they worked, happily chanting 'Om mani padme hum', 'all praise to the jewel in the lotus', a mantra that you will hear on people's lips all over the Himalaya as they walk past you on high mountain passes or as they bend to work in the fields. It is not a prayer but a magical formula or incantation and is based on a precise understanding of the occult power of sound. There is no such thing as prayer in the Buddhist faith since there are no gods to pray to. The word prayer, where it is used in the case of prayer-flags and prayer-wheels for example, is misleading. The flags and wheels are physical symbols of something much deeper than prayer.

There was a small collecting box on one wall with 'For Gompa' scrawled on it in English. I put ten rupees in the box and asked an old monk if it would be all right for me to take photographs of the gompa

The gompa at Manali hummed with the monks' happiness

and the monks. He smiled and nodded and called across to the monks. A little boy monk came over to us. He had a barrel chest and a slightly twisted spine. His face was clear and peaceful and when he spoke it was in excellent English. He was a Tibetan refugee and had been educated at the school in the village we had passed on our way up the valley. All his learning had been through the medium of English and in the Tibetan school he had learnt, after English, mathematics, science, geography, geometry, history and Hindi. He was obviously loved by the older monks who fussed over and touched him and joked with him all the time.

The whole place hummed with happiness.

Back at the John Bannon guest house we were drinking coffee when Mr Tickoo arrived to introduce us to our cook, Sultana, and thankfully, to our tent. Sultana, a slight wiry Kashmiri, struggled with us for half an hour to put the tent up on the front lawn of the guest house. A few of the other guests came out to watch, drinking whisky and making encouraging noises but wisely staying out of the way. It was a French tent of a type last used by Napoleon. When we finally got it up it looked very sad, as though it didn't really want to be coming with us. As with all tents we learnt more about putting it up by taking it down. May I suggest to all tent manufacturers that in future they sell their tents fully erected so that people can see what goes where. When a thing arrives as a lumpy, badly packed bundle of aluminium poles, fabric and string, how can anybody truly believe it will end up as a tent? We took the tent down again and packed it away. As always it looked twice as big as when we'd first unpacked it.

Sitting with Sultana over more coffee we told him what we would like to eat on the trek. He seemed disappointed that we didn't want porridge every day for breakfast and quite surprised when we told him that we liked Indian food. Sultana spoke very good English and had been a cook on many treks and expeditions. So he and Mr Tickoo went down into Manali to buy food for the trek and we sat on the veranda watching the sun drop below the far mountains and the night stars spattering the sky.

The next day dawned bright and clear with a few clouds swirling round the upper summits. We loaded all our gear on to the jeep and with John Bannon, Mr Tickoo and the other guests waving us off we lurched out of the grounds of the guest house towards the head of the valley. The road corkscrewed for miles towards the summit of the Rohtang Pass, past people waving in the fields and washday-white sheep in meadows, an indication of how clean the air was up here. A wrecked Punjabi lorry on its side at the edge of a five hundred foot drop didn't inspire us with much confidence but the jeep ploughed on up into the clouds which broke frequently to give us views back down the Kulu Valley and the way we'd come.

We stopped just below the col for tchai at a small tea house half-buried in the clouds. Prayer-flags cracked and flapped in the wind and three pairs of golden eagles circled far above. We climbed on up to the col through thick boiling clouds. Sudden breaks in the rolling grey world opened like windows on the valley and we saw, far below, waterfalls dropping hundreds of feet, spray blowing in the wind. Eagles cut silently out of the cloud so close above our heads we could almost have touched them and vanished as suddenly back into the mist. Then we were over the col and through the cloud that is held back by the ridge and ahead of us stretched the dry and stony Lahoul* Valley, the far wall a range of snowy peaks and summits.

We stopped the jeep and got out. We were on the watershed of the Himalaya. Beyond, in the direction our journey led, the land lay mainly in the Himalayan rain shadow. Little rain falls here although snow constantly forms on the highest peaks. It was strange to think that in literally a few hundred yards we had crossed from one climatic

*Lahoul is a Hindustani word meaning 'wilderness'.

The Rohtang Pass, the watershed of the Himalaya

zone to another. The view was overpowering. We had left behind a green mantled valley, before us stretched the snow mantled peaks of the Indian Himalaya while many hundreds of feet below us lay the road to Darsha. Now at thirteen thousand feet, we noticed for the first time the lack of oxygen. It was only a slight change but running from the edge of the crag where I had been taking a photograph back to the jeep left me a lot more breathless than it should have done.

We dropped slowly down from the pass to the checkpoint at Kyelang where in the early eighteen seventies an English explorer called Andrew Wilson founded a German Moravian mission. At Kyelang an army officer, obviously suffering from terminal boredom, got off his cot bed in the corner of the hut to write down our passport and visa particulars in a vast ledger. Indian bureaucracy never ceased to amaze me. They have the atom bomb yet everything runs on biros, paper, stamps and steam-driven telex machines.

We had tchai and dhal with rice in a little tchai house across from the checkpoint. We were the focus of interest for a troop of small boys who seemed to have appeared from out of the rocky ground. One of them fell in love with Pat and followed her round grinning.

Driving on along the dusty valley towards Darsha we passed road-gangs where women and girls worked alongside the men filling in holes and clearing landslides from the 'jeepable track'. On a bend high above the river the engine started making squealing noises and the driver, who'd been nursing the engine all the way over the pass, shook his head and cursed. We were only two miles from Darsha and the radiator was empty. The engine had overheated. The nearest water was a thousand feet below the road in the fast flowing river but luckily our water bottles were full so we poured them into the radiator and hobbled into Darsha.

That evening, one hundred and twenty-five miles and seven hours in a jeep from Manali, we sat down outside our tent on a boulder field by the river at Darsha. Around us were the Himalayan peaks flecked with snow, the dying light of the day tinting them a pale pink.

My journal reads:

> We have just met our ponyman, a laughing curly haired man from Darsha who has no English. We watched as our ponies were brought out and new shod. A Buddhist monk wearing a peaked yellow cap came out from the village to help and clicked and whoad and held them steady, a broad grin on his face, laughing his head off every time something went wrong or a horse bucked the Ponyman away.
>
> Sultana, or Cookie as he sometimes insisted on calling himself, called us to the cook tent for chicken curry, potato and cauliflower bhajia and rice followed by Persian tea which Cookie said was his speciality. It was a mixture of cinnamon, tea, cardamom and sugar and was delicious.

The sun moved far into the west, casting a cold black shadow over the arid landscape and as we sat inside the tent keeping warm we saw through the open door a pale pink stream of fine cloud bannering across the dark blue bowl of the night-coming sky. A gibbous moon lifted over the eastern rim of the plain and laid down its reflection, curved and shaking across the stream.

3

The 'Terrible' Shingo La

'Leave it alone. You'll never improve on it'.
– Roosevelt on the Grand Canyon

I AWOKE IN THE MORNING with a fair idea of what mountain sickness is really like. I had read in all the climbing books on the Himalaya how mountain sickness, or altitude sickness, was a painful and sometimes dangerous condition, resulting in some cases in death from pulmonary or cerebral oedema. What happens, apparently, is that the decrease in oxygen at high levels causes the lungs and brain to fill with water. It can happen anywhere above eight thousand feet although it doesn't normally make itself felt until a thousand feet or more higher.

The first symptoms of mountain sickness are: tingling in the fingers, swelling of the hands and face, loss of appetite, sleep disturbances, weakness, dizziness, headache and nausea.

Most times these symptoms are mild and usually go away with acclimatisation. As long as the symptoms are not too severe and don't persist, it's fairly safe to assume that you can continue climbing slowly, watching for signs that the sickness is not getting worse. Pushing yourself too high too quickly, however, can bring on acute mountain sickness. The symptoms of this are: marked shortness of breath with only gentle exertion, wet, bubbly breathing, low urine output (less than a pint a day), persistent vomiting, severe persistent headache, gross fatigue, delirium and loss of coordination leading to staggering and falling.

If you get any or all of these then you are in trouble and the only cure is a rapid descent. It is said that a descent of even five hundred feet will ameliorate some of the symptoms. But anybody affected by acute mountain sickness must descend as fast as possible and seek medical aid.

Having read all of this in Dr Stephen Bezruchka's admirable book *A Guide to Trekking in Nepal* was no comfort at all when I woke up that morning feeling as though a Punjabi lorry had run over my head. In retrospect I can see that we should have spent two days at least at Darsha at ten thousand feet acclimatising before continuing any higher, but at the time it seemed more important that we pushed on. As I wrote in my journal later that day, 'It's like having a hangover all the time.' I hadn't slept well anyway since we'd pitched camp on the only bit of grass we could find and the ponies had decided to have a four a.m. snack walking round the tent tripping over the guy ropes and crashing into the poles as they looked for the juiciest bits of grass.

It wasn't the best night I've spent under canvas. It was that day too that the real part of the trek was to begin. No more pussyfooting about on mountain roads in jeeps with washing-machine motors for engines. It was shanks's pony from now until Padum.

We had a light breakfast of Indian pancakes and honey and Cookie

The Copper Pot Man, a Zanskari who joined our party

gave us our lunch box, a green polythene affair with Little Miss Muffet on the front. How that got here I'll never know – I was too dumbfounded to ask. Lunch was cold chicken, boiled eggs, apples, chapattis and some terrible, sweet Indian biscuits. Pat filled the flasks with water and added the drops of iodine to them that were meant to kill all bacteria, tapeworms and other bugs and mites while I took the stupid tent down and packed it away.

The beauty of trekking with ponies is that they carry all the gear and in theory you just stroll along with a light day-pack containing your food, water and warm jacket. Being the excessive obsessive that I am, however, I'd brought along tons of photographic equipment, most of which I carried with me in two bags slung pannier-fashion. Pat carried the water bottles, food and down-lined jackets in a small rucksack. Once loaded up we set off behind the ponies, Pat with her Marks and Spencer umbrella that doubled as sunshade and walking-stick for crossing raging torrents, I with my bush hat from the Army and Navy store in Manchester and my snow goggles against the glare of the sun. At altitude the sun's rays are much stronger and the glare off the pale dust and rocks can be almost as strong as that off snow.

We left Darsha without any regrets. Apparently there is a pretty village with some pleasant people in it a short trek from the camp site but what we'd seen of the place hadn't made us long to linger there. It's a dirty dusty hole made further disagreeable by the presence of the army who are doing their best to destroy what wild beauty was there in the first place, leaving bits of muck and scrap metal everywhere. We presented our passports and papers to yet another bored looking Indian army officer who wrote our names in yet another ledger and looked at us suspiciously before waving us discourteously out of his hovel of an office. I know that India has border problems with both her neighbours but two English trekkers are hardly likely to be spies and a bit of pleasantry wouldn't have gone amiss, particularly since almost everybody else we met in India was hospitable and friendly.

As we left Darsha we were four strong, Pat and me and Cookie and our Ponyman who kept groaning and holding his head and saying 'chang', grinning sadly. Seven ponies and mules carried the tents and gear. I noticed as we climbed up out of Darsha that we'd picked up an extra traveller along the way, a Zanskari who was carrying the most immense copper cooking pot, the sort of thing you see witches seated round in *Macbeth* Act One Scene One. Cookie didn't seem to know much about him except that he had come all the way from Srinagar with the pot. He carried it slung across his back taking the weight on a tumpline round his forehead. It must have weighed somewhere round forty to fifty pounds and yet all the time he was with us he never flagged, jumping across wild mountain torrents and leaping from boulder to boulder as though he were walking on a cricket pitch.

Cookie walked ahead of us his oil lamp swinging from his hand. In all the time we were with him we were never to see him without it: he didn't trust the ponies with it, he said. So, like Demosthenes, the character from Greek mythology who walked the world with a lamp looking for an honest man, Sultana strode off towards the Shingo La with a hard boiled egg in one hand and his oil lamp swinging in the other.

Out of Darsha the unsurfaced track eventually becomes a trail climbing high above the valley following the Barai Nala River upstream as it flows strongly, milky-blue with dust, far below. This was the river we were going to have to cross that day and the following day and it looked big.

After a morning's walking the altitude began to tell and climbing anything but a moderate slope became a breathless affair. A short-cut through a tiny village of a few huddled houses and neat fields full of peas and barley meant cutting steeply across a series of switchback bends in the trail and, though it was only a couple of hundred yards of ascent, it left me feeling like I'd climbed Scafell in a rush.

The children of the next village ran out as we approached, many of them blowing bubble gum. They were shouting and laughing and waving at us and for the first time we heard the cry, '*Julay! Julay!*', which is Zanskari for 'Greetings', and the other cry we were to hear so much, '*Meetree! Meetree!*', which is a cry for sweets. Some misguided though no doubt good-hearted trekker a few years back thought it would be a good idea to carry loads of sweets to give out to children along the way. Now they often see every passing Westerner as a walking sweet-shop. Not only is it bad for their teeth but it is bad for their self esteem as well. Until the trekker came to these regions the people wouldn't have known what begging was.

At the last village along the trail, an hour or so further on, we stopped and had lunch from our Little Miss Muffet school lunch box, watched by lots of fascinated children who came to stare wide-eyed at the memsahib with the pink umbrella and the sahib with the white glasses and funny hat. And I can't say I can blame them.

While we were letting our lunch digest and trying to talk to the children in a mixture of sign language and simple English, there came strolling through the dust and muck and heat of the village, as though in a dream, an Indian army officer in full parade ground smart, with gleaming shoes, a perfectly groomed handlebar moustache, a Sam Browne belt and a revolver in a leather holster.

'Good afternoon, sir. Good afternoon, madam,' he said, saluting with a gloved hand.

'Have you come far?' were the only words I could form in my very fuddled brain.

'I am walking to Kyelang examining the track from Padum to Manali. Is there anything I can do to help you?'

His second-in-command arrived at that moment looking very hot, sweaty and rumpled and carrying a bulging briefcase full of maps, charts and money for the villagers who maintain the trail. Though it's a rough and dangerous route it is a direct way over into the Indo-Chinese border area from the Kulu Valley and could obviously

A Zanskari village near Darsha

be of some strategic importance to a would-be invader. Behind him stood the two local guides who had led them from Padum over the Shingo La looking quite worn out.

'I think we'll be fine,' I said. 'We're making for the Shingo La and then on to Padum and Kargil.'

'Have a pleasant journey,' he replied. He saluted and strode smartly off into the heat and dust, not a mote or beam on his shiny brown shoes, his trousers perfectly creased, his wrecked entourage struggling behind him. I was so numbed that I forgot to ask him if I could take his photograph and he walked out of my life for ever, leaving me still wondering how he did it. When we finally crossed the Shingo La ourselves we wondered all the more.

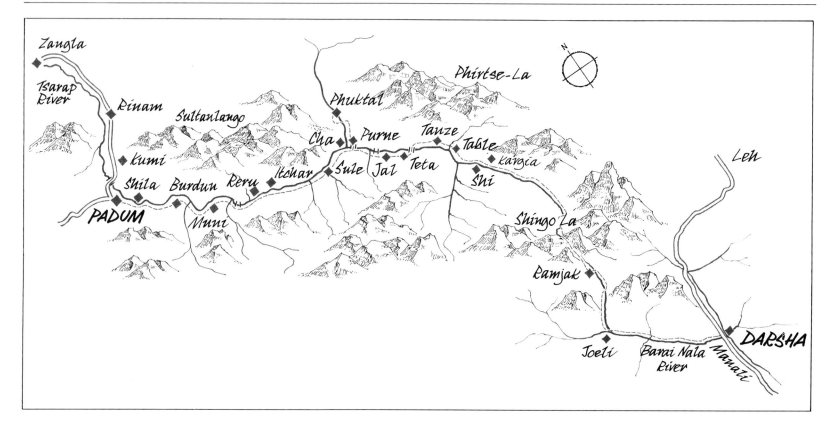

After lunch we climbed on along the rough trail, crossing scree slopes and ramshackle bridges over roaring streams through some truly amazing scenery. The river was well below us while above, across the valley, stretched dozens of unclimbed and nameless peaks that climbers would have been fighting over in Europe. Towards late afternoon we came to a gorge that was simply a vertical cleft in the valley floor sixty feet deep and perhaps twenty across. Through it the Barai Nala thundered and on its edge a 'chorten' stood crowned with prayer-flags, beating and flapping in the wind. Chortens are stone and rubble cairns that can range from a simple pile of rocks to the more ornate ones we were to meet around Kargia. The more ornate are often reliquaries containing the ashes of local saints or lamas. The simpler chortens usually contain little other than a prayer-scroll or the words 'Om mani padme hum' scratched on a pebble. Unadorned stone chortens with prayer-flags on them are found all over the Himalaya and are often put up on cols or river crossings to make the place specially holy and keep the demons and spirits of the mountain and the river at bay.

The prayer-flags, plain coloured muslin squares with mantras printed on them, are there to send the spirit of the devotions constantly to the four corners of the earth, carried there by the four winds. It's not a cheap and easy way of gaining grace but a way of giving praise to the Buddha.

I was glad that the chorten was there because we needed all the help we could get crossing the gorge. The bridge was a shaky affair of branches and planks lashed together without a handrail and a sixty-foot drop either side into the roaring river below.

Four miles further upstream on the west bank of the river we came up against our first snow-melt torrent.

Hardly any rain falls in these regions. Instead snow forms on the high peaks. During the heat of the day the snow melts and gushes down the mountains swelling the merest trickle into a full-blown dangerous mountain stream. That is why when trekking in this area it's often possible to wade across a river first thing in the morning quite comfortably when by mid afternoon it will sweep men and horses to their deaths.

We took our boots and socks off and by jumping from stone to stone led across by Cookie, the Ponyman and the Copper Pot Man we somehow made it the twenty or so feet to the other side.

From there it was a pleasant walk in the afternoon sun to the camp ground. Across the river we cold see another pack-horse train making its way downstream calling and waving, looking like tiny toys on the vast screes above the river.

I put the tent up and crawled inside, my head thumping from altitude sickness. I couldn't eat supper that night which was a shame

Prayer-flags by the gorge of the Barai Nala river

Crossing the snow-melt torrent by leaping, bare-footed, from rock to rock

since Cookie had made his speciality, Kashmiri lamb with rice. I just lay in the tent feeling that my head was going to explode. During the night I woke to hear rain thundering on the tent roof. I had read in all the books that we were now in the Himalayan Rain Shadow. Obviously these clouds were lost. I remember thinking at the time that the rain didn't bode well for the next day's river crossing.

The Copper Pot Man was still with us. God knows where he got the energy from. He ran off in the morning and gathered fodder for the horses from some mystery hillside, then slung the tumpline around his forehead and off he set. He seemed to be helping with the horses in return for eating with us but perhaps also it is the way of the mountains, that travellers come together and travel together. There are probably times when even hardened hillmen like these need all the help they can get.

I felt sorry for the horses. One of them had a large sore on its back and all of them, as soon as their loads came off at the end of the day's march, would roll in the dust kicking their legs in the air. We had two ponies and five donkeys or mules but Cookie called them all horses. The Ponyman had a terrible hacking cough. Each morning his whooping bark echoing around the mountains, together with Cookie calling 'Tea Sahib!' outside the tent as he pushed two mugs of tchai through the flap, would wake us. Yet he smoked whenever he could! Every stop to tighten the ponies cinches or to make a brew was an excuse to light up. Like most other people in the mountains he wore so little clothing that it was hard to tell whether his cough was a smoker's one or a permanent chest cold. Most of the people seemed to wear a shirt, a jacket or woollen sweater of some kind, pants and rough shoes and little else. Cookie, who came from the low lakeland area of Srinagar, walked the whole trek – desert, snowfields and rivers – in a pair of cheap plastic shoes.

Sultana looked about sixty and may well have been that age – I didn't like to ask. He told us that he had five young children ranging from two to ten years old back in Srinagar who missed him very much.

I felt a lot better in the morning and we were sitting on the ground after striking camp, eating a breakfast of chapattis and honey and Persian tea, when two shepherds arrived with their flock. High up in these mountains there are shepherd shelters where the men of the Upper Lahoul Valley live out while they are summering their stock. Food is brought up to them from the villages by young boys and women. Every bit of feed is precious here, so they have to drive the sheep up on to the upper limits of vegetation. The two shepherds squatted by the cook tent and took a cup of tea from Sultana. There was a lot of talking and pointing upstream followed by a lot more talking and pointing upstream and shaking of heads. After a little while they wandered off again, in pursuit of their flocks as they roamed the valley side baaing and bleating.

Cookie came across. He looked worried. 'Big problem. Is rain come very much in night. Sheepmen say river too high. Horses must go back to bridge and cross river then go up other side.'

This meant that the ponies would have to go all the way back to the bridge over the gorge that we had crossed yesterday and then make their way across the dangerous high screes on the other bank.

'And us?'

'I go with you to joeli.' (The word rhymes with holy.)

'Joeli?'

'Sheepman say is joeli,' and he indicated by hand signals a rope and a pulley, which meant that somehow we were going to be winched across the river.

'Horseman want two hundred rupees for horse to cross water. I tell him what for I pay two hundred rupees?'

So the horses went back on an hour's journey to cross by the bridge at the gorge and we travelled on slowly upstream. Both Pat and I got well out of breath as soon as we climbed any kind of slope at all. Thankfully there was a fair amount of cloud about so it was much cooler than the day before.

As we pushed on up the valley over boulder fields and rushing streams I was amazed by the numbers and variety of wild flowers that managed to survive at this altitude. Himalayan blue poppy peeped out from amongst the boulders and wild thyme and a kind of small yellow ragwort grew all around.

After half a day's further walking we dropped down to the river, which was now in full frenzied flood. Cookie said that it would normally only be up to our ankles. The water was at least chest high and running very, very fast. Footing would have been very difficult. One way of crossing rivers when they are like this is to wade across, keeping a horse on the downstream side, so that it takes the full brunt of the current. But I could see now why the horseman had asked so much more money for crossing the river. Even the horses might possibly not have made it.

But ahead of us lay salvation in the shape of a flying fox or bosun's chair and windlass slung across the river from two rough towers. It looked safe enough and there was no alternative anyway, so we crossed: one at a time, swinging above the swollen river. Two Zanskaris, a man and a boy who obviously ran this as some sort of business, hauled us over laughing and waving. It cost me twenty

Crossing the swollen river on a 'flying fox'

rupees. Less than a pound. I think if it had been two hundred rupees I would still have paid up. Apparently this was the last day that the joeli would be here. After that, the men were going to dismantle it and go home for the winter. We were by now at the very end of the season and just about as late as it can be to cross the Shingo La safely.

As we were grouping on the opposite bank the rain that had been threatening all day broke.

'Man said go there,' said Cookie pointing towards what looked like a roofless shepherd's shelter. 'There is fire and gompa.' The 'fire' and 'gompa' were two roofless rubble-walled enclosures huddled under a cliff.

And so with the sky for a roof we sheltered from a mixture of chilling rain and sleet in the home where the two men had spent the last four months winding people across the river. We had no waterproofs and no fibrepiles. Foolishly thinking that the day would be as hot and dry as it had been the day before we hadn't packed them. It became very cold. Luckily we had a silver-foil survival bag that we'd left in the rucksack in case of emergencies, which I wrapped round Pat.

The fire turned out to be a small pile of smoking pony turds and the gompa four boulder walls and a doorway. A Buddha in full lotus position was crudely but carefully painted on a stone by the entrance, with the words, 'Hole men. Welcome!' (All men are welcome!) scratched on it. Underneath the Buddha was a piece of paper with the words 'tea house' chalked on it with a burnt stick, while below were the prices of a few simple things like tea and pancakes. Obviously, in busier times, the men who ran the joeli also ran a sort of tea room for trekkers.

I scouted around and found some more bits of dung and a few pieces of wood and managed to get the fire going enough to warm all three of us up a little. Cookie put his lamp on the floor and squatted down beside it.

'We very good lucky,' said Cookie. 'After today is finish joeli.' Behind us the leather-faced man and the young boy had crossed to the opposite bank and were dismantling the joeli, making themselves a sort of camp and lighting a fire; to wait I assume for ponies to come and take their gear back home.

After a while the rain cleared and a watery sun warmed us a little. Hours passed and light was beginning to fail when we heard the sound of horses and shouting and the Ponyman and the Copper Pot Man appeared over a short rise below us. They forded an ice-cold, thigh-deep stream to get to our hovel. It was a tributary of the Barai Nala River that we would follow the next day up towards the Shingo La. We unloaded the ponies and gratefully pitched camp. We were about one mile from Ramjak which should have been our camp site that night but the Ponyman felt that the ponies had had enough for the day and so did we.

During the afternoon there had been terrible dust storms but now the wind died a little. The shadows crept up the valley as we ate our meal and all round us there was little but a wilderness of boulders and dust. The tent pegs were useless in this sort of terrain so we piled huge stones round the tent to keep it from blowing away in the night.

The horses wandered off up the hillside looking for something to eat. We'd brought a little fodder with us but the horses still needed to graze. Somehow, in amongst the boulders and dust, they seemed to be able to find a few blades of grass to munch on.

In the setting sun I looked back the way we had come. Bare, jagged valley sides led to ragged summits tipped with snow, and in the far distance I could see clearly the range of mountains that held the Rohtang Pass and the way back to Kulu.

We sat in the tent looking down the valley across the boulder field and the river we were to follow up to the Shingo La. Beyond my face and hands I hadn't washed for four days but since Pat was in the same boat she couldn't very well complain about the smell. Across the Barai Nala I could see the joeli men huddled round their fire as night fell. Dark clouds were racing up the valley, blotting out the evening sky and a few fine flakes of snow were falling. It didn't look good.

As dawn struggled over the nearest peaks the following day, I opened the tent door to mist and light snow. We dressed in everything we'd got, including waterproofs, and climbed out of the tent. The whole valley was shrouded in thick mist and through it a strong wind was blowing flurries of wet snow. It looked pretty miserable. We could just see the shape of the Copper Pot Man above us, making his way downhill carrying an armful of fodder. Somewhere he had managed to find vegetation more than three inches long.

The weather turned really nasty in minutes, the wind reached gale strength and thick flurries of snow rolled around the walls of the canyon ahead of us, but we set off, more in an attempt to keep warm than anything else.

'Do you think we will make it over the Shingo La?' I had asked Sultana at breakfast.

'Maybe we go now no problem,' he said. 'Maybe soon is too much snow and is closed.'

The freezing wind was numbing our faces and the whole scene was in ridiculous contrast to the first day when we had strolled along in burning sunlight under an open blue sky. We climbed steadily upwards through the cloud. Well below we could see Cookie and the

Ponyman dismantling the big cook tent while the Copper Pot Man was hurriedly throwing the blankets on the ponies' backs, getting them ready for loading.

The climb left us more and more breathless, forcing us to stop every hundred feet to get our breath back. The mist closed in until we could only just see the walls of the narrow craggy defile on either side, while above us the peaks vanished into the grey falling snow. After an hour or so of climbing we met four German trekkers, descending through the mist. They had crossed the Shingo La the day before and looked exhausted. They were pretty despondent when I told them that they'd got a river to cross at the bottom of the gorge. The Germans told us the Shingo La was just passable. There was a great deal of thick snow but the pass wasn't blocked.

About thirty minutes later we saw another group coming through the mist, blankets wrapped round them and looking very cold and miserable. They were the Germans' guides.

'Shingo La no good,' said the leader. 'Four, five people die there last year. Too much snow,' he added, indicating his waist. Then this harbinger of good fortune vanished with his mates into the mist leaving us wondering whom to believe. Pat hadn't liked the look of them. The leader had shifty eyes, she said. So we decided to believe the Germans.

We planned to carry on climbing until the ponies caught us up. Then, if the Ponyman was prepared to chance his ponies over the pass, we'd go with them.

Just as we heard the tinkling of the ponies' bells behind us the mist started to clear and, as though some giant or spirit of the mountains had sucked them out of the sky, the clouds and swirling snow melted away and the sun broke through. In minutes the most beautiful views stretched towards Ramjak ahead of us and back down the trail behind us. We pushed on ever higher, packing our waterproofs away and climbing steadily. The valley had widened out now, and we could see

Guides coming down from the Shingo La

high mountains all about us and a steady climb towards the pass ahead.

At Ramjak, which is nothing more than the remains of a hut and the debris of a few camp sites on some level ground below a cliff, our pony-train stopped to eat but we were feeling pretty good by then, cheered up by the warm sun and the mountains all about us, so we climbed away from the camp following the trail.

As we were climbing I saw something out of the corner of my eye that made me stop and take a better look. On a ledge a few yards up the cliff face, a monk was seated cross-legged, chanting and bowing, his whole body moving to and fro in rhythm with the chant.

Solitary meditation in caves is one of the ways in which monks and

The hermit monk who sat cross-legged on the ledge, chanting and bowing

lamas hope to achieve 'Samadhi', a deep state of contemplation that is just one step on the path to Buddhahood. When I asked Sultana afterwards he said that this hermit had been here for some time and that he survived on very little food, largely on what people brought him in passing, perhaps some tsampa or some rice. Notwithstanding the mental strength of the hermit, bearing all that cold and privation is simply incredible. With nothing but his robes, bare armed and living off gifts, he would stay there meditating until the big snows came when he would make the crossing over the Shingo La and along the Tsarap Gorge to the Phuktal Gompa. To those who live in it the Himalaya is an accessible world because the common Tibetan language enables them to travel thousands of miles and still be understood. From Afghanistan to Burma monks travel the mountain passes. They need little or no money because monks are always welcome wherever they go and people along the trail will share their food with them.

In winter the temperature drops to below thirty degrees centigrade and packs of hungry wolves come close to the snowbound villages of Zanskar. The villagers have an ingenious method of dealing with them. They build a circular stone trap about twelve feet in diameter and eight feet high, the top stones sloping steeply inwards. A young kid is tied inside as a bait and a ramp leads the wolves over the lip of the pit. Once inside the wolves can't get out and the villagers stone them to death. Since wolves hunt in packs, it is an effective way of dealing with them. Cruel, of course, but what else can you do if wolves are taking the food that will keep you alive all winter?

The valley closed in for a while then opened out again on to a moraine jumble and a flat plain which helped us to make good time. We stopped to eat our food in the sun at what looked like a shepherd's camp site and as we were eating the horses caught up with us.

'Camp only half hour,' said Cookie as he strolled past swinging his lamp. We were moving fairly quickly but in the event it was more

than an hour and a half further to the camp. The valley narrowed again as we pushed upwards, climbing steadily and coming at last to our halt for the night, a ponyman's shelter and a sloping rubble field with sparse fodder for the horses.

We unpacked and set up the tent. Sultana soon had our meal cooked on his primitive but effective kerosene stove, but when we saw what was happening to the meat we decided to ask for vegetarian meals only from now on. The shepherd's shelter was a roofed-in affair, a sort of igloo made of flat stones, and the first thing Sultana did while pitching camp was to spread all our meat out to dry on the roof of the hut. It didn't look good and it smelt even worse.

While we were eating, a pack-horse train pulled into our camp with eight or nine fully-loaded ponies and five men and a boy. One of the men was the jolly Buddhist monk who had helped with the horses at Darsha. In five minutes the packs were turned into the wall of their shelter for the night and a tarpaulin made the roof. The monk wandered round picking up pony turds left here by previous pack-trains to make a fire. He had a skin bellows which he used to get the turds flaming and in minutes the horsemen and the monk were eating rice and dhal. I wouldn't have imagined that turds made a very good fuel source but a French priest called Father Huc who travelled from China to Lhasa in Tibet and back in 1856 said that the best fuel of all was camel turd, followed by sheep, then in descending order of calorific value by yak, cow and horse. At high altitudes it's difficult to get much heat out of anything, but yak or pony dung does give just enough heat to cook by and its smell is not unpleasant. I thought it was a little like the smell of the peat fires of the west of Ireland.

The monk travelling with the ponymen was using the bellows because of the lack of oxygen. The bellows themselves were made from the skin of a whole sheep, legs and all. The skin had been sewn back together and a pipe inserted into the neck. When the sack was pulled open it filled with air which entered through a small hole with some sort of valve in it. I'll leave you to guess where the hole was.

It grew very cold towards nightfall and a full moon rolled over the high peak to the south-east as we climbed into the tent. The monk and the Zanskaris were singing round their fire, lit by its flames and sheltered from the wind by their baggage and rough-roofed tent. It was a scene that could have taken place a thousand years ago: the ponies moving on the steep valley side in the fading light, the bells around their necks gently clanking, the fire burning brightly against the dark and the cold and the travellers and pilgrim monk singing round its glow.

My journal for that night records:

> It is very cold here and a strong wind has just struck up from out of nowhere. The moon is shining in a clear sky and over the sound of the men singing I can hear the river rushing south. With luck tomorrow we should be over into Zanskar.
> They all say 'Shingo La no problem'. We are now ten men and one woman strong and many ponies. Maybe there's safety in numbers.

The height of the Shingo La has been put variously at between 15,000 and 16,722 feet. In retrospect, and having climbed in Nepal to well over 18,000, I'd guess that the latter is more correct. Michel Peissel, one of the first French travellers in this area, called the pass *'The Terrible Shingo La'* and even Mr Tickoo had been a little worried about our crossing. It is normally open during the summer months only and is closed by snow by mid-September. We were very close to that thin line. The name Shingo La comes from 'Shing Kur', meaning 'to carry wood', because in order to cross it safely you have to carry wood. If you are stranded there is nothing to make a fire and without fire you die.

It was freezing cold when we awoke the next morning, the water in the pail was ice and our breath had frozen in thick sheets on the inside of the tent. We dressed in a hurry and ate and packed as quickly as we could. The rising sun was making its way slowly over the rim of the eastern high peaks but, though it was now seven o'clock and a good few hours after dawn, it would be a while before it got to us. Stamping our feet in our cold boots to get the blood flowing we looked at the sky. It looked settled so we decided to leave our waterproofs on the ponies and take just our fibrepiles and duvet jackets. Even the horsemen were feeling the cold this morning, moving quickly with blankets thrown around them, their breath steaming in the icy air. Cookie had somehow found a thin torn jacket which he pulled on, his sole concession to the sub-zero temperature.

So we set out for the Shingo La, well in advance of the ponies. It was a cloudless day with an incredibly deep blue sky. The air is so

Cairn on the Shingo La, resembling Nine Standards Rigg

clear at this altitude that it gives an unreal sharpness to everything. Tiny daisies and stitchwort-like flowers seem to be able to live right up to the limit of the col, only petering out a hundred yards or so below it.

After an hour's walking the sun came out and the valley opened into yet another boulder plain with low peaks away to the west and east of us. We stuffed our duvet jackets into the rucksack and drank in the warm sun. By the side of the river was a cairn exactly like one of those you find on Nine Standards Rigg in the Yorkshire Dales and on some of the Lakeland summits, perfectly made and standing alone by the rushing water. I wondered if there was some sort of common ancestry that linked the builders of the Yorkshire cairns to the people who lived on these high mountains? The early Dalesfolk were Celts who are said to have come originally from the Middle East. Could migration eastwards have brought a branch of the same people here into Zanskar? Some of the symbols found in Buddhist paintings, in particular the spiral and the swastika, are also found in Celtic art. But perhaps this is all fancy.*

One of the interesting things about this cairn was that it contained a number of lovingly carved mani stones, showing the Buddha in the lotus position. Other stones carried the words again and again 'Om mani padme hum'.

A few minutes upriver from the cairn we started climbing again until rounding a spur, we saw a huge snow bridge, the tail end of a glacier, ahead of us. The ponies were already there and from this distance we watched the men and horses crossing and they looked minute. At this height the snow bridges are so thick that they never melt even in the hottest sun. We followed and crossed over, a little breathless now, our boots biting deep into the snow.

*I later found that Andrew Wilson, who crossed the Shingo La in the eighteen seventies, came to the same sort of conclusion.

Cookie hung back for us at the snow bridge and we went on together. I was managing fine although my head was beginning to pound a little. Pat, however, seemed to be going slower than she should have been. Then we met with a succession of false cols: there must have been about eleven in all. Sometimes, climbing in the mountains can be infuriating almost to the point of despair because often, near the summit of a hill or pass, there seems to be a succession of steps a couple of hundred feet high. Of course all you can see at the time is the top of the step that you are on, which you wrongly assume to be the summit of the hill or pass. Only when you gain it do you realise that it wasn't the top at all but the bottom of another climb.

So it was on this day. My head was now banging like a temple gong and even climbing slowly and steadily we were both struggling. Every hundred feet or so we stopped for a few minutes to get our breath back. It became a gradual torture. We drank as much and as often as we could because at this height you sweat copiously but the dry air absorbs it immediately so that you are dehydrating all the time. You only notice this when you go for a pee and nothing happens.

We hit another snowfield and paused again. Pat was really slowing down now and I was beginning to get worried. The monk and the other pony-train passed us on the snow, waving and calling, and headed off towards what I prayed was the last col, five hundred feet or so higher beyond a massive ice bank. The endurance of these people is amazing. I was wearing thermals, a tracksuit, a fibrepile jacket and a duvet jacket, boots and mittens. The monk was just wearing his robes and a pair of thin shoes and yet was striding out as though he were walking the flatlands of East Anglia.

Then Pat began to really suffer badly from kidney pains. In retrospect it was probably a combination of the Diamox tablets we had taken that morning 'just in case' and dehydration. Diamox, the recommended drug for mountain sickness, acts as a diuretic so that a build up of salt crystals in her kidneys could have caused the pain. She became weak and lethargic and could move only a few paces at a time before having to stop. In this condition we staggered on, never seeming to get any nearer to the summit of the pass. I had virtually to push her up the last stretch. I took her rucksack and Cookie carried one of my camera bags and we did the only thing we could, which was to push on. We were going incredibly slowly now and I was particularly worried because the afternoon was wearing on. Once over the col we still had some way to go before we made camp and if anything did happen it was a long way there and back with a horse. We pushed on a few steps at a time, climbing steadily, with Pat having to stop more and more and for longer periods. Carrying her would have been impossible at this height.

The col turned out to be yet another mirage and ahead of us was a broad sheer-sided snowbank a hundred feet high. The trail climbed it from the left, continued along its top then disappeared. If it hadn't been for Cookie we would have been in serious trouble. Pat was getting very close to exhaustion, her speech was slurred and she was becoming increasingly listless. If I'd had to carry all the bags I think I would have been in trouble too. We dragged up and on and it really seemed as though we would never reach the top, pulling on up the snowbank, our aching lungs vainly sucking at the thin air for oxygen.

Then, almost as an anticlimax, we left the snowfield behind, climbed a small scree slope that led on to a ridge and found ourselves looking down into the kingdom of Zanskar.

The monk on the Shingo La

Below on our left was a high mountain lake, behind us the peaks of Lahoul and ahead the arid great valley of Zanskar. Prayer-flags on long wands flapped in the wind and before us was the trail winding down for miles to the valley floor. At that moment there was no more welcome sight in the world.

4

The Desert at the Top of the World

'I believe that only by being in the presence of beauty and the great things in the world around us can man eventually get the goddam hatred of wanting to kill each other out of his system. We begin to understand that we're only in this world such a short time it's incredible we should spend these few years hating and killing each other.'

– American Dreams Lost and Found by Studs Terkel

WE SAT DOWN BY the prayer flags on the col for a while until Pat had recovered enough to continue. She was still suffering from terrible pains in the region of her kidneys and each step jarred even more, doubling her misery, but gradually, taking it easy, we dropped downwards through the most barren but incredibly beautiful landscape. High cliffs and mountains were all round us in tints of mauve and pink, ochre and yellow. Below, far below, the Shingo River, a pale turquoise, threaded its way through this great dustbowl towards its eventual confluence with the Indus – one of the four holy rivers of India.

We descended slowly down the ridge of a long spur that thrust into the head of the valley as the sun lowered towards the western rim. To our right I could see, several hundred feet below, a fast-flowing mountain stream lying right across our path. Even from there it looked wide. After two hours we got to the stream. It was well up, waist deep and running fast. After the struggle over the pass and the pain of the descent, it was a very low moment and we were steeling ourselves for the inevitable, taking our boots and socks off and

looking at the freezing cold water with disgust when the cavalry arrived in the guise of our Ponyman, who rode across the stream on the back of the strongest of the ponies and carried us all across one by one, dry and warm. The next day we gave the horse our apple ration. It was the least we could do.

I managed to get the tent up with a throbbing head, feeling dizzy and a bit sick. Pat sat against a low wall drinking tea and recovering in the afternoon sun. She gradually felt better and managed to eat some curried vegetables and rice.

Pat recovered amazingly quickly so I think that her pains must have been caused by dehydration. There is so much going on in your head, with the scenery all about you and the strain of knowing that you have a difficult pass to cross, that you forget to notice simple things such as how little liquid you pee.

Lying by the tent that night as the last of the sun moved up the valley walls across the river we saw a pair of eagles high in the air circling slowly gilded by sun. A few yards away the river rolled noisily over its rocky bed.

Pat, with her M & S umbrella, beside the Shingo River

We woke to sunshine and everywhere the smell of wild thyme. We were now officially in Zanskar – 'The Land of White Copper'; so called because it is said to be plentifully supplied with that metal ore. According to the books, Zanskar is a true kingdom. Established in AD930 it remained independent for nine hundred years. It has its own language, history and traditions and still has its own rulers. The king of Zanskar lives at Zangla although it seems that the Indian government largely ignore his existence.

That day's trek was supposed to be easy but in fact it turned out to be quite hard. We were well above twelve thousand feet and anything more than a mild saunter left you breathless, added to which the last night had been incredibly cold – so cold that the water froze in our water bottles inside the tent. So neither of us had slept particularly well. Pat's pains had disappeared but, although we were feeling much fitter than when we started the trek, we were still noticing the effects of the thin air.

We breakfasted on chapattis with honey and Persian tea. It may seem a monotonous diet but it wasn't. Walking for long hours at this altitude you need lots of carbohydrate. Rice, chapattis and potatoes are the ideal food. In some parts of Nepal, porters work out their journey according to how much food they have to consume along the way so

Zanskari nomad milking a dzo

that distances are measured not in miles but in bowls of rice.

Our journey towards Padum took us first of all through a jumble of fallen boulders, some as big as a small car. How the horses got over them I'll never know. I had heard that the hill ponies and mules of this region were powerful and sure footed but it still amazed me that they never fell or faltered.

Once over the maze of tumbled rocks we were able to look back the way we had come and see that the wall of the valley we had travelled through was the western flank of the fang-shaped mountain, Gumburanjon, rising like a tusk straight from the valley floor, looking more majestic the further down the valley we travelled.

Rounding a bend in the river hours later we came upon an encampment of Zanskari nomads, their homes rough stone shelters roofed in skin. On the land around, their animals, dzomo (a cross between a cow and a yak) and dzo (a cross between a buffalo and a yak) were grazing on the scant vegetation. A young girl was milking one of the dzo, catching the milk in a wooden pail. A tiny child in a yellow cap stood watching her and us.

I've always felt guilty when coming across indigenous peoples in that I wonder at my motives for wanting to be there and more importantly for wanting to take photographs. Partly this comes from my dislike of tourism and the diminishing and degrading effect it has on other peoples' cultures. You don't have to look any further than Greece, Spain and Portugal and the Cherokee reservations in the Smoky Mountains of America to see what I mean. Tourism destroys because it introduces great numbers of foreigners, who have too much money and too little understanding of the culture, into a vulnerable community. I've always tried to travel either alone or in very small groups and at least to spend some time with the people, learn a few words of their language, show them that I appreciate their way of life and don't in any way denigrate it. I think that is what I mean when I talk about the difference between the tourist and the traveller.

The traveller doesn't expect to be provided with the comforts he has left behind. He tries to journey amongst the people, meeting them and living to some extent as they do, for a while at least. He will never become one with them because his cultural background and language are so different that there will always be a gap between himself and the people he is travelling amongst but he is trying to see and experience their world without changing it. In his travels through Arabia Wilfred Thesiger lived amongst the Arabs speaking their language, eating, drinking and sleeping exactly as they did. He is a good example of what I mean by a traveller. The tourist, on the other hand, is jetted round the world, bent double with Pentax stoop, his fists full of touro-dollars, his video camera rolling. His sole object is to collect images, T-shirts, antiquities and 'experiences'. Because he is too stupid to try and understand it, the culture is debased and packaged for him. From undersized Irishmen dressed as leprechauns at 'Medieval' banquets in the west of Ireland to stuffed bears and fibreglass Cherokee Indians in the Smoky Mountains, the world is becoming a stage where the rare and beautiful is corrupted for the grinning fools who don't seek to understand but want only to go home with a camera full of Kodachromes for the neighbours to gawp at, tut over, marvel at and squeal 'How could you stand it?' It is at base a *mondo cane* approach to other peoples' cultures.

We did spend some little time with the herdsmen. Our communication was limited since Cookie spoke Hindi and a little Zanskari and the Ponyman spoke the dialect of the Lahoul Valley. The Copper Pot Man was Zanskari but he told us that the herdsmen spoke a dialect that even he found hard to understand. They gave us some curds to drink and I took some photographs before we left, still with the same mixed feelings. If my photographs were to encourage too many people to go there it would destroy the very special nature of the land and people. I suffered the same sort of doubt when writing my book on the Dales. Would this encourage coach-trippers, the people who just want to walk around looking for gift shops and postcards, I often asked myself. It isn't elitism that makes me worry like this. It's a belief that some things are very special and that there are ways in which we can and should approach them that will leave them unspoilt, and ways that will destroy them. The beauty of the Lake District and the lives of these herdsmen are not a world apart. Both are equally fragile.

For a long time Gumburanjon was still there behind us, a lone pike rearing itself up into the blue sky. The whole great valley was so barren, stony and dusty and yet the emptiness itself and the dusky pink cliffs and crags gave it enormous beauty.

For the rest of the day we strolled gently through this desert at the top of the world, pausing every so often to take a photograph or rest, until, in the late afternoon we reached the top of a hump and came upon a snow-white chorten twenty feet high, the first in a long series that led down from the high crest of ground towards the river.

The line of chortens, pure white on the ochre soil, meant that we were close to Kargia, the village that was to be our stop for the night. These chortens were bigger than any we had seen before and were in four sections. A square base was surmounted by a rounded dome, then by a spire and finally by a few twigs with prayer flags flying from them. The square base represents Earth, the dome, Water, and the spire, Fire. In Nepal and at lower altitudes in Buddhist India the spire is capped by a

The lone pike of Gumburanjon rearing up into the blue sky

The first of the chortens on the approach to Kargia

crescent moon cupping the sun which represents Ether, so that the chorten thus represents the four elements of all existence. The spire, normally in the shape of thirteen diminishing rings and said to represent the thirteen stages of enlightenment before Nirvana is reached, is missing in Zanskar because it is normally carved in wood and most of Zanskar is above the treeline. One of the chortens had a small door in the base and inside we could see a collection of small grey tablets made from clay mixed with the ashes of some long-dead lama or saint.

We followed the line of chortens and ahead of us we could see the cluster of whitewashed houses that was Kargia and below the village, by the river, the cook tent already up with the smoke curling from the Ponyman's fire, which meant that Cookie would already have a brew going on the kerosene stove and would be peeling the onions and garlic ready for the evening meal.

Kargia camp site was a mess. My journal reads:

It's a shame, the place is full of shit, pink toilet paper and discarded cans.
Children beg for sweets and though they don't pester you it's dispiriting to see them already putting on a beggar's hurt face. It changes in an instant

when they realise you aren't going to give them any sweets and they smile again.

As we were putting up our tent and stowing the gear two little girls came to watch us. They must have been aged about ten or eleven, perhaps a little older. Their hands were as dry and wrinkled as old women's.

Pat sat down with a crowd of children and showed them some photographs she had brought with her of our daughters Sarah and Emma. The children were fascinated by the way the girls were dressed and kept passing the pictures round, pointing at them and chattering amongst themselves. We shared out a packet of biscuits and while

Pat showing photographs to the village children

they were sitting with us one of the little girls noticed the tin whistle sticking out of one of the packs. I suffer withdrawal symptoms if I'm away from a musical instrument for too long so I'd brought a blues harmonica and a tin whistle with me as the smallest things I could carry. I played some Irish tunes for them and they sang some songs for us in Zanskari, chanting in their high voices. Then they treated us to a version of 'Frère Jacques', which they had obviously learned in school.

As we lay in our sleeping bags later that night writing up our journals, the tent flap opened and two little girls stuck their heads in and sang 'Frère Jacques' again.

In the morning as we packed and stamped our feet to warm them, an old man with a basket on his back ran down from the village and moved around the camp gathering the fresh dung, picking it up and throwing it into the basket in one movement.

We ate and moved off on the trek which was to take us further north to Purne where we were to have a rest day. We left Kargia, climbing up to the village from the camp site and dropping down again to the river by white-limed houses with winter fodder or 'prangos' piled on the flat roofs and fields full of barley.

The Englishman, Moorcroft, who explored Ladakh in 1820 took a great interest in the yaks and other animals of the Himalaya. He found that the Ladakhis fed their yaks on a fodder which was so rich that small quantities were enough to fatten cattle and keep them going through a long winter. It is this prangos which is piled high on the rooftops of the Kargia houses.

In autumn the farmers in Zanskar and Ladakh make mounds of earth in the middle of the fields. Then in spring they take the earth that has been piled up over the winter and spread it on the snow. The dark earth absorbs the sun's rays and melts the snow, allowing them to plant seeds much earlier than otherwise.

Walking by the chortens, we saw across the river a village high on the ridge and above it an already waning moon. Against the brilliant blue sky, it was a superb sight and made me think yet again what a beautiful country this was.

At Table there was a huge wolf trap and a small village while the track led on past chorten after chorten and mani wall after mani wall. The latter vary in length from a few feet to hundreds. They contain thousands of mani stones with their mantras and what the guidebook called 'xoanon', which I later found meant 'crude religious carvings'. In many cases, however, the carvings were simple, though far from crude, and had great delicacy and beauty. You should always pass a mani wall keeping it to your right for this way you gain all the benefit from the devotions upon it.

The villages of the Zanskar Valley seem to have perched themselves wherever a flattened truncated spur has given them enough level land to survive. Water from the snow-melt is channelled through the fields, often in very elaborate and ingenious irrigation systems feeding good crops of barley. The villages stand out like semi-precious stones, gold and emerald in the rust-red, desiccated moonscape.

Just before Purne we passed through two pretty villages where pleasant walled lanes ran by neat whitewashed houses. Kuru is a major village for livestock breeders and Teta, where water seemed to be flowing everywhere in a maze of ditches, was alive with yapping dogs and running children.

The valley narrowed gradually until it closed in, dark-red and shadowy round us, bringing a chill to the afternoon. Rounding a bend we saw our goal, Purne, on a truncated spur far below us across the river, burning green-gold in the sun. Descending quickly we came to a well-built suspension bridge in a spectacular gorge.

We had just crossed the river and climbed up to Purne when I saw something that will remain engraved on my mind for as long as I live. We heard horses' hoofs behind us and looking back we saw a rider

The chorten's shape represents Earth, Water and Fire

approaching. It was an extremely beautiful Zanskari woman in traditional dress, turquoise jewels on the breast of her dark blouse, her long black hair pulled back from her face in a thick plait. She rode proudly past us on a fine chestnut mare nodding to us as she passed, brightly lit against the black walls of the gorge.

Purne has a small gompa, a line of chortens that stand above water-driven prayer wheels and a small, semi-official camping ground which is surrounded by small trees and very pleasant.

We pitched the tent, washed our hair at the spring, our heads throbbing from the ice-cold water, ate our meal and crashed out. It had been a long day.

Purne, far below us, burning green-gold in the sun

The line of chortens and prayer-flags at Purne

5

The Dancing Monk

'The Universe is sacred.
You cannot improve it.
If you try to change it you will ruin it.
If you try to hold it you will lose it.'
– Loa Tsu 'Tao Le Ching'

WE WERE NOW DUE an official rest day so we did some washing at the spring in a small bowl that Sultana lent us, hanging our clothes between the trees on the rope we had brought to see us across raging rivers and up craggy scrambles. It was the only time it was used.

We seemed to have become unofficial doctors to the whole area. Just before breakfast, the Ponyman emerged from the cook tent where he and Cookie slept, complaining of bad guts and a headache, rubbing his belly and pulling faces to show how bad he felt. I knew the feeling. It was a hangover, a result of his going on the rant last night in the local 'hotel', that is, the only house of any size in the village. According to Cookie he had drunk two bottles of chang.

Chang is a sort of rice beer and is found all over the Himalaya. Normally, it is only mildly alcoholic though some brews are stronger than others and at this height it can pack quite a punch. Dervla Murphy describes it as 'alcoholic porridge', which is pretty accurate. I didn't think that chang alone could have upset him so badly. I rather suspected that he'd been hitting the 'rakshi' – a sort of moonshine,

arak, or potheen made from distilled grain. That stuff is really serious and at this altitude a thimbleful will get you roaring.

'Half past eleven he come back,' said Cookie, the tone of his voice a mixture of offence and disgust since, as a Muslim, he never drank. 'I inside he outside. He want chow. I put him chow outside. I tell him chow outside. I not make him chow inside. He drink plenty chang. He sick now.'

How Cookie knew that it was half past eleven when he came back I don't know since Cookie had no watch and where the word 'chow' came from is another mystery. I'd always thought of it as a Chinese-American expression coined by the railroad builders. Perhaps the British Army brought it to India. We gave the Ponyman two sachets of antacid powder and half an hour later he was in the tent joking with Cookie. I wish I could recover from a hangover as quickly.

The first thing Pat had to do after breakfast was to treat a Zanskari granny with a baby on her back for a cut finger. The cut wasn't deep but it was wrapped in a filthy rag. We washed it, put some antiseptic cream on it and then a plaster.

In the early sun and dry air the clothes were already beginning to dry when, after breakfast, we left Cookie sorting out his kitchen and the Ponyman mending tackle and set off up the bank of the Tsarap river to visit the Phuktal Gompa, one of the highest and most inaccessible monasteries in the world.

In the Phuktal Gompa there is a stone that bears the inscription: 'Csomo de Koros lived here 1825–6. Pioneer of Tibetan Studies.'

De Koros was a very strange man. He was a young Hungarian student who had wandered across Asia to Ladakh alone. He changed his name while travelling to Sikander Beg (Gentleman Alexander) and came to Zangla, near Padum, where he stayed for nearly a year learning Tibetan and studying Buddhist texts. He was the first European to visit the gompa, spending the winter of 1825 at Phuktal and the plaque, which he carved himself, is still there to commemorate his visit.

The path to Phuktal goes from Purne along the narrow and stony Tsarap Gorge, climbing up cliff-faces and dodging round gullies. A strange collection of wind- and water-worn 'castles' of moraine clay, each crowned by a flat stone, lines the path, as far below the Tsarap, an unbelievable turquoise blue, rushes beneath sheer blood-red cliffs. The colours in the landscape are beyond anything I've ever seen before, even in the deserts of

Wind- and water-worn 'castles' of moraine clay

Arabia. The colour of the river here, which truly has to be seen to be believed, is said to be caused by all the copper salts in the rocks of the gorge. It was the exact colour of the copper sulphate solution we've all messed with in the school chemistry lab.

It was a beautiful morning, warm and sunny, and we strolled along knowing that we'd plenty of time and not far to go. A little way along the path we met a Frenchman running like a madman back towards Purne, cameras swinging and rucksack bumping. We stopped to let him past on the narrow track.

'How far is it to the Phuktal Gompa?' we asked.

'I go in one hour,' he panted, running backwards so that he could answer without stopping. 'I try to return in less.'

Why? was all I could think of.

I couldn't for the life of me see the point of it and his red face and heaving chest looked so out of place in such a quiet land. It reminded me of a story I'd once heard about an Englishwoman in the thirties who met the Dalai Lama. Running out of conversation and unable to appreciate the silence, she tried to impress him with the achievements of Western technology by telling him that a woman called Amy Johnson had just flown from England to Australia in nineteen days. The Dalai Lama paused and then asked, 'Why was she in such a hurry?'

The old monk and the small boy on the path beside the turquoise-coloured Tsarap River

The Frenchman vanished round a bend huffing and blowing, the sound of his footsteps soon drowned by the river, and we walked slowly on up the gorge. It grew narrower and steeper until, from time to time, we found ourselves treading a thin ledge with a thousand-foot cliff above and the bright blue river hundreds of feet below.

Along the trail we got caught on a twist in the path by a band of dzomo or dzo (surely only a mountain man can tell the difference). There's only one thing you can do in such circumstances and that is to get out of the way. Charging dzos stop for no one. We clung to the edge of the path as they thundered past. After them, whooping and calling, went the two men who were driving them down the gorge, grinning and waving to us and shouting 'Julay! Julay!' as they scurried by.

A little further on, as I stopped to take a photograph, an old monk and a small boy on his way to join the monastery overtook us. The boy had a lovely face, open, clear and bright, and they walked on ahead of us for much of the way hand in hand, each taking care of the other.

The path got quite hairy at times, becoming not much more than a narrow ledge scratched into the cliff face high above the river. It is funny but we were calmly walking paths here that, had they been in the Lake District or Scotland, would have had me a little shaky and

Pat crossing the gorge by the worst bridge we'd ever seen

Pat cursing and casting doubts on my intelligence and parentage.

Just before the Phuktal Gompa the gorge narrows, the Tsarap rushes through stone gates, and spanning the river is the worst bridge I have ever seen. It is suspended from two stone towers and is basically just a collection of cables. Two cables form a handrail and three below support what should be a walkway of woven hurdle but is often just three cables. There's a bit of brushwood every so often and a stone slab or two but most of the time you're treading the central wire and looking down on the thundering turquoise flood sixty or so feet below. If you fell you'd almost certainly die. Not from drowning but from being hurled against the massive rocks in the river. However, there was nothing we could do. We'd come all this way to see the gompa; the monk and the little boy had obviously gone across and I reasoned that if they could do it so could we.

I stepped on to the cable and inched carefully forwards. One problem was that as the bridge took my weight it seemed to spread out so that the handrails went lower and lower the further I went. By the middle of the bridge they were almost knee high and what stones and brushwood there were had largely given out so that I was walking solely on the central cable like a tightrope walker. Underneath, the waters swirled and rolled and, one foot after the other, I moved slowly along

The row of chortens leading to the gompa at Phuktal which is just visible on the cliffs ahead

the wire. Pat followed me very gingerly and very quietly and didn't curse me once. It must have been the proximity of the monastery.

From the bridge the path climbed steeply up the cliff to round a headland to give us our first view of the gompa. It is truly like the imagined Shangri-La, clinging to the cliff like a cluster of swallows' nests. The name Phuktal, or Phugtal as it is sometimes spelt, comes from the Zanskari word 'Phug', meaning cave, and the gompa is built into a massive cave in the cliff face, spilling out in a cascade of whitewashed cells and buildings. Above the terraced buildings, stretching across the mouth of the massive cave, was a line of prayer-flags streaming in the wind. Ravens turned and wheeled in the updraught while in a wind-battered tower on the cliff edge above the cave a lone tree grew like a symbol of life.

A row of white chortens lined the winding path to the gompa, like the approach to a medieval castle, and we followed it to a huge stone gate surmounted by a chorten that led us into a narrow earth-floored alleyway. We called out to see if anybody was about and almost immediately two smiling monks appeared from one of the little white cells. 'Julay! Julay!' they shouted.

'Julay! Julay!' we called back.

'Tchai?' they asked.

Our lack of common language didn't seem to make for any great problems in our communicating the basics. Yes, we nodded, and we followed them through the web of lanes, wooden ladders and stone steps that were the thoroughfares of the monastery complex. One of the monks disappeared to make some tea; the other, a young monk with close-cropped hair, showed us round the shrines of the monastery, four beautiful temples set well into the cool of the cave.

The monastery is said to have been founded by the saint Lama Chansen Cherap Zampo. Three holy men were living in the cave, which has a sacred spring of pure water at its heart. The lama suggested to the holy men that they should build a monastery in the

The gompa hanging on the cliff-face like swallows' nests

cave. The cave is too small, he was told. So the lama performed a miracle that caused the cave to grow to its present size.

In the shrines we saw statues of the Buddha in front of which lamps of yak-butter oil burned and small chalices of pure water shone and shimmered. Balls of yak butter were laid before the statues as offerings and round the necks of many of the statues was the thin white scarf that is a sign of respect universal to the Buddhist peoples of the Himalaya.

Lining the red-painted walls of one of the shrines were pigeonholes in which were kept the hundreds of sacred texts that comprised the gompa's library. These books are often kept in a higher position than the statues and when they are taken down the monk first of all places them upon his forehead to show that the words of the Buddha are higher than everything. The library books are printed in Tibet on woodblocks, approximately two foot long and five inches wide. They are unbound, the loose leaves being kept between two wooden boards and wrapped in elaborate silk cloths. I asked a monk to take out a book and he began chanting, continuing for many minutes until the end of the devotion, for to halt in the middle would have been sacrilegious.

We came out of one of the higher shrines and stood looking down at the cluster of buildings and narrow alleys. A sudden movement below caught my eye. It was a shaven-headed monk dancing on a flat roof. Totally unaware that we were watching, he danced wildly round in the sunlight, singing and jumping, flinging his robes in the air, spinning round and leaping. The young monk we were with pointed and chuckled. Then the dancing monk, realising that somebody was watching, turned round, waved, kicked his legs in the air and vanished into his cell.

In the chapels we saw some amazing 'thankas'. It is hard for us to imagine the importance or power of these paintings. Some are so powerful that they are exposed only on the holiest of holy days. Constantly surrounded as we are in the West by pictures on television, on hoardings, in magazines and in art galleries, it is almost impossible for us to understand the impact of the thankas on the minds of the local people. But imagine an almost pre-imagistic society, one where the vision takes in the mountains, the world, the rivers, the sky, the trees, animals, one's friends and family but little else. There is no art in the Himalaya other than religious art. Imagine then the impact of the gold statues of the Buddha and the thankas, the chants, the incense, the masks of the Mani Rimdu dances we saw later in Nepal. In *The Doors of Perception and Heaven and Hell* Aldous Huxley tried to visualise the effect of stained-glass windows and religious paintings on the non-imagistic peoples of medieval Chartres. He concluded that the

Detail of a thanka at the Phuktal gompa

result (as in Zanskar and Ladakh) can only have been one of heightened religious awareness, perhaps even of ecstasy.

All the chapels were built into the natural alcoves in the cave wall. In the main chapel, one statue of the Buddha was far up above us in the wall. Another, way back behind glass, shrouded, too terrible to see, was the manifestation 'Avalokiteshvara', the thousand-headed Buddha.

The monk led us from the gompa to a courtyard that looked out over monks' cells and then down to the river nine hundred feet below. In all, eighty monks live at Phuktal which is quite a lot for somewhere as isolated as this and indicates how important and how holy a place it is. Across the river was a small village with fields of ripening tsampa, the mainstay of the monks' diet. Tsampa is added to the salt and butter tea that they drink constantly. It has been reckoned that a monk will drink more than fifty cups of yak-butter tea a day. Occasionally there will be a feast, and rice, nuts and vegetables may be added to the diet but basically, for month after month, a monk will live on little other than tsampa and 'gur gur' tea, tea with salt and rancid yak-butter in it, called after the churn or gur gur that it is made in. It may be a plain diet but it seems to give them all that they need because they all looked healthy with strong, muscular arms.

We climbed a wooden ladder, crossed the roof of another cell and went up some steps to what I took to be a guest room: a plain, dark, smoke-filled room with a stove in the middle on which a big kettle was boiling. A little boy monk was poking some twigs into the stove and an old monk was chatting with him in between smiling at us and motioning us to sit down. We squatted on a few thin cushions against the wall and took tea from the same bald-headed monk who had danced on the roof below and who had just burst into the room laughing and joking.

After drinking the tea we made a small donation to the monastery and went out on to the roof of the building below. The monks took photos of us with our cameras and the bald monk took my snow goggles and put them on. Another wrapped Pat's scarf around his head like a bonnet which made the rest double up with laughter. We didn't speak a word of each other's languages beyond 'tea' (a corruption of tchai in any case) but we loved each other's company.

Buddhism seems such a happy religion. I can't imagine Benedictine monks dancing on a monastery roof because to me Christianity has always seemed such a po-faced religion, particularly in its more Calvinistic and Lutheran manifestations. Did Christ never sing, laugh, dance, get tipsy, perhaps even fall in love?

Buddhism is founded upon the life of the Buddha or 'enlightened one'. A historical being, Siddhartha Gotama was 'born of the Aryan

The bald monk in the borrowed snow goggles

race in the Kshatriya caste of the Sakya clan whose country lay along the south edge of Nepal.' His mother, Maya, gave birth to him in what is now the Lumbini Gardens, which lie just over the border from India in the Nepal Terai.

The story goes that he was the son of wealthy Rajah and, being brought up in a rich, powerful family, he was cushioned from the world and pampered in everything he desired. One day the young Prince, out riding in his chariot from the palace of his father, saw first an old man, then a sick man and finally a dead man. He asked the charioteer the meaning of what he had just seen. 'This comes to us all,' was the reply.

The Prince was so troubled that he went back to the palace and began the contemplations which compelled him to renounce all worldly goods and to set out on a life of meditation and travelling in an attempt to destroy the constant cravings of the Self, which be believed causes us all to be reborn time and again on to the wheel of life. After years of wandering and contemplation he achieved enlightenment while fasting and meditating under the Bodhi Tree, the sacred pipal tree, a sapling of which still grows on the same spot today.

Then, like Jesus Christ, the Buddha went through a period of ministry and preaching which resulted in the conversion of thousands to the faith. Eventually he died in India, his last words being 'Decay is inherent in all component things! Work out your own salvation with diligence.' He was cremated and his ashes were divided and put in ten 'stupas', or holy shrines, spread out amongst the places he had visited and ministered in. These places soon became sites of pilgrimage, something the Buddha himself would have deplored.

The dates of the Buddha's birth are controversial but most students of Buddhism have agreed that it is probable that he was born in 563 BC, left home at the age of twenty-nine and attained enlightenment at the age of thirty-five. When he died in 483 BC, he was eighty years old.

There are two forms of Buddhism practised in Zanskar, basically classified into the Red-Hat sect and the Yellow-Hat sect. The Yellow-Hat monks belong to the reformed Gelugpa sect of which the Dalai Lama is the head. In Zanskar all monasteries belong either to this one or to the Red-Hat Drukpa Kargyupa sect. You can tell which sect a village is part of by the colour of the bonnets worn by the little girls. At Kargia, for example, they wore yellow bonnets.

The Gelugpa sect follows the reformed teachings of a Buddhist saint, Tsong Khapa. The older Red-Hat sects, in particular the Tibetan Nyingmapa, believe not only in the classical Buddhist texts but also in the 'Revealed' texts that were found in certain holy caves by lamas. The Nyingmapa sect incorporates many of the beliefs of the ancient animistic Bon religion which once dominated the whole of Central Asia. The sects are in no way antagonistic to each other and often share chapels. One strange facet of Buddhism I found hard to understand is that a religion so tolerant and all-embracing should be peopled by a subworld of demons and monsters that are truly horrifying. It must be a hangover from the older Bon religions.

Buddhists believe in reincarnation, the transmigration of the soul into another earthly body after death. That is why a Buddhist will do all he can to avoid killing any living thing since he is then condemning it to be reborn as another, perhaps more lowly, animal. Life is seen as something to be endured and worked through; and in this life you must try to improve yourself by good work, by compassion and understanding and by love. By doing this you should achieve, in your next life, a higher plane of existence. The ultimate aim of the Buddhist is to reach, through the accumulation of merit in all these various lives, a state of Nirvana, or Nothingness, the fusion of one's soul with the Absolute which is what is meant by the attaining of enlightenment. In Buddhism there are no gods; thus Buddha was not a god but one of the Enlightened Ones and as such was assumed at death into Nirvana, leaving the tortuous world of life and becoming one with perfection.

Buddhism is a very humble religion in which compassion and understanding are constantly stressed. Western man's battle with nature is seen as mere foolishness and his preoccupation with wealth and possessions as something that is increasingly coming between an understanding of his own position in the world and himself. They view our attempts to possess the Earth as folly. Since we must all die – how can we take what we possess with us – how can we be said to really possess anything, even ourselves?

To achieve perfection takes a very long time. One of the common Buddhist thankas shows the wheel of life and Man's struggle through aeons of time to achieve perfection. The Buddha, when asked how long an aeon is, answered, 'Just as if, brother, there was a mighty mountain crag, four leagues in length breadth and height, without a crack or cranny, not hollowed out, one solid mass of rock, and a man should come at the end of every century and with a cloth of Benares, should once on each occasion stroke that rock; sooner, brother, would that mighty mountain crag be worn away by this method, sooner be used up, than the aeon.'

Every village is affiliated to a monastery and families that have two or more sons send all but the eldest to the monastery to be educated. There, although they do not become monks, their heads are shaven and they are dressed like little monks.

For those who take orders life changes and each monk becomes responsible for providing for himself. Often, his family provide him with some money or food: often, a field will be set aside for his upkeep. As well as his religious duties, in the monastery he will be expected to work in the fields or perhaps cook or, if he is specially gifted, he might work as a scribe.

Like universities, the monasteries give titles similar to degrees. They sit public cross-examinations. Questions are hurled at the monk and he is expected to answer them without hesitation. Sitting in a chair in the courtyard the questions are thrown at him in a ritual way. The adept monks rush towards him shouting 'KA-YE!' and making mock throwing gestures. The monk is expected to answer questions on doctrine or the various intricacies and names of the divinities.

Monks take vows of celibacy and other ones such as not to steal, not to drink alcohol and to say prayers daily. But monks are allowed to leave the monastery and re-enter it at will. Some monks leave to get married, never to return to the monastery. There is no stigma attached to this at all as there has been in Western Christian societies where, particularly in the Catholic church, leaving the priesthood, or becoming a 'spoilt priest' as it was known, was seen as a slur not just on the man but on his whole family.

*

It's quite a long walk up to the Phuktal Gompa, which, together with the very hairy bridge-crossing, makes me think that it will be a while before it gets spoilt. The whole valley from Purne to Phuktal has a very strange, almost mystical air about it. The only other place I've felt the same is on the Dingle Peninsula in the far West of Ireland where there are so many Celtic and Early Christian remains that the whole land rings with an odd sort of energy. I think it may also have something to do with the light because I've always had trouble taking photographs there too. There is a bright edge to the light, particularly in early spring, that produces dark black shadows and almost burns out the light tones. The same thing happens in Zanskar. The difference I suppose is that in Ireland you get the most wonderful sunsets, particularly from Slea Head with the Blaskets sculpted in the near distance. In Zanskar there are no sunsets. The high mountains cut out the dying sun and the sky above the valley darkens from blue to indigo with just the faintest wisp of ruby and yellow vapour streaking across the sky.

We said goodbye to the monks, crossed the terrifying bridge again and set off back towards Purne. It grew cold in the dark gorge and we were glad when, after a couple of hours of walking, we saw the barley fields of Purne ahead of us and the line of chortens with the stream flowing through. When we arrived at camp Cookie had made pokhoras for us which we ate luxuriously in the last hours of sunlight.

We were woken at six the next morning by the Ponyman singing his head off. Either he had kept off the chang the night before or else he was still drunk. We were packed and ready for off by just after eight and I asked Cookie what time we would get to Itchar.

'We not go Itchar,' he said. 'Ponyman say horses too tired.'

'Where are we making camp then?' I asked, puzzled because Itchar didn't look too far away at all on the map and according to the guide was quite interesting with a rope bridge and a gompa.

The Tsarap River meeting the Shingo River

'We go People Hotel,' muttered Cookie, obviously miffed at the Ponyman. We were to find out later why the Ponyman had gone for two short days' trek.

We left Purne, crossed the bridge between the cliffs and followed a stony narrow track, climbing up above the river. Looking down we could see quite clearly where the Tsarap River, bright turquoise, met the Shingo River, whose muddy-blue waters swirled into and finally overcame the smaller, less powerful tributary.

Just before Sule the path drops down into a stupendous gorge with overhanging cliffs and a bridge at the bottom that was little more than a boulder choke with stones laid on it. Crossing the bridge we met an Israeli girl trekking alone towards the Shingo La with no tent, no sleeping bag and no cold-weather gear. The Shingo La is a lot easier from the Zanskar Valley side in that you get eight or nine days' acclimatisation on the way through, but it's still no doddle and any day now the heavy snows would come. If she died, there would be nothing left of her but a simple pile of boulders and a longhand report in some little police hut in Darsha or Padum.

Slung across the path at intervals we saw flags and banners that were not the usual prayer-flags with the tiny Tibetan prayers printed on the thin and fading muslin but the sort of bunting you would normally associate with festivals. Below one village was a board with something scrawled on it and many more flags and banners. Soon all became clear when we saw coming towards us a pony-train carrying folding chairs and tables and behind the ponies a team of bureaucrats talking and laughing, all wearing little white beanie hats on their heads. We found later that they were on their way to inspect the gompa at Phuktal for what I can only think were taxation purposes. Unless they were going to mend the bridge. They passed us by like a medieval procession, smiling and waving, disappearing in a haze of dust and afternoon light.

The People Hotel turned out to be a rough and filthy stone shack on a pebble bank by the river side. The hotel owner sold us a cup of tchai, then huddled in conversation with the Ponyman round a dung fire. We put up the tent, which by now was looking as though it might not last out the trip. The rubber bands which the ingenious French had designed to hold inner tent to fly and pole had almost all snapped and we were keeping it up with a few bits of string and prayer. We fell asleep that night on our lumpy bed, our heads only a few feet from the river muttering on its way to the Indus.

6

Tea Soup and a Baby Horse

'As the dew is dried up by the morning sun, so are the sins of mankind by the sight of the Himalaya.'
— Anon

WITHOUT ANY REGRETS we left the People Hotel behind just after breakfast the next morning and headed down river. After an hour and a half we saw Itchar on the opposite bank, and, far below, the long rope-bridge across the river. The track now became very narrow and at times was a hardly discernible line across scree slopes that shot straight down into the river. On these it was a question of moving very quickly and as lightly as possible. Ponies are often lost at this point on the trail.

The sun was well up and the air in the narrow canyon was warm and pleasant. We were moving quite quickly, enjoying the day when, coming towards us, we saw something that really annoyed me. A trekker, wearing nothing but a little pair of running shorts and a pair of boots, was strolling along as though he was on the beach at Ibiza. In Zanskar, as in most of the Himalaya, it is considered immodest to expose the body. The only bare-legged men, apart from trekkers, that I saw in two and a half months in the Himalaya were the porters in Nepal amongst whom such dress is accepted since they are seen as lower caste anyway. Baring your legs, particularly if you are a woman, is seen as lewd by these people and they either laugh at you and look down on you or are offended. Bearing the upper part of the body is never done. In Nepal a woman would only expose her breasts

to feed a child, never at any other time. A man would bare his chest only while bathing in the river and then in privacy. The insensitivity and ignorance of some trekkers amazed me. Many Western women hikers upset locals by stripping to the waist to sunbathe or to wash in public. I normally believe in minding my own business and leaving other people to get on with their own lives but this bloke's attitude really irritated me. Yet when I told him that by walking round showing so much bare flesh he was insulting the local people, he just shrugged his shoulders, looked down his nose at me, mumbled something in German and strolled on.

The trail dropped down to river-level just as the valley opened out into a wide bowl surrounded by hills. For the first time in days we didn't feel hemmed in by the mountains and we could see ahead of us a range of dark-red hills that I thought lay about a day beyond Reru and were probably close to Padum where our trek would end.

It was quite a grind from the valley bottom to Reru, about a thousand feet of rough track and then a level trail leading to the village. The school had just closed for the day and thirty or so children of various shapes and sizes ran towards us shouting 'Meetree!', 'Skulpen!' and 'Bon Bon!' We managed to get through the village by telling the children 'No Bon Bon! No Meetree! No Skulpen!' and by

The village of Itchar perched on the opposite bank

A monk from the Muni gompa

The young monk who now has my harmonica

getting them to repeat it after us in a sort of chant which they thought was very funny. They insisted on having their photo taken.

From Reru we crossed the searing-hot plain heading for Muni, getting lost more than once in the fields of barley that seemed to stretch half-way across the plain. Ahead of us towered a range of peaks, the highest tipped with snow. Then, cresting a rise, to the right we saw the village of Muni with the gompa standing above it and to the left our camp with Cookie waving at us.

We pitched our tent next to the cook tent and almost immediately were surrounded by a group of monks from the gompa who had come along to see what we were doing. They watched while we put the tent up, insisted we take their photographs, then took photographs of each other. They hooted with laughter at the sight of each other in the camera's viewfinder.

A young monk from the village who was being educated at a Buddhist monastery in the south of India was home on holiday to see his family. He spoke very good English and was able to translate for us. As we stood round talking and laughing, a low horn sounded out across the valley and on the roof of the gompa we could see a monk blowing a brass horn that signalled the beginning of evening prayers.

'Puja! Puja!' said one of the monks and eagerly taking our hands he led us into the gompa where we sat to listen to the monks chanting.

They knelt, facing each other, in two lines. At the end of each line by the door were two horn players and a drummer. Each of the monks had a bell in one hand and a small sceptre, 'the 'dorje', in the other. The dorje is the symbol of the thunderbolt and together with the bell represents wisdom and method. The horns and drums played together and then the monks shook the bells and chanted ensemble. They were chanting 'sutras', 'discourses put into the mouth of Buddha'. The drums and horns began again followed by the bells and yet another sutra. The whole ceremony lasted, I suppose, an hour and a half, and all the time small boys ran round with huge teapots, filling the silver-rimmed wooden bowls that were the monks' teacups. As guests we were given some too. It was, of course, gur gur tea.

It tastes just as you would imagine, but it has an added smoky flavour. The thing to do is not to think of it as tea at all but as a soup or *bouillon*. The minute you think of it as tea you are finished and you can't drink another drop. Regard it as soup and you'll get on fine. Pat couldn't get on with it at all but I quite liked it, though not as much as the monks did, keeping the boys running about like bees round a bed of flowers all during the ceremony. There was a lot of talking and laughing during the ceremony too. As long as enough people were keeping the chant going it didn't seem to matter too much if a monk wanted to yawn or scratch himself or talk to his neighbour.

One of the little boys who was pouring the tea followed us across to the tent after puja. He noticed the harmonica that I had brought with me lying on the floor of the tent so I picked it up and played it for him. Fascinated, he stared open-mouthed as I played some blues runs. He looked around to see if anyone was looking and pulled a copper bracelet from under his tunic.

'Want buy?' he asked.

'No thank you,' I said.

He pointed at the mouth-organ. 'How much?' he asked.

'Nothing,' I replied.

I gave it him and he ran off grinning. Pat reckoned he'd get thrown out of the monastery for playing it in the middle of the night and disturbing the monks' beauty sleep.

While walking round the village we met the Head Lama, a friendly smiling man carrying an armful of sacred scrolls and bells. He'd been

The head lama from the Muni gompa

Small boys ran round with huge teapots

down to Reru to carry out a special blessing ceremony in the home of one of the villagers, something I was to come across later on in Nepal on the way back from Everest.

Before bed we spent an hour playing doctor to one of the older monks who had several large mouth ulcers on his gum and inside his lower lip. We gave him some TCP mouth pastilles and got the young monk to translate that he was to suck one slowly three times a day.

The Copper Pot mystery had been solved that evening at Muni. As we arrived, a crowd of people had gathered round the Copper Pot Man laughing and cheering. The pot was a replacement for the village chang pot that had collapsed after years of use. No wonder he'd gone to so much trouble to carry it all the way here. The village had been dry for two months! The following night they were going to kill a goat and hold a big party to celebrate the arrival of the chang pot. Chang is a very important element of life in both Zanskar and Ladakh. 'Good chang makes good religion', is an old Zanskari proverb. Most festivals and feast days, weddings and homecomings are accompanied by feasting and chang.

The next morning we were also to discover why the Ponyman had wanted to give the ponies a rest at the People Hotel. When we climbed out of the tent the first thing Cookie did as he fetched the morning brew was to shout, 'Horse has baby in night!' and he pointed to the large grey mare that had carried the heaviest load from Darsha. I had thought she might have been in foal but, since my knowledge of horses is second only to my ability to break-dance, I had pushed the idea to the back of my mind.

'He had child up dere,' said Cookie, 'in jungle', the jungle being the bare shrubs and scrubby bushes above the camp. Blood still on her hocks, the mare munched contentedly on a bag of tsampa while the weak legged foal tottered against her side and looked at the new world about it, neighing faintly. The mare and foal were to be left at Muni village to be looked after by one of the farmers until the Ponyman

The mare and her new-born foal

returned from Padum and the foal was strong enough to travel over the Shingo La.

The lama with the mouth ulcer reappeared and asked for more medicine. Apparently the soluble aspirin we had given him with the pastilles had taken away some of the pain. I gave him two more and, saying goodbye to the little boy monk and the young one from Southern India, we set off, waving to them all. Dropping down from the rock bluff to the riverside, we followed the river for most of the morning until, shortly before noon, we came to the Burdun Gompa suspended high on a bluff three hundred feet above the water. We climbed the track towards the gompa where there was not a living soul about except for a fierce dog on the end of a chain that yapped and snarled furiously as we entered through a low door, and went up into the courtyard.

A young novice monk appeared to show us round. All the other twenty-five Bhutan lama monks were out working in the fields. This was a Red-Hat monastery and its position above the river would, I imagined, have made it unassailable. Not so. It had been ransacked on more than one occasion, the last being in 1947 when, during the troubles that followed Partition, Pakistani troops stole all the jewel-studded and gold divinities that had once been the set pieces of the massive altar.

At one side of the courtyard is a small stone hut housing an enormous brass-covered prayer-wheel some six or seven feet high and said to be one of the biggest in the Buddhist world. The wheel is full of hundreds of paper prayer-scrolls and took some effort to turn. At each turn a bell rang to signal a revolution of the wheel. People have said erroneously that prayer-wheels are turned so that the person gets the merit from all the prayers inside. This is not so. The wheel is an important symbol in the Buddhist world and turning it is symbolic itself, reminding the person who turns it of the passage of time. The merit obtained from turning prayer-wheels, either huge ones like the one at Burdun or smaller personal hand-held wheels, is obtained because of the physical act, in the same way that genuflecting before an altar or making the sign of the cross is practised as a physical act of devotion.

The interior of the gompa was very interesting. As well as some beautiful thankas it also contained a huge drum and many ceremonial masks. There was a back room we were not allowed to see where the devil masks are kept, many with the third eye, that are used in a form of witchcraft and sorcery, said to be much practised by the Red Hats. I don't know whether it was this or the abandoned air of the gompa that made me think that the Yellow Hat Muni Gompa was a much warmer and friendlier place.

We braved the dog once again (the dogs of Burdun, by the way, are mentioned in the letters and journals of almost every Westerner who has visited this region since the earliest days) and left the gompa

behind. It is even more impressive when seen from river level than it is when seen from the plain.

The track widened out after a while to become what is obviously the beginnings of a road and seemed to point to the end of our trek and the beginning of some sort of civilisation. Sure enough a few miles on we met a symbol of Indian road construction: six men squatting in the dust, one holding a screwdriver, having a top-level meeting over a broken pneumatic drill.

We walked on in the sun, the track eventually becoming a dusty, rough 'jeepable' road, until at last the great bowl of the plain opened up in front of us and we meandered into Padum, the capital of Zanskar, our trek over.

There are said by officials to be twenty-eight villages in Zanskar and the population is in the order of twelve thousand. Yet this small number of people have their own language (dialect really), their own traditions and their own history.

The high altitude, the extreme cold and the ultra violet rays are said to decrease male fertility. Polyandry is practised in Zanskar as a means of keeping the population stable. The same thing occurs to some extent in Ladakh where there is quite high mortality amongst infants. Children of polyandrous triples call their eldest father big daddy and the youngest small daddy. Nobody seems to mind who the genetic father is and in terms of the culture it doesn't matter.

Children are shown a tremendous amount of love. Men and women take turns looking after the children and it was very warming to see men with babies in their arms singing to them. Quite a contrast with what we were to see later in Muslim Kargil.

Zanskari women play a role equal to that of the men and this attitude goes hand in hand with the general respect for the individual within society. It is largely a result of the Buddhist teaching and the lack of any real hierarchy in Zanskar. The kings of Zanskar are kings

The gompa at Burdun, a Red-Hat monastery

in name only, they are hardly richer than the poorest of their subjects.

The people are all independent landowners so there is no serfdom. When an elder son marries he immediately inherits the family land and house. The father and mother go to live in a little house and the son takes over the management of the land. This has ensured that the land has not been split into small unsustainable units. Other brothers become monks or marry into families without sons. There are, of course, casualties of a sort in that there may be unmarried men or women who find no partner and who don't enter a monastery, but everyone is cared for and helps on the land. The intelligence and wisdom of the people is fostered by their struggle with the climate and the land and by their religion. Perhaps no other religion but Buddhism could survive in these barren heights. Trade and travel have long been an important part of the culture, and looking at life here it's possible to understand a little of what life must have been like in medieval Europe. Then, if you wanted lace from Bruges or cutlery from Sheffield, you would have had to send for it, perhaps hundreds of miles, and the journey would have had to be made on foot or with ponies. A man would have been dispatched with the money and after weeks or months would have returned with the goods. Trade routes were established and along them the traders and monks moved during the open months. The Copper Pot Man had travelled a huge distance with the pot for his village. He had been glad to join our party not because he feared the journey but because Zanskaris generally enjoy company. It's a way of hearing news, of meeting people, of telling old stories and learning new ones.

Zanskar was an independent Kingdom for nearly a thousand years until the Hindu Rajahs conquered it in 1836. Then, in 1846, the British signed the Treaty of Lahore with the Hindu ruler of the kingdom, and at a pen-stroke they got control of Jammu and Kashmir and the kingdoms of Baltistan, Ladakh and Zanskar. With a word on a strip of paper the nine-hundred-year-old independence of Zanskar was ended.

Unhindered by the British, Zanskar went back to its old way of life. Too remote to justify interference, too poor to be worth developing, it has stayed much as it was until the recent past.

Military problems on the Indo-Pakistan border and possible mineral finds are threatening Zanskar from the north. Already a road is being driven in as far as Burdun Gompa. It's hard to see a road ever being built over the Shingo La but perhaps much the same thing was said about the Rohtang and Zoji passes, where the Indian military road builders have pushed the West into the mountains.

So far the mineral wealth of Zanskar has not been exploited because of the religious belief that to plunder the earth is evil. This, together with a lack of monetary sense, has made the attitude of the Himalaya Buddhists to metals, even precious metals like gold, incomprehensible to most Westerners who see the earth merely as something to develop and use. There are many gold mines in Tibet and many gold- and copper-bearing rivers in Zanskar but the local population has done very little to take advantage of them. The working of metal is considered sinful and the blacksmiths of Zanskar belong to a low caste. The same is true in the Khumbu Valley. The caste system is not as strong as that of the Hindus but they do consider butchers, blacksmiths and even musicians as separate communities and custom does not allow intermarriage. I hope that the world-wide usage of fibre optics will eventually cut the need for copper down to a minimum, for only if this happens has Zanskar any real hope of surviving.

I don't for a minute believe that Zanskar will be able to hold back the tide of the West any more than any other emergent or newly discovered nation has been able to. But there is an element of harmony in life in Zanskar that it would be tragic to destroy. Do we really want to supplant happiness with greed and misery?

The Zanskaris you see working the fields don't look on it as work. It may be something they have to do to live but so is breathing. They

The fertile plain on the approach to Padum

only work as long as the job takes. Men and women work together, there is singing and laughing and, when the work is done, people sit and do nothing. In these mountains there is not the Protestant work ethic that drives us on to buy goods and time. The crazy thing is that in order to afford time-saving devices, we give up forty hours or more of our lives each week, forty-eight weeks of the year. If we want heat we have to buy it from the electricity or coal board, or petrol from the gasoline company or food from the supermarket.

We cannot exist without a massive superstructure. The Zanskari or Ladakhi with his horse or yak and his few fields and four walls has no nervous breakdown; stock exchange crashes don't worry him: he has no mortgage debts or hire-purchase or insurance. There is nobody behind him brown-nosing his way up the company ladder, dagger in hand. Murder, suicide and theft are unknown to him and in his old age he will be cared for by his children. We have cities full of crazies with Kalashnikovs, lonely bag people, muggers and criminals. Who are we to look down on the 'peasants' of the Himalaya?

Forty-five is the usual retirement age in Zanskar. This follows the Tibetan system so condemned by the Chinese who claimed that the Tibetans had no respect for their old. This is in fact totally untrue since the Tibetans, Zanskaris and Ladakhis have tremendous respect for their old people whom they cherish as a valuable part of the community. The custom of government by the young stems from the first ruler of Tibet, Songsten Gampo, whose armies settled Zanskar in the seventh century. He saw as a soldier that his young men had energy and imagination and that if he didn't allow them the reins of power then society would stagnate and there would also be a very real danger of dissent and revolt.

In the West old men and women often cling grudgingly and greedily to their authority and power. In some cases, old age does bring wisdom and many decisions are rightly based on the advice of the old, but I think it is generally healthier for them to be made by men and women who are going to be around long enough to see the results instead of their being made by people who are never going to see the long-term effects of their bungling.

In Padum there is a 'hotel' of sorts, run by a spiv-like character who seems to attract the 'freaks' of the world. We took a room for the night at a satellite hotel of his down the Kargil road, one mile from town and close by the camp site. The hotel was unfinished: four rough concrete walls and two iron beds with plastic mesh mattresses was all our room had to offer, but since we had to be up early in the morning to catch a lorry ride to Kargil it didn't really matter all that much.

We saw Cookie, and he set about organising a truck for five o'clock the following morning for Kargil. We had a wash in a stream that was driving six tsampa mills, all with grindstones churning round and each with a handful of small children seated by it, feeding the barley into the hopper and filling the bags beneath. The mills are communal to the village.

We walked into town after dumping our gear and wandered round the market buying provisions for the lorry ride the next day. It is normally a two-day journey to Kargil across terrible roads but the driver Cookie had fixed a ride with was going to try and make it in one day.

We bought apples, biscuits and chocolate from little wooden cabins that are the shops of Padum and went to eat in the 'hotel'.

The dining-room was bare and simple with long tables and plain wooden chairs. The food was hot and good and after the unvaried diet of the last two weeks it was very tasty. We feasted on egg biriyani, tomato soup and chapattis.

At our table was a motley assortment of Westerners and trekkers. Three Dutch hippies, man, wife and teenage daughter, and a fat, bearded German who smoked and wheezed and pontificated. I wasn't having much luck with the Germans on this trip, I decided. The

Dutch family, looking like a throwback from the sixties, were going to Darsha via the Shingo La.

'It's going to be really peaceful, man,' he told me. 'No hassles, stop in the villages, sleep in the gompas, man, no problem, yeah?' They had no tent and no experience. They were not going to take a ponyman, a guide or a cook. 'Too much hassle, man! We want to be like totally free – you know.' They were taking a bag of tsampa to last the trek and were expecting to get food at the villages along the way.

'But for two days either side of the Shingo La there are no villages,' I said helpfully.

'That's OK, man, we'll work it out.'

Later that night I saw him trying to haggle over the price of a bag of apples at a small stall with a very bored and very unimpressed Balti merchant to whom the sight of aged hippies with suicidal tendencies was obviously nothing new. The German, on the other hand, was a real Captain Oates. I don't think I've ever met anybody so arrogant and ill informed.

We paid for our meal and set off for our hotel, wandering down the road under a star filled sky, to sleep on our rickety beds in a room full of dust, a bulb with a glowing dull-red filament and a corner full of rubbish.

My journal for that night, written while shivering in my sleeping bag on a thin, plastic-mesh mattress, reads:

> Ze German 'I like to trek in my own vay mit der sleepink beg unter der stars. I go long vay Padum to Phurtal Gompa. No ponies I am beckpecking all day this way to trek.'

7

The Jalabi Bends to Leh

'Truly this is something that does have to be seen to be believed, and that once seen must be constantly yearned for when left behind, becoming as incurable a fever of the spirit as of the body.'
— Dervla Murphy

WE WOKE UP in our concrete cell at about 3.15 a.m. and watched a thumbnail paring of moon gleaming over the plain.

It was still dark by the time we had dressed and dragged our kit out by the side of the road. A lone figure passed us in the dark going towards Padum; he waved and called 'Julay! Julay!' and disappeared into the darkness. We cleaned our teeth by the roadside by the light of our Petzl headtorches and sat on the bags waiting for the lorry. Cookie arrived shortly before five o'clock and with him was the Ponyman who had come to say goodbye. Relationships in the hills are short-lived but intense and we said goodbye to each other with genuine affection. He had led us across the Shingo La and seen us through raging rivers and dusty trails and now he was making his way back to his home village. We would probably never see him again. We shook hands, shouted many Julays and he walked off towards his horses and gear. Cookie had the tents and cooking equipment that were going on the lorry with us as far as Kargil, then he was going west to Srinagar while we headed east over the Fotu La to Leh in Ladakh.

We waited and waited, the dawn rose over the plain and no truck came. We were beginning to get a little worried and Cookie had started to walk towards Padum to see what had happened when a cloud of dust in the pink morning light told us the lorry was on its way.

Nobody who has ever travelled in a Punjabi lorry will ever forget it. They are regularly blowing up, falling over sheer drops and running into each other. Their drivers, in the main, are wild-eyed Sikhs and Baltis sustained, so it is said, on their incredibly long journeys (often up to four days of constant driving) by a combination of fanaticism, drink and in some cases drugs. Every truck driver has a mate who is responsible for loading people and goods on and off, filling the tank and the radiator, cleaning the windscreen at every opportunity (even while driving) and lighting the driver's cigarettes whether straight tobacco or 'wacky backy'. The lorries travel all over India carrying every kind of produce. Initially from the Punjab, such a large pool of trucks has been built up that they have also become the official carriers for the whole of the continent. Thousands are employed by the government to keep the army and the road builders supplied and these trucks are painted proudly with their names and licence details. Many of them also carry slogans such as 'King of the Road' and 'Wind of Shiva'. They are almost universally painted a bright orange with gold and turquoise trimmings and their cabs are often fringed with silver and gold tassles. A cross between a gypsy caravan and a cattle truck, they roar down the road belching thick, black, choking, noxious smoke, a result of the poor quality fuel oil they use.

We had managed to bribe the driver to let us sit in the cab since the roads are so dusty that riding on top is even more of a nightmare. Pat and I and a French couple called Jean Marc and Catherine who were going to Kargil too, crammed in the cab with Cookie, the driver and his mate – seven of us stuck like pickles in a jar. If you shifted your left buttock to ease the numbness caused by the constant juddering, someone else's right buttock immediately took up the space.

We rumbled beyond the last fields of Padum, the plain flying away behind us, stopping every so often to pick up every Tom, Dick and Tsering who was waving at the side of the road. At one time I counted eighteen people on the back of the lorry, together with all sorts of kit and equipment. Some of them were going all the way to Kargil. Others were only going as far as the Rangdum Gompa.

The road was unsurfaced and full of potholes that caused the driver to swerve and curse. His assistant, who chain-smoked, filled the cab with nicotine and scratched his balls enthusiastically and constantly. Opening the window would have meant covering us all with dust so we had to sit it out, lurching across fords and bumping over landfalls, getting secondary lung cancer, and totally losing any feeling in our bums.

We left behind the last of the villages of the plain, as the men and women were going to work in the fields and the children were walking to school, and climbed slowly up a seemingly never-ending series of hairpin bends that left you one moment looking out over nothing but space back towards Padum and the next looking at a windscreen filled with sky where the occasional raven was the only sign that we hadn't in fact driven into infinity.

I soon became convinced that the driver was some sort of genius because not only did he keep us on the road but he managed to coax

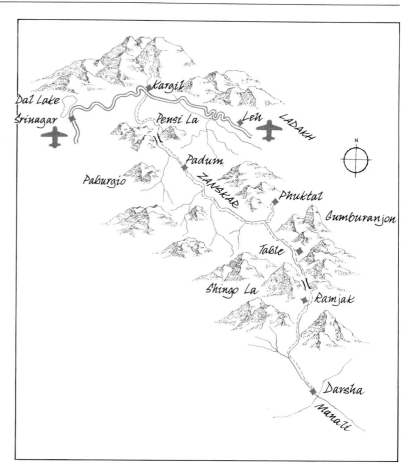

the fully-loaded and overheating lorry forward up the pass, slamming the clutch in and whipping the stick through the gears, his co-pilot clambering on the bonnet to wipe the dust off the windscreen, holding

The magnificent Pensi La Glacier, a sweeping river of ice

on with one hand and scratching his balls with the other and intermittently rubbing the glass.

Just below the summit of the Pensi La, the lorry stopped and everyone got off to take a leak and stretch their legs. The people on the top, including two Israelis who had laughed at us and told us we would see nothing of the landscape from the cab, were so covered in dust they looked like snowmen and spent most of the halt coughing and beating themselves and trying to clean their cameras enough to take a picture because across the col from us was the magnificent Pensi La Glacier, a sweeping river of ice between commanding peaks.

The road down from the pass was even worse than the road up, potholed, washed away and partly blocked by landslides. Every so often we were forced to stop by oncoming trucks whose drivers would skim past, waving and shouting greetings in Punjabi or Balti because we were now getting close to the end of Buddhist Zanskar. Then at last we dropped swiftly down to the great plain where we could see, in the far distance, on a perfect conical hill, the Rangdum Gompa. Behind it was the most amazing range of hills with multi-coloured and layered stone, twisted so that they looked like layers of toffee, folded and kinked, more like caramel whips than mountains.

We stopped at a 'hotel' in a small village below the gompa for dhal and rice. Later I wandered out on to the plain. A line of chortens led the eye to the distant hills. A way off, a horseman was galloping, driving a herd of ponies before him, leaving a cloud of dust a hundred feet high in his train. In the far distance, lorries crawled towards the Pensi La and squatting in the dust near the chortens was an old man mending a boot, watched closely by his two little grandsons.

On a wall behind him curds were drying, laid out in curled strips on stone slabs. A crow flapped down, stole a strip and flapped away again. While I was looking at the crow a young Indian in his twenties approached me and we got talking. He was a bureaucrat employed by the government to check on the food supply at the gompa which in

this case really means the food supply for the whole village. He spends one month here at harvest time to check on any shortfall which is then made up by the government. In winter on this plain the temperature drops to minus forty degrees Fahrenheit and the wind-chill factor must be incredible.

From Rangdum we moved on, grinding our way out of Zanskar and, as light failed, we passed under the twin peaks of Nun and Kun, (23,400 and 23,250 feet respectively) into the Islamic Suru Valley. The chortens gave way to the black flags of Islam and the faces of the people changed from the Mongol features of Zanskar to those of the Afghanistani or Baltistani Eurasian type. We could have been in Saudi.

The harvest was being gathered in and as we passed everybody was at work carrying, stacking and winnowing, but here there were no smiles, only the watchful eyes of the women looking over their veils. The people here are Baltis who came from Baltistan in the Western Himalaya. They were originally Buddhists but converted to Islam fairly recently.

We stopped to have our papers checked at a police post in a miserable-looking village called Pakarchik, which also gave us an opportunity to stretch our legs and buy some dried apricots and tins of fruit juice from a dusty store that sold everything from sickles to eggs.

After passport control night fell and, as thick darkness cloaked the land, we entered Kargil, said to be the most flea-ridden place in the Himalaya. Our stuff was dumped off the lorry. Cookie went off in search of a ride to Srinagar and we said goodbye, knowing we'd meet him again there.

A youth approached out of the black night.
'Hotel?'
'We got hotel. Hotel Siachen.'
'I carry bag ten rupees.'
'Two bag ten rupees.'

The multicoloured hills, looking like caramel whips, behind the Rangdum gompa which sits on top of the small hill in the centre

'No, one bag. I not strong.'

So I gave him the heaviest bag of all to carry for ten rupees and we carried the rest ourselves for no rupees.

We arrived at the hotel, a pleasant enough two-storeyed place built largely of wood around a courtyard, checked in and for the first time in weeks we were able to have a shower. Lukewarm though it was, it was wonderful.

It was ten-thirty, but one or two places were still open so we ate at a small Tibetan eating house which had an enormous menu of which almost everything was off; 'Not tonight sorr'' the manager/waiter/chef/owner apologised. So we had what was 'on', 'mo mos' (meat-filled dumplings) and rice. And so to bed after sixteen hours on a bum-numbing lorry. Let the fleas, I thought, do their worst.

There were in fact no fleas in the Siachen Hotel, or if there were it was their day off because we slept like unmolested logs. Breakfast the next day was soggy cornflakes and plastic cow followed by a walk round Kargil. The Muslims of Kargil are noted for their extreme orthodoxy. They follow the Shiite form of Islam, the same that is followed in Iran. They frown on all forms of entertainment and alcohol and women are conspicuously absent from the streets.

Everywhere we looked there were posters of the Ayatollah with denunciations of the Americans and all other imperialist Western dogs underneath. It didn't make you feel very welcome. It felt a very glum town and we certainly didn't feel that we were respected there. I had found, travelling in Arabia, that the Islamic attitude to Westerners, which sees us as unclean and almost sub-human, can be depressing, not to say threatening. It wasn't quite as heavy here as in Sharjah or Bahrain but it was still heavy enough. Pat didn't like it at all. As a woman she felt, dressed modestly as she was by European standards, the object of a lot of unwelcome stares. She was quite happy to stay in the hotel room while I went out wandering round the town.

A shoemender and his child in Kargil

There were many open stalls selling everything from jewellery to kerosene stoves. A butcher was cutting up a goat on the sidewalk while further along a man was indulging in what I suppose you'd call 'Pollymancy'. He had a parakeet on a little table that pulled envelopes from a bundle with various fortunes typed out inside them. You paid one rupee for the privilege. My horoscope told me: '*You ar in luck,with health and well meet the parson of your desire to be happiness for long time. Watch for your eye trouble.*' Since my eyesight has always been lousy following an attack of measles when I was ten years old and since I had no intention of going to bed with a vicar I didn't feel that the future held much new or exciting for me.

Back at the hotel I met Mr Bhutt who was supposed to be looking after us on our trip to Leh. I'm afraid I didn't like Mr Bhutt very much, and I'm also afraid that I formed my opinion on first sight. I've always believed that, like animals, we have a sixth sense, an ability to feel atmospheres and sense the true nature of people but that, unlike animals, we spend a great deal of time and effort telling ourselves that our senses are wrong. They are rarely wrong. I've often met people that I haven't liked on first meeting, gone out of my way to give them the benefit of the doubt and then found some time later that my first impression was right. It isn't infallible but I do think we don't give ourselves enough credit for being intuitively smart.

Mr Bhutt looked sly and shifty. He told us that the jeep for Leh would be ready for us at 7 am , so at 6.30 am we were up and ready and waiting.

A jeep eventually came about 7.50 am.

'He been for petrol,' explained Mr Bhutt unconvincingly. We loaded the jeep with gear and Mr Bhutt indicated with waving arms that we should get into the back.

'We'll sit in front,' I said, looking at the windowless rear of the vehicle. 'We'll see nothing in the back.'

Mr Bhutt looked at the front seat. There was room for Pat and me beside the driver but not for three of us.

'No room,' he said,

'Plenty room,' I said, reminding Mr Bhutt who was paying, and we got in the front with the driver, leaving Mr Bhutt and two strangers who had somehow attached themselves to our party to squash up in the back. With much muttering in the rear we set off. The jeep sounded very unhealthy, as though it was firing on three cylinders and badly at that. We climbed away from Kargil on what a sign told us was The Beacon Highway and after a quarter of a mile or so stopped at a petrol station.

'I thought he filled up before he came, Mr Bhutt?'

Mr Bhutt murmured something about no power and then we watched as a man came out from a hut scratching his balls and began hand-cranking a pump to fill a Punjabi truck. The pump we were waiting at had no handle. There was it seems only one handle on the whole petrol station. Somebody sent for another handle. A quarter of an hour later it arrived, brought by another man scratching his balls. We fastened the handle on the pump, cranked it, filled the tank, stuck some of our gear on top of the jeep and set off again.

After an hour it became apparent that we'd won the village idiot with the rubber-band driven jeep. We passed Mulbekh with its great stone statue of the Maitreya, or 'future' Buddha, carved into the solid rock and headed away from the valley towards the Namika La. Within a few minutes Pat was screaming at the driver when, approaching the pass, he overtook on blind bends with sheer drops looming beneath and took similarly exposed corners far too fast.

The driver took no notice, skidding out of the way of oncoming lorries at the very last minute, charging at bends as though he wanted to see if they were in fact a mirage, and then only just cornering in time. On one occasion both offside wheels were inches from a five hundred foot drop. I was just about to say something when Pat exploded.

It was all to do with having children and family back home that we might possibly want to see again and it also had a lot to do with the driver's parentage and his possible performance in an IQ test. Mr Bhutt translated for her and the driver slowed down enough to make the rest of the ride bearable, if not comfortable.

My journal for that night reads:

> The military road from Kargil to Leh is a miracle of modern road building. It also gives you the screaming abdabs, especially when you're being driven by a Muslim fanatic called Hassan who believes the fate of us all is in the hands of Allah, and if he dies he goes straight to heaven. With all due respect to Allah – I'd rather be in the hands of a careful driver.

We stopped for tchai at a place called Bodhkharbu where there were two tchai houses and a huge military camp where dozens of soldiers

The landscape approaching the Fotu La is like the surface of the moon

were bathing and doing their laundry under a stop tap at the side of the road. The driver and one of the strangers in the back were busy throwing water on the engine to cool it down. The engine seemed to overheat every fifteen miles or so particularly when there was a hill, which was most of the time. This meant that so far we'd stopped seven times. A can was kept in the back and whenever we came to a halt one of the men ran down to the river or to a mountain stream and then threw water on the engine.

From the tea house we headed towards the Fotu La, the highest point on the highway, 13,479 feet above sea level. The Fotu La is also perhaps the crowning point of the whole of the Beacon Highway.

Beacon is the code name of the particular section of the paramilitary organisation that builds and maintains the border roads. The whole highway is an incredible piece of engineering and all along it from Sonamarg to Leh are plaques commemorating workers who died building the road.

It is a dangerous road and deaths occur on it every year. There had been a terrible tragedy on the Zoji La (a name, by the way, that seemed to frighten everybody) the previous winter when a convoy of buses and lorries had been forced to stop on the pass while returning to Srinagar at the end of the season and just before the snows that block the pass normally came. The snows, however, came early and the people in the buses and lorries were trapped for days as first blizzards howled and then avalanches and landslides built up. It is difficult to get any real information. Government figures put the deaths at three hundred but local sources say there were many more than that, some putting it as high as two thousand, claiming that over three hundred lorries and buses were lost with people hit by landslides and avalanches or frozen to death when they tried to escape.

The road was built for the military and the fact that it is strategically important can be seen by the great number of lorries and military vehicles that roll along it night and day. Trouble on India's borders with both Pakistan and China has meant that the entire road from Srinagar to Leh has to be maintained constantly. All along the side of the road are signs painted by the road builders carrying such legends as:

> If you drive like hell you may get there; Drive carefree, Beacon toils night and day; Liquor and driving make a catastrophic cocktail; My curves are gorgeous but watch out for my bends.

Ladakh was at one time covered in lakes and rivers and the great upheavals that formed this present-day arid land must have been incredible for the lakes are all drained away now and the landscape approaching the Fotu La is like the surface of the moon. Only in Death Valley in America have I seen such barren and lifeless landscape as well as one so terrifyingly beautiful. The colours of the rocks are banded in golds, pinks, purples, greens and pale ochres and the moonscape stretches away towards the high mountains.

As we fell below the pass the road straightened for a while before curving sharply to the left, giving an incredible view of a cluster of houses surmounted by a gompa perched way across the valley to our right. This was Lamayuru, surely one of the most dramatically perched villages in the world. There we stopped to eat lunch at a roadside tea house and wandered into the gompa, while the driver threw more water on his engine.

The gompa has become very commercial since it is on what is now fast becoming a tourist route from Srinagar to Leh. The monks were quite unfriendly, charged for admission to every part of the monastery and even tried to charge for each photograph I took. The gompa was very impressive, though, and looking from its many windows down to the valley far below across a moonscape of dust and rock, you got some idea of what life must be like there in winter – cold and grim.

From Lamayuru the road dropped 3,600 feet in about one mile, twisting and coiling back on itself in a series of curves that the drivers of the Punjabi lorries call the Jalabi Bends, after the curled Indian sweetmeat with its orange twirls and whorls. Our driver, whose memory span was less than three hours, immediately saw the Jalabi Bends as a wonderful excuse to show his mates in the back how close to oblivion he could get without actually getting there. I did manage to remind him in fairly strong language that we were hoping to reach Leh in a jeep and not in a box. He slowed down a bit.

We were still stopping every twenty minutes to throw water on the engine. At one village, at the bottom of the bends, I talked for a bit to the village schoolmaster, a gentle soft-spoken man who taught forty pupils of all ages everything from mathematics to English.

The villages along the Indus banks running like a string of oases from the foot of the Fotu La to Leh, are famous for their dried apricots and at a late afternoon tea stop we bought a bag of them to eat in the jeep. Because we had lost so much time there was no knowing when we would arrive in Leh. We seemed to be either tearing through the dust at breakneck speed or standing stationary at the roadside throwing water on the engine.

Dusk came. On a narrow stretch of the road we passed an overturned Punjabi lorry, the driver and his mate sitting on top, cross legged, waiting for help. They had been there ten days. A few miles further on we saw, down below us in the river, an oil tanker, its driver dead in the cab while from the banks men were trying to get a line across to recover the body from the swollen waters. In all, before dusk turned into night, we saw six crashed, overturned or burnt-out trucks. The most common cause of all the accidents is brake failure caused by poor maintenance and overheating.

Night fell and we were still twenty or thirty miles from Leh. The whole of the plain around Leh is one vast military camp. Trucks are constantly on the move by night, their lights threading the vast plain like glow-worms. The nightmare turned into a double nightmare as convoy after convoy of trucks roared towards us through the dark.

A detail of the pitted surface of the rocks

The jeep's headlights were as feeble as its engine and when the lights of the lorries were beamed full on us we were blinded. Our driver, who had been driving for twelve hours, was now becoming even more erratic.

We climbed a narrow road on to the plateau that lies before Leh and, after half an hour or so, we saw the lights of the town ahead of us. After that we got lost only once in an army camp and drove round the town six times before finding the guest house where we were to stay, a few hundred yards from the town centre. We said goodbye to the driver (never was parting less sweet sorrow), checked into the guest house, showered, ate and crashed out.

All night I dreamed that I was driving my own car over the Jalabi Bends looking for a pub in Manchester called the Old House At Home. I couldn't understand in my dream why none of the Punjabi truck drivers I asked knew where it was.

The line of chortens in the moonscape of dust and rocks below the Lamayuru gompa

The Jalabi Bends, so-named after the curled and twirled Indian sweetmeat

8

Land of the Broken Moon

'The stupa echoes the mountains and the mountains are stupas also. Everything in this world is linked.'
–Andrew Harvey, *A Journey in Ladakh*

LADAKH, LIKE ZANSKAR, WAS an independent kingdom and, though it now comes under the jurisdiction of Jammu and Kashmir, it still has a Queen who lives in the Royal Palace at Stok and who has a seat in the Indian Parliament. Until recently Ladakh was closed to the West, largely for security reasons. Now, though there are still many places where Westerners are prohibited, it has been open to trekkers and travellers since 1974.

Ladakh has a number of names; amongst the nicest are 'The Land of Smiles', because of the friendliness of the people and 'The Land of the Broken Moon', the derivation of which still eludes me.

It is more often called 'Little Tibet' because, although it was never ruled by Tibet, it has long been a part of the Tibetan religious and cultural world. After the Chinese invasion of Tibet, the destruction of almost all its monasteries and the flight of the Dalai Lama into India, it is in Ladakh more than anywhere in the Himalaya that you will see the last remnants of this culture.

Geographically and climatically Ladakh bears more than a fleeting resemblance to Tibet. Like Tibet most of Ladakh is high plateau country (all over twelve thousand feet) and like Tibet it is a climate of extremes and aridity; less rain falls here than in the Sahara Desert. Hot dry summers are followed by freezing winters. During the summer the heat of the day is quickly followed by cool nights for there is no cloud cover to keep the warmth in. In winter, though, even on the coldest days the sun is warm and it is said to be possible for a man to sit with his head in the sun and his feet in the shade and suffer from frost-bite and sunstroke at the same time. The first European to cross the Zoji La was an illiterate Portuguese merchant called Diogo d'Almeida who came there in 1600 or 1602 and in fact thought he was in China.

The next visitors were Jesuit missionaries *en route* to their Tibetan missions. It is amazing to think that Christian missions existed in Tibet from 1630 until 1745. After the Jesuits no other European came this way until the arrival of William Moorcroft, the first English veterinary surgeon, who came over the Zoji La and entered Ladakh via Kargil in 1820. He came to Ladakh on his way to Central Asia to search for horses for the East India Company's stud farm of which he was the superintendent. He and his companion George Trebeck were kept at Leh for two years waiting for permission to travel north into Yarkand. He never got permission and it is doubtful that any Westerner would get permission to travel there today because it would mean crossing the Indo-Chinese border, which of course is closed.

The Royal Palace at Leh, eight storeys high and now in a sad and sorry state

The Zanskar mountains beyond Leh, from the Royal Palace

Breakfast at the hotel the next morning was eggs and Ladakhi bread, which was excellent, a sort of round naan-type bread. After breakfast we went to the Indian airline office with Mr Bhutt to try and get our flights confirmed from Leh to Srinagar. Leh Airport has a lot of problems. It is surrounded by the highest hills in the world and this creates strange weather patterns. The airport is often closed because of low cloud, and when planes do take off they have to climb very quickly to clear the peaks. Consequently flights are often delayed or cancelled and people have been known to be stranded there for days. There was a chance that we could have our flights confirmed at the airline office. It was closed. 'Open 10 a.m.' said a notice on the door. So we walked round the market and looked at the stalls and the people buying and selling. It looks as though Ladakhis are largely being ousted from business in Leh by an influx of Kashmiris, quick to cash in on a recent tourist boom that has meant that Leh now has two small hotels. Most of the stuff on the stalls was described as 'genuine' antiques by the stall holders but looked like reproductions to me. There were prayer-wheels, pipes, cymbals and horns from gompas and many elaborate Tibetan locks and keys.

Leh is simply beautiful. Overlooking the town stands the old Royal Palace, eight storeys high and until the Kashmiri invasions of the last century inhabited by the Royal Family. It is now in a sad and sorry state and if anywhere qualifies for a world cultural grant for renovation then surely this is it. Built at the same time as the Potola of Lhasa in Tibet and every bit as impressive, it stands high above the town on a rocky bluff, prayer-flags fluttering all around. It is tragic to think that, unless something is done, the whole building will tumble down through neglect.

Walking through the maze of streets and alleyways that led to the Palace we passed women with children on their backs, old ladies in gaggles, old men with prayer-wheels squatting and chatting to each other and, framed in his doorway, a man shaving in the morning sun.

We slowly wound our way up to the Palace and walked in through the open gates, stepping from the hot sun into the cool dark. Many of the rooms in the Palace are closed off because they are too dangerous and ceilings, floors and walls are all caving in. But the chapel was open, under the care of a young Ladakhi who showed us round. A huge statue of the Buddha stands on the altar while all round the room are thankas and parasols, gongs and bowls of butter oil. The chapel is still in use and outside on one of the flat roofs, we met a young boy monk and an older lama who were living there. But like the rest of the Palace, it is badly in need of some loving care. We walked down from the Palace and back through the old town to our hotel. Mr Bhutt still hadn't managed to sort out our plane tickets.

'What happens if there is no plane?' I asked.

'Maybe you take lorry,' he suggested.

The thought of a day's journey back to Kargil in a lorry followed by another day's journey through notorious Dras and over the Zoji La was just too much.

'If there is no plane then we go by taxi.'

'Taxi?' asked Mr Bhutt, even more open-mouthed than usual.

'Yes, taxi. The plane fare we save by not flying will more than cover the taxi fare.'

Mr Bhutt looked glum and muttered something about buses and jeeps and then went off to do his thing, whatever that was, while we hired a cab to visit the gompas of Phyang and Spitok.

At Phyang, about fifteen miles from Leh, we met a young monk who spoke good English and showed us round. The monks were at midday 'puja' when we arrived so we sat in the cool of the gompa and watched the ceremony. Like the prayers at Muni Gompa these were accompanied by bells and trumpets. The music is quite strange to our Western ears and seems to have a limited tonal range yet I dare say if you studied it you would find it has great subtlety and complexity.

The noises the monks made during puja were remarkable. The first

A silver-rimmed human cranium at the Phyang gompa

hundred years old, where, amongst other things, we were shown some ancient ritual masks and a collection of Mongol armour and weaponry. Most interesting of all was a silver-rimmed, human cranium used by the monks as a chang bowl; a real *memento mori*, to drink from Death itself.

From Phyang we travelled back along the highway to Spitok where the gompa stands high on a conical hill just at the end of the airport runway close to Leh. The monks of Spitok were building a new temple, so that getting into the courtyard was a bit like wading through a building site. Once inside a little boy asked for twenty-six rupees. Most gompas charge a small admission fee that goes towards the upkeep of the monastery. In this way some monasteries like Thikse have been able to renew paintings and build wonderful new statues. But normally prices are between five and ten rupees per person. Twenty-six rupees made the admission to Spitok thirteen rupees each, which made it the most expensive gompa yet. I didn't mind the price at all. I just wondered why it cost more than the others.

'Ah,' said an old monk, 'new gompa many rupees. Rupees no, gompa no.' Which is fair enough.

The little boy monk took us by the hand and led us past a line of prayer-wheels mounted in the wall into a sort of anteroom where a lama sat meditating and counting his beads. 'Sit,' he said indicating the floor and so we did. Another monk came in with some gur gur tea and I drank a cup while Pat very politely managed to say no.

Another older monk, who we later discovered was the head lama, came in and sat at tea with us. The two older monks teased the boy monk continuously and playfully. They got him to read his lessons for them, threatening him jokingly when he made a mistake. There was a great amount of love and affection between the monks, especially between the older monks and the little boy. Later, the boy took us to see the room that the Dalai Lama used when he came to Leh and then onto the roof of the building where a young monk was blowing the

kind of chant consisted mainly of a sort of throat clearing and sighing. This was followed by a series of low booming noises interspersed with what sounded like random finger clicks and claps. The music was fierce and loud and echoed round the gompa, woven from the sounds of bells, big drums, hand drums, cymbals and trumpets. It all seemed to be improvised but it also seemed as though everybody knew what they were doing.

After puja we crossed the courtyard to a chapel in which there was a statue of the thousand-headed Avalokiteshvara and another protector divinity which is so fearsome to look at that it is only uncovered on one day in the year and that only after days of fasting and meditation.

Before leaving, we went to the monastery museum, said to be nine

The conch-blower at Spitok gompa

horn for afternoon puja. The horn was a beautiful conch wrapped with brass and silver and studded with turquoise.

Again there was a distinct difference in the atmosphere of Spitok and Phyang monasteries and I put this down to the fact that the monks at the Spitok gompa were Yellow-Hat while those at Phyang were Red-Hat; I'd felt the same difference between Muni and Burdun gompas. It's hard to explain but it just seemed that the Yellow-Hat monks of Spitok were much friendlier and more open.

Far below the monastery the last of the barley harvest was being gathered and a lone woman walked across the mown fields. A group of musicians were playing in one of the meadows to celebrate the end of harvest and before them villagers were singing and dancing. Every

lane and byway was full of men and women, boys and girls carrying bundles of barley to the winnowing floors. As they walked they chanted some round or refrain that reached up from the plains to the eyrie of the horn-blower.

From the journal:

> I really enjoy meeting the monks and feel very at ease with them. We sat for some time saying nothing at all and yet it didn't seem to matter at all. It's not a directly spiritual thing, more that they are not clamouring for your appreciation, attention, respect, or whatever and so you don't feel that you have to do so either. The mask or masque of words can be left well behind. Instead you just sit there sensing what is all around you, the peace, the quiet and the feeling of years of religious worship soaked into the gompa walls.

From Spitok we drove back to Leh where Mr Bhutt, Tickoo's secret agent, had been a failure. There was still no confirmation of our seats on the flight. We were numbers twelve and thirteen on the waiting list which didn't give us much of a chance at all. There were 'buffer' days written into the whole journey but the main problem was that if we did fail to get a flight we'd have a nightmarish two days' journey along the dangerous Leh-Srinagar highway shortly before it was to be closed by the army and also near the time when the blizzard wiped out so many people the year before. Mr Bhutt merely shrugged his shoulders and sucked his teeth saying, 'It's very difficult.'

We spent the evening walking round Leh as the lights came on, looking at the stalls and the markets. There is a diesel generator on the outskirts of town and in many of the shops a single bulb burnt over piles of dried fruits, nuts, shoes and new electrical goods, transistor radios, cassette players and watches. The last were for the thousands of soldiers that were stationed here to strengthen the border defences. They were in town in their dozens, walking hand in hand round the streets, looking in the shops and listening to Hindi music blaring out of the shop that sells and mends transistors. The town was fascinating:

all darkness and lamplit shops; oases of yellow light; goods piled high; smells; shouting; dark figures in native costume moving from pool to pool of light; a cow with its head stuck in an overturned dustbin; Punjabi lorries looming out of the dark covered in Christmas tree fairy lights; men roasting peas on hot sand in big woks; men cooking kebabs over charcoal and a boy on the market's edge selling dhal and frittered potato cakes.

Before dawn the next morning I went again to Spitok Gompa; there was something about the place that fascinated me. Climbing the stairs I met again the head lama in the courtyard. He came across and threw his arms round me as though I'd been away for years and we just stood there holding each other and laughing for several minutes.

He went in to prepare for puja and I climbed on to the roof where two horn-blowers wearing high fringed caps were preparing to sound their long brass horns. They took deep breaths, their cheeks rounded, and a primitive low sound like nothing I have ever heard before rolled sustenato across the valley to the mountains. The music of the gompas of Ladakh is not so much music as pure elemental sound that strikes to the root of things.

Tsering Mutup ('Tsering' means 'long life'), the driver who had brought me to the gompa, had a sister who lived close by who still wore the local dress and after puja we went down the monastery steps to the village below. His sister's was a typical Leh house with the stove at the heart of the room and rows of shining copper and brass pots all round the walls. Tsering's brother-in-law was rocking a little baby on his knee while his sister was bent over the stove making gur gur tea which we all drank constantly. Tsering's sister was wearing the 'perak' a long head-dress made from hundreds of turquoise beads reaching from the forehead down between the shoulder blades. They are family heirlooms and are passed down from mother to daughter. The one we were looking at was hundreds of years old. There is a theory that the head-dress originated in the serpent costume worn by dancers in the old Bon religious ceremonies that Buddhism largely supplanted here.

The place was spotlessly clean and neat and while we were drinking tea another girl came in and took the baby, the biggest, fattest six-month-old baby I had ever seen. Mutup nursed him and then I too held him for a while. All this meant, of course, that I was late back to see the airport station manager to get our tickets confirmed. He had again disappeared. 'He back two, two fifteen, two thirty maybe,' said the man with the broom, sweeping the office which was now closed for lunch. There was nothing to be done so we set off down the road to the gompas of Shey and Thikse.

As we drove past the Tibetan refugee camp I could see clouds above the plateau and a high wind was rolling in from Zanskar, and I wondered if that meant snow on the Shingo La. If it did then the Dutch hippies were in serious trouble and a lot of badly prepared people were going to come unstuck.

Thikse, like most of the other Ladakhi monasteries is on a rocky bluff. It's more than five hundred years old and houses more than a hundred Yellow-Hat monks, which makes it the biggest monastery in Ladakh. When we had climbed the winding way to the gompa it seemed deserted. Then from nowhere a monk appeared with the usual book of tickets and quickly took twenty rupees off us. The main temple seemed unremarkable to me, though there is an anteroom with a beautiful statue of Buddha standing on a dim, barely lit altar.

We went on to a new shrine where there is a forty-two-feet-high statue of the Maitreya Buddha. It looks very new and garish compared to the older Buddhas; perhaps it will mellow with age. It certainly seems as though religion in Ladakh is in a healthy state: another gompa is being built somewhere in Leh by a Japanese designer. Spitok has a new gompa and there's the Future Buddha of Thikse which took three years to build and house – they were all paid for by tourist rupees. A young monk was seated cross-legged before the new statue,

Horn-blowers at Spitok make music, a low primitive sound that rolled across the valley to the mountains

The golden Buddha at Shey, the largest in Ladakh

massive and beautiful old Buddha. It is the largest golden Buddha in Ladakh, standing thirty-six feet high and is worked out of gold and gilded sheets of copper. It was built in the mid-seventeenth century and, like the Thikse Buddha, has powerful staring eyes. The most important event in the building of such a Buddha is the moment when the eyes are painted in. Until then the Buddha cannot see. But no artist or monk would dare to look the Buddha in the eye so the artist paints the eyes by standing with his back to the statue and painting over his shoulder using, I can only assume, a mirror.

A vast prayer-wheel outside was still spinning on its smooth well-oiled axle, a bell clanging with every turn. The noise of the wind howling through the gompa and prayer-flags mingling with the sound of the bell sounded so wild and lonely. Shey also has an oracle held in even higher regard than the oracle of Thikse, revered as a living god who has achieved the highest level of existence.

Back in Leh I went with Mr Bhutt to the airport station manager's house, trying to beard the liar in his den. 'He in office,' said his housekeeper, but he wasn't there either.

That night we went for a drink in the Ibex bar, a sort of watering hole for the younger Ladakhi business people and intellectuals. Talking to them was very enlightening. To a man they turned out to be pro-Ladakhi and anti-Indian.

'We will not change. India invaded us in 1835. We're still Ladakhis. We may change outside, wear jeans and Western dress, but inside we are as always. We do not count the Red-Hats, they are not really religious. It is the Yellow-Hats who are the most religious. The two most spiritual places in Ladakh are Risdong and Alchi.'

We also met India's most decorated soldier, a jolly Raj-type colonel. He was the officer in overall charge of the airport. I explained our problem to him over a drink. He sipped his gin and tonic and smiled.

'There will be no problem. I think you will fly tomorrow.'

chanting from an open book. He carried on singing while we stood there, finished his devotions and then, jumping up, asked our names. When we told him he turned them into a kind of chant and skipped around us scat-singing. I wondered if there wasn't a bottle of chang hidden somewhere under his robes.

Thikse is remarkable in that it is one of the few places in Ladakh to have an oracle. An old man in the village who is supposed to have supernatural powers passes into a trance and in Tibetan, a language he has no knowledge of whatsoever, condemns wrongdoers, prophesies the future and is able to cure both men and animals using a small tube with which he 'sucks' diseases from the bodies of the sick.

At Shey the wind moaned eerily round the gompa which houses a

9

By the Zoji La to Dal Lake

'The road we had ascended was in many places rather trying to the nerves, being very steep, and sometimes consisting merely of a platform of brushwood attached to the face of the precipice.'
— Sir Thomas Forsyth, 1871

THE NEXT MORNING dawned and we were still without any flight confirmation. We went out to the airport just in case. There I managed to buy another ticket, already confirmed, for a fictitious Dutch woman called Desiree de Jong which meant that Pat was all right unless they looked at her passport. She said that she'd never felt less like a Desiree in her life. After bribing one of the airline officials I managed to get my ticket confirmed so that we both now had boarding-cards and our luggage was on the trolley which meant that if the plane flew we would be on it. The spectre of the Zoji La seemed to fade into that land of terrible shadows whence come all fears, nightmares and dry-mouthed guilts.

We went through security and waited in the departure lounge. A group of high-ranking Indian army officials sporting bushy moustaches and pukka uniforms were looking out at the sky.

'No problem. We will surely fly today.'

We waited, and waited, and waited, and the plane didn't come. Rumour flew. She's left Srinagar. She's left Delhi. One hour, maybe half an hour.

'Char and biskewits,' said a voice and some men brought round tea and those terrible sweet Indian biscuits. Something like a hundred people ate the biscuits and drank the sweetened tea staring glumly at a cloudless sky. And still nothing came.

The hearsay and misinformation that are so much a part of Indian life flew round the airport. The plane has left. The plane hasn't left. The plane has engine trouble at Srinagar. The plane has left Srinagar. The plane hasn't even left Delhi yet. Someone heard a plane engine.

'Here she is!' shouted one of the important army types who must have been at least a lieutenant-colonel. All our noses pressed on the window. A little military plane touched down and taxied to a halt. Everybody looked at the lieutenant-colonel who had just failed his aircraft spotter's badge. He stared ahead and tugged at his moustache.

Then the clouds rolled in. There is a problem peculiar to Leh Airport. There is no radar on the station which means that planes have to fly in and out on visual fixes. If there is low cloud then there is no window and the planes can neither land nor take off. As a pilot once remarked looking at a sea of cloud that contained several peaks at over twenty thousand feet, 'Some of them clouds got rocks in 'em.'

Miraculously the cloud broke and rolled back over the bowl of hills.

'There must be no problem,' said the lieutenant-colonel. 'Surely we must fly.'

The luggage lay on the runway. More hours passed. It was now past noon. Still nothing happened. The Indian airline officials had all gone behind closed doors presumably to elect a new Pope. No one told us anything. We stood in limbo in the lounge.

Suddenly one of the baggage handlers in a pair of grubby overalls stuck his head round the door.

'Flight cancelled!' he shouted. Then he ran for it.

Through the window we could see all the airline employees and officials, and anybody else who thought they might be lynched, jumping on their bicycles, fumbling with their car locks or simply walking away as fast as they could. We had been deserted.

No reason was given, no explanation, no directions, no apologies. It was basically, 'Right you lot, you can bugger off now, it's your problem.'

While standing around in the airport waiting to be 'dropped in the brown and nasty' as the Australians would have put it, we had been talking to a rangy young Scots journalist called Robin who looked like an anorexic Jungle Jim. He was dressed in a photographer's jacket with hundreds of pockets, a pair of slacks, a jungle hat and a pair of desert boots. His luggage seemed to consist of a large Bellingham camera-bag and a small camera-bag. Everything about him was khaki except his nose which was red and his scarf which was long and white. He was the archetypal world traveller. At first I had taken him to be a photographer and thought that we could at least while the hours away boring each other with f-stops, focal lengths and *contre-jours*. But the large camera-bag contained nothing more than a few shirts, a couple of changes of underwear, a bottle of malt whisky and a bottle of Malvern water. The small camera-bag contained an idiot-proof automatic camera and a book on moral philosophy. This was all the luggage he had. I stood back in awe and admiration.

He was working for a travel trade paper doing a bit on all-India travel. He was to become our travelling companion.

We had also during the course of the last few days got to know a young Ladakhi who was running a trekking agency in Leh and a Kashmiri, Mr Habibi, who had travelled to Leh from Srinagar with a party of Western craftspeople who were here to look at the Tibetan weavers out at the refugee camp and at the local crafts of Leh. There were something like thirteen Western craftspeople of various ages stranded by the flight cancellation. Very kindly they let us throw in our lot with then and both Mr Habibi and the young Ladakhi set about organising a convoy of taxis, because we now had no other alternative than to cross the dreaded Zoji La.

Suddenly, from nowhere, Mr Bhutt appeared. 'You lift me to Kargil?' he insinuated, his oily face fixed in a grin. What I said to him was all to do with sex and travel.

While arrangements for the convoy were being finalised we went to the Dreamland Restaurant for a dinner of mo mos and vegetables. There I examined Robin's coat of many pockets. It had everything a traveller could desire, each in its own little compartment; a whistle, a knife, fork and spoon, a stick of lip salve, a Swiss army knife, a tiny but powerful torch, his passport and travel documents and a folding silver goblet for his whisky.

We loaded the vehicles and set off in convoy. In our car were Robin, Pat, Mr Habibi, our driver Ishmael and me.

As we left Leh behind, people were carrying barley in from the fields and children on their way home from school stopped to look at the line of taxis roaring out of town.

We drove at some speed up on to the plateau above Leh and on towards Kargil. Ahead of us was a line of lorries and buses; behind us another line of lorries and buses; coming towards us, yet another line of lorries and buses.

Ishmael proved a fast but careful driver, weaving skilfully in and

Women gathering the barley stooks outside Leh

smoke and flames coming from nose. Howls of pain coming from mouth. Entrance of waiter with fire extinguisher. Father's nose saved from cremation.

The surrealism of the situation gradually dawned on me. Here we were being driven by a man called Ishmael through the dark Ladakhi night, Punjabi lorries threatening to wipe us off the face of creation at any minute, drinking fine malt whisky and listening to the life story of a Scots Münchhausen.

We made it over the Fotu La and the Namika La and arrived in Kargil shortly before midnight. We were the first of the convoy to arrive and we checked into a small, neat hotel where smiling people somehow managed to conjure up a meal for twenty at that time of the night. We had a night-cap of Robin's excellent malt and crashed out. That was the easy bit over, the Zoji La was for the morrow.

We were awake at four a.m. and in the moving cars half an hour later. I could sense that Mr Habibi was worried about the Zoji La. A well to do Kashmiri businessman in his fifties, shrewd and intelligent, he was nevertheless very tense and very insistent that we should quickly get going. The reasoning behind this was that we were to try and avoid any congestion at Dras where there was an army checkpoint and where there could often be delays of several hours. Leaving at this time, he felt, would get us there just before the checkpoint opened. The Zoji La is only open from mid-May to mid-October and the state of the road varies depending upon the severity of the previous winter. The mid-October date is also arbitrary since it was very early in October the year before that the snows came and wiped out all those people. We were now right at the end of September. Snow had been known to come that early. Travel over the Zoji La is normally restricted to daytime, with only army convoys allowed to travel at night. As we left Kargil the dawn crept slowly over the hills and we saw the sunrise just tipping the high peaks of the Suru Valley. Everything was going fine and we were looking forward to being in

out of the traffic until, by the time we reached the foot of the Fotu La, we were out of the congestion and climbing smoothly. It was then that Robin decided to calm our nerves by telling us a string of very funny stories. One told how his father set his nose on fire. In synopsis it was basically this:

Family on holiday in Italy. Father takes Robin and mother out for meal. At end of meal Father decides liqueur good idea. Father orders Zambuca. Father does not know that Zambuca is served 'au flambé'. Father has inordinately hairy nostrils, 'two tunnels filled with brushwood', expounds Robin graphically. Father picks up Zambuca, looks at it, admires colour, etc. Does not see flames. Sniffs it to savour bouquet. Father's nose on fire. Collapse of staid Scotsman backwards,

Srinagar for lunch. Then our stomachs sank when we reached the army checkpoint of Dras and we saw miles and miles of stationary Punjabi lorries ahead of us.

In my journal I wrote as we travelled:

> Everywhere there are thick, choking black clouds of smoke from the lorries. There must be somewhere around five hundred of them here. There are many buses and something like fifty or so cars and jeeps.
>
> Sun is tipping the snow-gloved peaks, shark's teeth fringing the valley. Hundreds of jogging Sikhs from the nearby army camp fill the road.
>
> It's terrifying to see the Punjabi drivers lighting fires under their diesel tanks to thaw out the frozen fuel. They are flinging bundles of burning rags soaked in kerosene beneath them. Orange flames, black oily smoke, flames spilling on the tarmac running like water. A bundle of waste and rags is burning under the diesel tank of a lorry with four petrol tankers either side. If that goes up we're all finished.

The roadblock to end all roadblocks at Dras

> All along the road men are cooking and washing. This is obviously an everyday event. We wait. Nothing happens. It is 7 a.m. The checkpoint normally opens at 6 a.m.

Dras is the second coldest inhabited place outside Siberia. All traffic halts here because the Zoji La is so narrow and deadly that traffic is one way. Two control posts, one at Dras, the other at Sonamarg, keep in telephone contact and traffic is sent westwards in the morning and eastwards in the afternoon. The road is at times less than six miles from the cease-fire line with Pakistan. It is a bleak and unremittingly dreary place, famous for being hot and shelterless in summer and for its fantastic snowfalls in winter. The local dialect spoken here is called 'Hambabs' which means 'snowfall'. So these are the Snowfall People. It's no wonder it's such a dismal place.

The journal continues:

> By 9.30 a.m. we've heard:
> 1. That 700 lorries have left Srinagar.
> 2. That 300 have left but they're trying to stop half at another check-point to let us through.
>
> Rumoured we might be leaving Dras by 1 p.m. If not then by 6 p.m. Around us is a Rag Tag and Bobtail army of badly dressed slovenly looking soldiers. There don't seem to be any commands. They walk around, slouching, scratching their balls and spitting. No system. No news. The universal squat and wait. Now the rumours are:
> 1. There has been a landslide on the pass.
> 2. Two lorries have been in collision and the army are trying to clear it.
>
> According to another rumour we're being held up because the Indians and Pakistanis are fighting over a glacier in Ladakh the name of which nobody can remember. It's a good way of tying the Sikhs up. You recruit all the fit young fighting men you can get your hands on from the Punjab and send them up here to fight the Pakistanis. That way you take out several thousand potential extremists.
>
> More than one person said today that the border skirmishes are the Indian government's way of maintaining support amongst the population. It's the old philosophy of making a common enemy to unite a population

and divert attention from the real political issues: while they're up here fighting over a glacier at 20,000 feet the rest of India is starving.

I heard a rumour that more than eight hundred soldiers die each year in border incidents and that 1,800 Punjabi lorries as well as hundreds of army lorries are tied up along this border road maintaining the supply line.

Two Sikh soldiers walk past holding hands.

10.30 a.m. They've taken the sign down that says convoys leave here 6 a.m. for Sonamarg, in case we lynch them. A soldier goes past with a dirty Sten gun slung across his shoulder and wanders towards the tea stall scratching his balls. A Sikh in a red turban lets the occasional army lorry through. And nothing happens.

A colonel arrives in a jeep, beside him a major. They smile and when I ask them what is happening they just say courteously, 'There must be some problem. Perhaps a lorry has overturned. There is no radio contact you see, once they have left Sonamarg,' and they smile politely and move away. I am asking too many questions.

Hot, dry and dusty. By the roadside, stalls have appeared selling nuts, dried apricots and packets of those terrible biscuits. Sikhs are cooking meals in their cabs, squatting by their lorries peeling vegetables.

Some of the Sikhs use this as an opportunity to clean up their lorries of which they are fiercely proud. They fill jerry cans with water at the river and begin washing their trucks. The orange paintwork and chrome begins to gleam in the sun. Wheels and tyres are washed.

I see a man asleep, bare feet planted on the windscreen. And nothing happens. People repeatedly wander up to the control post and ask the military what is happening. But nothing happens. No news. The only military type who doesn't scratch his balls is the colonel. He probably has somebody to do it for him. Still nothing happens.

By 1 a.m. a truck comes through – everybody cheers. Then for another hour nothing happens. Rumours – there is a landslide. Many people have been killed – there is no landslide but a lorry has burst into flames – there is no burning lorry, it is four lorries that have fallen over the side and landed on the road below blocking it. There is a fiction factory somewhere at the front of this queue where rumours are being created.

Some of Mr Habibi's craftspeople in the other cars are elderly and are feeling sick from the heat. There is no shelter here and just one stinking, fly-thick, hole-in-the-floor thunderbox toilet for hundreds of people.

We might go at eight o'clock tonight. We might go at seven o'clock.

A convoy of eastbound trucks began to pour through belching smoke and shouting rumours from their cabs.

'How many behind you?' we asked.

'Hundreds,' one of them said. 'Five,' said another. 'Twenty said yet another. For nearly two hours the convoy rolled through. They must have been stuck all night on the pass. It was obvious that something important was going on.

In the end it was 6.30 p.m., after more than twelve hours of waiting, that we got away. Without saying anything a red-turbaned Sikh corporal with a wonderful white handlebar moustache lifted the barrier and hundreds of lorry drivers ran to their cabs. Imagine if you can a Le Mans start involving hundreds of lorries, cars and buses and you get some idea what happened. Luckily Ishmael was quickly off the mark and we were in the first dozen or so cars to roar under the barrier and, eating the dust of the cars in front, we motored towards the Zoji La.

The sun was falling behind the mountains as we raced along the valley bottom. At one point there was a cleft in the near hills that brought into sight a beautiful snowcapped peak, perfectly cone shaped. By the time we began our climb up to the Zoji La darkness had spread over the mountains and we could see little other than the road ahead and the dust wake of the vehicle in front. Occasionally, stranded at the side of the track with barely enough room for another vehicle to pass, were Punjabi lorries burnt out, wrecked or broken down, their drivers squatting in the dust before fires they had lit to ward off the cold of the night.

We only just squeezed round them, our headlights shooting out into empty space. The worst thing was that there was nothing below us but hundreds of feet of blackness.

In the dark a few miles from the summit was a roadside hoarding put up by the Beacon workers saying, 'You can now have a dialogue with God. Beacon wishes you a safe journey.'

Sunrise over Dal Lake, a great bowl of burning gold; fish eagles circle overhead before dropping down to catch their breakfast

The Zoji La has claimed, so it is said, 1,000 lives in one year. All we see ahead of us is dust and a sort of ledge on which we're driving. The dust is so bad that from time to time we have to stop completely and wait for it to clear. Although it's night and you can't see it, nevertheless you're conscious of not so much a yawning void as a grinning void just at the side of you. The road is basically a one-vehicle-wide ledge, above a 10,685 feet deep empty space that would kill you if you tried to drive on it. Mr Habibi, who has kept up an interesting conversation so far in amongst Robin's banter, has been silent for the last hour, his fingers gripping the dashboard. Even Robin has gone quiet. He claims he's conserving energy.

Pat is either asleep or catatonic, it's hard to tell which. I'm trying to pretend I'm not worried by writing in my journal by the light of my headlamp. It's only after a while that I realise I've got the book upside down and am writing from the back forwards.

Eventually we cleared the pass and spiralled down the other side towards Sonamarg. It was almost as bad going down since the cars were travelling bumper to bumper at what seemed reckless speeds through a constant fog of dust. Below the pass the road surface improved and at eleven o'clock we rolled into Sonamarg where we stopped for tchai and pokhoras. We prised Mr Habibi's fingers free and helped him across the road.

Sonamarg was a blaze of lights after the black pass and all the roadside stalls were serving food and drink. We were well ahead of most of the other traffic so we had a quiet half hour before jumping back into the car for the last leg of the journey.

From Sonamarg to Srinagar is fifty-two miles and that night all of them seemed to be full of shepherds and their sheep. They were moving down from the high pastures because any day now the first snows of winter could come. The road flattened out and, once past the sheep, we sped through the darkness of Srinagar, driving over the causeway and arriving at the lakeside in the early hours.

My last memory of that night is of being rowed gently across the lake to our houseboat under a sky full of stars and an old boatman singing softly to himself. After the rattling, banging, dust and frustration of the last two days it was as though we'd suddenly been transported into some kind of watery heaven.

I got up at six o'clock the next morning to watch the sunrise over Dal Lake; fishermen were casting their nets from small boats, looking in the far distance like scratches on a burnished brass mirror as the sun caught the whole lake and turned it into one great bowl of burning gold cupped by the shadowy hills. Across the water a muezzin was calling the holy to prayer from the tower of the mosque as the sun tipped the far peaks. Kingfishers swooped and kites circled over the lake before dropping down to catch small fish from the water.

A boat passed slowly before me, a bird perched expectantly on the boom, eyeing the fisherman's catch. A 'shikara' or water-taxi, crossed the lake to a far houseboat, a veiled woman seated under the canopy. Across the still water a woman paddled a boatful of water-weed that would be used as fertiliser on one of the floating gardens.

After a while the city came to life and the noise of honking taxis and an airliner grumbling overhead for Delhi brought me back to the twentieth century.

The Dal Lake was for long a summer retreat of the Moghul emperors who built many beautiful gardens on the shores of the lake. It attracted the British in India who summered up here in the cool amongst the green fertile hills. The Moghuls refused them permission to build, however, hoping in this way to prevent Srinagar becoming yet another British hill station like Simla or Gulamarg. A very clever Scot hit on the idea of building a houseboat on the lake which was not, of course, a permanent dwelling. He copied the design of the old Thames houseboat and soon hundreds of other houseboats were built by Brits anxious to have a place on the lake. They are very Victorian in feeling. A large open lounge leads out to the veranda at the front while behind are the bedrooms and bathroom and behind that the kitchen and servants' quarters.

A flower-seller, one of the many floating businesses on the lake

They are constructed entirely of wood and are panelled throughout. The veranda usually has an ornate carved awning in pine while some of the better class of houseboats have walnut ceilings and panelling.

Mr Tickoo arrived as we were having breakfast and looked very pleased to see us alive and still in one piece.

'How was the Shingo La?' he asked. I told him that we hadn't really had any problems but had found it hard going.

'That was the only thing I was worried about. The Shingo La can be very dangerous. Two people died there last week.'

After breakfast we went for a trip round the lake on the houseboat shikara. Our boatman had only one eye and spoke no English at all. He, the cook and the houseboat 'boy' (both in their early sixties) had been with the houseboat when the British still governed India and had stayed with it ever since. The food served on the boat was basic English boarding school fare. Well cooked but plain. It's a shame that the English left India with little other than a legal, parliamentary and educational system that has produced a massive bureaucracy and a belief that all Westerners like meat and two veg and some sort of sticky pudding for 'afters'.

The side canals of Dal Lake are fascinating. Kashmiri women queue at a floating butcher's shop and there are all manner of floating businesses rocking gently on the water; boat builders, a hardware stall, chapatti shops; there is a floating market and shikaras pass by piled high with all kinds of goods. The lake is constantly on the move.

All life is lived on the water and the smallest child learns to hold a paddle as soon as it is big enough. For much of our stay we were paddled around by two young brothers of ten and twelve.

The floating gardens really are floating. They are huge reed rafts three yards wide on average and of varying length. Soil is piled on top compounded with manure and rotting weeds from the lake bed. They make a very fertile base on which the lake people grow vegetables of all kinds including melons.

We took a shikara across the lake and then went by taxi from the waterside to the Moghul Gardens of Shalimar and Nishat. The gardens were laid down by the Moghuls as a part of their summer palaces and are formal and harmonic – Persian carpets in flower and stone. The Moghuls exploited the many springs and fountains that rise on the hillside above the lake and led them, through underground conduits, to hundreds of fountains whose water cooled the air. You can just imagine the princes and their princesses walking through the gardens drinking sherberts in the midday cool. The Nishat Gardens (the Gardens of Pleasure) were built in 1633 by Asaf Khan. Against a mountain backdrop, the ten terraces fall dramatically, the spring water running through the centre and being fed off by side ducts to flowerbeds and lawns where the thick-leaved chinar trees provide shade from the sun.

The Shalimar Gardens (the Gardens of Love) stand at the eastern end of the lake. They were built in 1619 by the Emperor Jehanigar for his queen Nur Jehan and are in a poor state of repair, partly through neglect and partly through bad management.

'They much better when British are here,' said the houseboat 'boy', looking sadly at the gardens. Many of the fountains no longer work. They have been wired for a son-et-lumière presentation and everywhere the cables crawl and badly concealed lights spoil the appearance of the flowerbeds and pools.

Thousands of Indians were visiting the gardens, here on holiday from further down country. They strolled in family groups, children splashing excitedly in the fountains, their parents photographing each other proudly before the terraces and flowers.

The influence of the Persians in Kashmir is particularly strong here at Srinagar. The Persian tea that Cookie served us – sweetened and flavoured with cinnamon and served with milk – is very popular here. There is a strong Moghul influence in Kashmiri art, from the carpets that are constantly thrust at you as you stroll past the shops to the

Manasbal Lake where not a breath stirred

papier-mâché work so finely made and painted; and, of course, there is the Islamic faith.

One disturbing thing about Srinagar is the great number of police. They are largely Hindu and are there to prevent any rioting. At partition Kashmir, a Muslim state, was ceded to India. It is the only Muslim state in India and many of its inhabitants identify strongly with Islamic Pakistan. This has produced all sorts of tensions and difficulties.

As our boatman rowed us home that night the lake was still and quiet and above the sound of the paddle dipping rhythmically in the dark waters we could hear, floating across the water, the voices of young girls singing. The next day the daughter of the owner of the houseboat next to ours was to be married and all her sisters and girl-friends were gathering at her house to sing songs to the bride-to-be, most of which seemed to be about how lovely she was and how lucky the boy was to be getting her. What sweet romance. It's the same the world over.

Kingfisher on a lotus flower

Manasarowar that is found at the foot of the Holy Mount Kailas in Tibet, regarded by Buddhists as the centre of the universe, round which rise the four holiest rivers in the world; the Sutlej, the Indus, the Ganges and the Brahmaputra. Very peaceful and undeveloped, Manasbal Lake has no houseboats on it and only a handful of shikaras. We hired the one boatman we could find to row us across the lake's still waters. Not a breath stirred and through the clear water we could see underlying mats of weed. In July and August the lake is a mass of lotus blossoms and, though it was now September, there were still a few flowers standing high above the surface. On one a kingfisher, to me the most beautiful of all birds, perched looking down into the depths. As we approached he flew off, his short silky wings shimmering in the sunlight.

We travelled back to Srinagar past fields where villagers were busy with the rice harvest. As we went by, the golden-yellow paddies were being cut by hand and laid in swathes on the mud, to be carted back to the village on back-slings, very much as the people of Leh had been doing on the day we left.

The Vale of Kashmir is one of the most fertile places in India; the plentiful rainfall and the constant sunshine of the summer months mean that the Vale is rich in rice and vegetables, fruits and nuts and peppers.

Early the next day we took a cab from the lakeside to Manasbal Lake some seventeen miles from Srinagar. It is named after Lake

Back at the houseboat a legion of salesmen selling papier-mâché, leather, saffron, Kashmiri shawls, sweets, wood carving and tailoring were waiting to take us in their shikaras to their factories. These traders are the plague of the lake, refusing to take no for an answer and coming day after day trying to wear you down by pestering.

Rice fields on the way back from Manasbal Lake

Above Pahalgum, a hill-station where Indians now retreat to for their summer holidays

One very fat man lounging in the back of a scruffy-looking shikara being paddled by a tiny boy arrived as we sat on the veranda. He had a swatch of cloth on his knee.

'I make you suit,' he shouted.

'I never wear suits,' I shouted back.

'I make you nice jacket,' he replied.

'I don't want one, thank you,' I replied.

'Why don't you let me make you a nice pair of slacks?'

'I have no money left,' I said, thinking to get rid of him. 'I spent it all on papier-mâché and wood carvings.'

He pulled out a credit card machine and waved it at me.

'I take all plastics!' he called. If nothing else you have to admire their determination.

We spent the next day driving up into the hills to Pahalgum, a hill station where the Indians from the cities now spend their summer holidays. The 'boy' was quite upset that we went into a Hindu restaurant and ate curry and chapattis with some truck drivers. He was trying to steer us towards a very Raj-looking tea shop, all sticky buns and silver teapots.

On our last afternoon we went to see Cookie and his family on the houseboat and sat on the clean scrubbed floor talking to him and his wife and children. The smallest boy had a rope round his waist and as he toddled around the boat all the other children kept an eye on him and if he got too near the edge out went a foot on to the rope and he plopped down on his bottom. We thanked Sultana for looking after us so well on the trail and said goodbye realising we would probably never see him again. As evening crept over the city we went by

Cookie's family

motor-rickshaw back to the landing stage from where our shikara took us back to the houseboat. Early the next morning we were flying to Delhi, from where Pat would return to England while I flew on to Nepal for the second leg of my Himalayan journey.

We watched the sunset and, as the last crimson glow left the sky and the first stars appeared, a rocket from the wedding boat shot into the sky and exploded in a burst of falling stars over the lake.

BOOK TWO
To the Roof of the World

1   Freak Street and Beyond

2   In Search of the Fish Tail

3   Electric Soup and the Last Boat Home

4   Kathmandu No Can Do

5   To Namche Bazar

6   Chinese Sing Song

7   Turn Left for Shangri-La

8   Sherpa Beer and Lama Pee

9   The Bearded Man in my Room

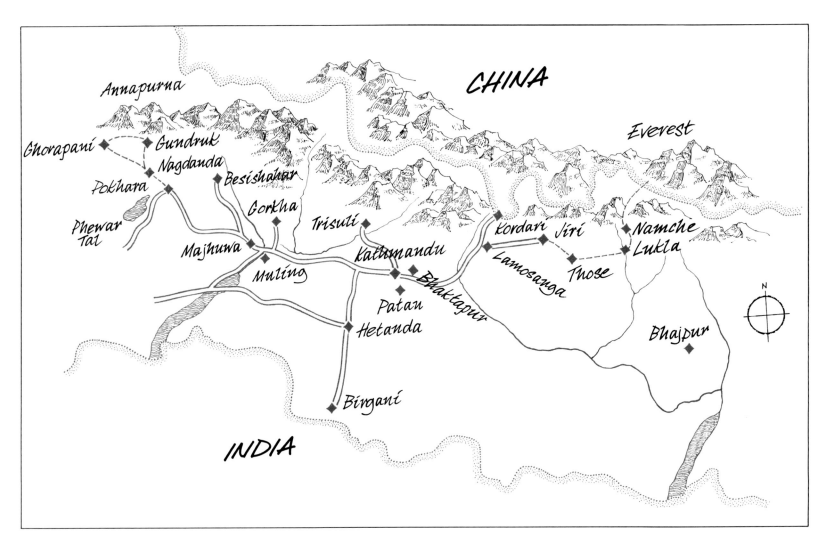

Freak Street and Beyond

'From a sanitary point of view Kathmandu may be said to be built on a dunghill in the middle of latrines.'
– Dr David Wright, surgeon to the British Residency in 1877

ABOUT TO LEAVE FOR Kathmandu, in the breakfast room of the Hotel Kanishka, New Delhi, I read in the *Hindustani Times* that there had been a serious skirmish on the Indo-Pakistani border on a glacier called the Siachen. Two hundred Pakistani troops were claimed dead for the loss of only eighteen Indians.

'This is very bad for the cricket!' said the manager, the very same gentleman who had told me to 'jigger them up' when KLM left my baggage at Amsterdam Airport more than a month ago.

It was obvious that the hold-up at Dras had been caused by the fighting. The road is no more than a few miles from where the battle must have taken place in the high mountains to the north. It also explained the immense amount of military activity we saw along the Leh-Srinagar road.

It seemed to me the ultimate in madness that men were killing each other for a few hundred yards of glacier at twenty thousand feet in those beautiful icy mountains while their countries were playing cricket together. But you mustn't expect anything but madness from politicians and the military.

There was the usual bunfight and cattle market at the Royal Nepal Airlines check-in desk at Delhi Airport, because a new plane with forty per cent more seating supposed to come into service that day hadn't in fact arrived and the airline had overbooked the flight. Twenty people had already been turned away and rumours were flying round that even more people were going to be stranded.

I had been amongst the first half-dozen people to arrive at the empty check-in desk and had waited there for nearly two hours staring at nothing. Behind me a crowd gathered; trekkers with rucksacks, more people with cardboard boxes and bin-liners and a team of twenty or more American students, led by a lovely Tibetan lady, who were on their way to Nepal to study Buddhism for two months. There were also a dozen business types in suits who looked increasingly anxious as the aircraft departure time got ever closer and still no official arrived at the desk.

An ad hoc, shapeless queue formed. I was fourth from the front. A female official appeared at the desk. The queue disappeared in a forest of knees and elbows with tickets thrust out and I suddenly found myself on the outside of the scrum looking in. India had prepared me for this and, elbows flying, I made my way to the front of the queue, got my baggage through, picked up my boarding card and, only thirty-five minutes after its scheduled departure time, the plane flew into the clouds and headed for Kathmandu.

It was cloudy all the way so that I peered out of the windows looking hopelessly for a view of the Himalaya. Just as we were coming in over the valley I saw them to the north, snow-headed and looming magnificent above the bed of clouds. Two Gurkha soldiers next to me going home on leave from their regiment in India played cards all the way, cheerfully cheating each other and slapping the cards on the fold-down table with loud amusement.

As we dropped below the clouds to begin our approach to Kathmandu, I saw the valley far below, an intricate landscape of fields and terraces stretching away to the distant hills. Villages of wooden and ochre-brick houses surrounded high temples that grew majestically from the plain and as the aircraft lined up with the runway I saw below the minutiae of the landscape, the dusty roads leading between the villages, people at work in the fields, bending and straightening under our swooping cruciform shadow, carts and bullocks on the road, a lone water-buffalo standing in a wallow and people in bright clothes threshing. Then came the sudden rush of tarmac and the scream of rubber as the plane braked and taxied to its stand.

Walking across the tarmac I already sensed a difference between Nepal and India. There was not as much tension, the people seemed more relaxed, they smiled more. There was less of the sense of a nation under siege, a feeling that was all too obvious at times in Ladakh and in the various airports in India where security had been so strict. What soldiers there were looked smart and clean and seemed to look at us with interest rather than suspicion. I also noticed that they seemed to have fewer problems with their private parts.

All the luggage came through without any hitch and the man at customs took a brief look at the camera gear and put a chalk cross on everything. I'd booked into one of the better hotels in the city and was going to wait there the three or four days it took John to arrive from England with the film stock and the camera equipment. I crossed the road to the taxi stand and half an hour later I had dumped my kit in the hotel and was walking the streets of the city.

I'd first heard of Kathmandu in the early part of the sixties when I met a priest from New Zealand who'd spent five years working there. He had been deeply impressed by everything he saw, particularly the warmth and generosity of the people. 'And the temples,' he said. 'I've never seen such temples.'

I walked round the corner from the hotel and along the road past a still, calm lake with a magnificent white shrine, looking like a miniature palace, set in the centre. Built on the site of an earlier sixteenth-century shrine, the Rani Pokhari had been erected by the wife of one of the rulers, Pratap Malla, in memory of her son who died young. The shrine is still used and a ceremony takes place there once a year. It is a wonderful expanse of quiet water in the heart of a noisy city. The old town of Kathmandu is a jumbled mixture of brass-doored temples in madly busy squares, shrines, statues, shops and roadside stalls. The buildings are mainly three-storeys, the bottom floor usually being an open shop front while the upper storeys are divided into dwellings or offices. Handwritten cards on the doorways advertise English lessons, tailors and tooth-pullers. Overhead run hundreds of cables and wires connecting poles and pylons, the electricity supply humming inches above the heads of flute sellers.

The buildings are, in the main, of timber and red-brick with carved wooden window-frames and doorways and the narrow streets are jammed with a maelstrom of people and traffic. Tricycle rickshaws are pedalled furiously past by scrawny young men who ring their bells constantly while plump European women clutch the sides of their seats in alarm. A flute seller, a hundred and more bamboo flutes splayed out on his pole like the spines of a porcupine, plays a wild and stirring tune and shouts his wares. A curd seller with his red earthenware bowls of white curds squats in the corner of a square while women bargain at stalls for the red wool strands they weave in their long dark hair. On the pavement baskets of fruit and vegetables, piles of cloth, boxes of spices and bags of rice are dumped all of a jumble.

Kathmandu: the shrine in the middle of the lake

In the sixties Kathmandu, like Marrakesh, was the goal of the Magic Bus, the overland trippers and 'trip-outers' heading for the alternative life-style. Cat Stevens wrote a song about Kathmandu and, with the Beatles, Jimmy Hendrix and the newly risen maharishis, came a generation looking for the infinite in a grain of hash.

Hash, as I said before, had long been a normal part of local everyday life. It was used mainly by the old folk and was seen as a social drug in the same way that alcohol is in the West. In Kathmandu it was easily available from licensed shops.

The news spread and the buses came. Painted in all the colours of psychedelia they trundled across Europe and Asia looking for the

Flute sellers displaying their wares

ultimate high. So many came that one of the buses was even known as the Chapatti Express. Thus, in a narrow alleyway close by a square called Basantapur in the old part of the city, Freak Street was born. There were head shops, smoke shops, pie shops, bookshops. Cafés with names like 'The August Moon' and 'The Hungry Eye' appeared seemingly overnight and on to the street came the dropouts, the weirdos and the college kids trying to be hip but who later went back home, cut their hair and got jobs working for IBM. Acid Rock blared out into the street, and the air was thick with the scent of the local hashish, known in Europe as Nepalese Black.

Then overnight Freak Street disappeared. It was partly due to the

authorities adopting a less tolerant attitude and partly to the country wanting to clean up its act following the coronation of King Mehindra in 1975 which, amongst other things, brought about the prohibition of hashish and other drugs.

Visas were refused and people without means were offered a free trip out of the country. Like a cloud of hash smoke, the hippies faded away into the blue Kathmandu skies.

A few, a very few, remain. A throwback to the sixties, you can see them walking the streets. One man, his head completely emptied by acid, is reputed to be the son of a California millionaire who is paying him to stay out in Nepal because he would be an embarrassment back home. He walks the streets in a grubby kaftan and flared loon pants, still covered in beads, a red tikka mark on his forehead. When you talk to him it's like talking to the sea – there comes back at you simply the noise of waves breaking on a beach; he makes wave-like motions with his hands and then he's gone.

Another wanders the streets in a khaki suit playing a bamboo flute. The music he's extemporising as he walks weaves through the streets and mingles with the noises of car horns, people shouting and the constant ringing of the pedal rickshaw bells.

The Thamel at the north end of the Old City is now the area where trekkers and what are now called 'trippies' congregate. There are the bookshops and trekking shops, the craft shops and the hotels that point to a new direction in Nepal's growth, tourism. The 'trippies' are largely from Australia and New Zealand, on a round trip to Bali and Thailand, catching as much of the East as they can. They very often include in their holiday a week in Kathmandu or an easy trek in the Annapurna area. Walking through the Thamel at night the boys approach you from the shadows calling softly, 'Change sah? You want hash? I make you good price. You want flute? You want make fuck? I know good girls sah.'

That night, drunk on the sounds and smells of Kathmandu, I ate mo mos in a Tibetan restaurant in the Thamel before riding back to the hotel in a pedal rickshaw playing a flute I'd just bought on the street. The rickshaw boy's friend, when he found that he couldn't sell me any hash or a woman, pulled out a mouth organ and accompanied very spasmodically the 'Harvest Home Hornpipe' in the wrong key, all the way back. In my hotel bedroom that night I found not just Gideon's Bible but the Bhagavad-Gita as well.

The next morning I awoke to a curious scene. Looking out of my window I saw the Gurkha doorman in full uniform trying to frighten a mouse away from the foyer. He wouldn't kill it since it was against his religion so he simply stood there, waving his arms and shouting at it. The confused mouse scurried round in circles, running in terror up against the cliff of the high kerb-stone. Eventually it climbed the kerb and got away.

Ganesh, the Elephant-headed God of Hindu mythology, rides on a mouse so perhaps that's another reason why the doorman didn't kill it.

I had arrived in Kathmandu at a very special time, the Badh Dashain, the biggest and most important festival in Nepal. There are, by the way, almost as many festivals in Nepal as there are days in the year. It was the fifteenth day of Dashain, the day of ritual slaughter, when people brought animals – mainly ducks, chickens and goats – to be killed in the temple courtyards and before the shrines around Durbar Square, the main temple area of the city. Walking through the crowded streets I saw two beautiful Nepali girls feeding rice to a duck from a plate full of peeled and coloured hard-boiled eggs, marigolds, salt, saffron rice and green fresh herbs, before handing it over to be slaughtered.

A barefoot man, his trousers rolled up to the knee to avoid the blood he was splashing about in, was obviously acting as a semi-official slaughterman. He took the duck and bending its neck back so that its throat was stretched into a curve, he quickly slashed its throat and shook the spurting blood over the bronze statue at the temple door, adding to the thick crust of red paste, marigold petals and congealing blood with which it was already coated. Then, severing the head completely, he threw the poor thing on the floor. I had forgotten that fowl killed like this twitch for so long afterwards: for at least three or four minutes the wings half fluttered pitifully and the webbed feet trod the reeking air before the blood-pooled temple stones.

At another temple, beneath a canopy of carpets and shawls, two men were blessing a young white goat ceremonially with water before killing it. All its orifices were sprinkled and then the little kid's neck was stretched over a wooden log and its head lopped off in one blow from a kukri. Again the blood was splashed on to the temple doorposts and four soldiers standing in the crowd fired old muskets into the air.

During the festival everybody wears a decorative crimson tikka, a spot of paste on their forehead, for red is the dominant colour, from the blood on the streets to the hair bindings and saris of the women. The mark on the forehead reminded me of the mark made with ashes that Catholics wear on Ash Wednesday. The third eye or pineal gland seems to be a common link in both. More than a thousand animals from small chickens to massive water buffalo are killed during the

Women queuing to receive their tikkas and the Royal blessing

to drink the water. I ran an inch and a half of water into a glass to wash down the malaria tablets I had been taking since Manali (stupidly probably, since the only malarial mosquitoes around are in the Terai of Nepal and I wasn't going there) and I threw it down in one.

A few hours later whatever was in there invaded my system and wiped me out completely; I felt dizzy and weak, and dangerous at both ends. But I still dragged myself round the town, there was so much to see and I didn't want to miss any of it. The hotel was only a couple of hundred yards from Durbar Square so I was rarely more than a ten- or fifteen-minute dash from sanctuary. Anything I ate came straight back but I drank plenty of fresh lime juice and soda water because I knew it was important that I shouldn't dehydrate and that I keep up my salt and blood-sugar levels.

My journal for the next day reads:

> Up and down like a dysenteric yo yo. How weak we human beings
> ultimately are. A small thing like an amoeba gets into your gut and the
> whole world comes to an end. The trouble is it's your end it comes to.

I spent a lot of time that day in bed or on the bog reading *The Heart of the Matter* by Graham Greene, which I feel is one of the best novels ever written. It helps to understand it if you are a Catholic, even a lapsed one. There's a shop in the Thamel that sells and exchanges second-hand books and later that day, when the volcanoes at either end had lain dormant for a while, I took a rickshaw there to change some books. There was a mile-long queue of Nepalis either side of the Royal Palace, men on one side, women on the other. They were waiting to get their tikkas from the King and Queen because on this day the Royal Palace gates are opened and the people of Kathmandu file past to receive the Royal blessing. There were light-skinned people from the lowlands, Gurkhas, Gurongs and Tamangs from the hill villages and Indian-looking peoples from the Terai.

At breakfast the next morning I met three English lads from

festival and in the warm, post-monsoon air the smell of blood mingles with the scent of marigolds and the smoke from burning incense.

I was having some difficulty walking through the streets since I had developed a fully-blown case of the Delhi Belly, the Green Apple Quickstep or Kathmandu Cancan. All through India we had doctored our drinking water with iodine, unless we were really high up and knew there was no habitation above the stream. So apart from the occasional twinge, I hadn't suffered any ill effects. Kathmandu is notorious for its water problems. The water supply system is old and runs alongside much of the sewerage. The wooden pipes and ducts often break and raw sewage runs into the water supply. I made the mistake of not reading the notice above the washbasin telling me not

Manchester and Sheffield who'd just returned from an unsuccessful attempt to climb Ama Dablam in the Khumbu Valley near Everest. The rest of the team had stayed on the mountain. Glandular fever and amoebic dysentery had struck and they had pulled off the climb rather than be dead weight on the team. They were disappointed at having had to give up but were greatly impressed by the things they had seen along the way, raving about the beauty of the Dudh Kosi Valley and the friendliness of the Sherpa people. We arranged to have a drink together in the bar that night and they promised to bring along a Sherpa, Pema Dorje, who had helped them on the walk there. They felt Pema would be a good contact and might be able to fix up our Annapurna and Everest trips.

I bought some postcards and sat on the terrace for a while before I felt sufficiently brave to stray far enough away from the toilet to go to the monkey temple at Swayambunath, one of the two major Buddhist temples in the valley.

The journey there took me about four miles out of town over the river and on past fields, tiny farmers' houses and then through a small village at the foot of the hill that the gompa stands on. Children played barefoot on the streets, a man turned a prayer-wheel, sitting on his house steps, women walked with babies in their arms, chatting.

I climbed the stairs past a little beggar girl, about five years old, who was chasing the monkeys away from the coins she had collected with a stick. The gompa is less impressive than the massive stupa with its golden spire, its four sets of eyes looking at the four corners of the earth and its prayer-flags fluttering in the wind, while pigeons fly to land and hawks circle above. At the base of the stupa stand four shrines, a line of prayer-wheels connecting them. Here, as in other parts of the Kathmandu Valley, there is a strange mix of Hindu and Buddhist religions so that Ganesh, the elephant god, is found on the approach to the temple and Hindu gods are found in the compound, Hindus walk round the stupa and worship at the shrines while

A worshipper at Swayambunath, the monkey temple

Buddhist monks walk round the base turning the prayer-wheels and chanting as they go. There has never been any animosity between the two religions and it is said that if you ask a Nepali if he is Hindu or Buddhist he will answer 'yes'.

That night in the bar of the hotel I met the three English lads and Pema Dorje. Like all the Sherpas we were to meet Pema seemed gentle and friendly, always full of fun and yet proud. There is nothing subservient or shifty about Sherpas and I found them honest and direct, without any edge at all, in sharp contrast to some of the people I had come across at Srinagar. They also tend to be very intelligent; several Sherpas, educated at Hillary schools, have gone on to university to study subjects like forestry and national park management. I met one Sherpa in Namche Bazar who spoke Sherpa, Nepali, Tibetan, English, French, German and enough Japanese and Polish for him to have been a sirdar on some of the major climbing expeditions. Pema Dorje originally had another name but he had been ill as a small child, so the medicine man in his village changed his name and he recovered, a common way of dealing with childhood sickness in the Khumbu Valley.

Pema's brother was at Lhotse base camp with two Americans and the two famous Englishmen, the Burgess twins, the Tweedledum and Tweedledee of climbing. The team was attempting Lhotse Middle Peak, the last unclimbed twenty-four-thousand foot peak in the Everest group. A newsflash on the radio that afternoon had talked of an accident on the Lhotse climb and reported some climbers killed. Pema, who has summited Everest twice – once on Bonington's successful expedition – knew all four of the Western climbers and was quite upset. They wouldn't know any more until the next day.

Pema is a handsome young man with a thin moustache and laughing eyes. He has a great sense of humour and told me a very funny story about an English climber's adventures with a young Sherpani after a night on the chang that will not bear repeating here. Pema said he couldn't wait to see the baby; the thought of a Sherpa baby with fair hair and blue eyes amused him greatly.

There is no stigma, by the way, attached to children born out of wedlock in a Sherpa community. Pema himself had only just married the mother of his two children. It is normal for a couple to live apart until they have a house or until the husband has finished his big travels, which in Pema's case meant that he no longer considered himself eligible for major expedition work but was now concentrating on leading treks for a large company in Nepal. Before we parted that night, Pema said he would try and arrange his schedule so that he could lead our treks into the Annapurna area and to Everest base camp.

John arrived the next afternoon and it was good to see him, though he was shocked at how much weight I had lost. A beard I had grown while in the mountains made me look even wilder and more wrecked. Though he didn't say anything I could tell he was a little concerned. I was still very weak and wasted and was going to the toilet a couple of times an hour, sometimes more, round the clock.

The more people I met, the more horror stories I heard about Kathmandu: apparently there was a hepatitis epidemic and two Israeli girls had been flown home with typhoid that week. I was thankful that all I seemed to have was some acute form of dysentery. My journal for the next ten days reads like the writings of a deranged man, who doesn't know whether he is caught up in a comedy, nightmare or fantasy. The dysentery seemed to lie low every couple of days only to flare up again just when I was beginning to relax. I got even weaker and thinner. I just kept on hoping that it would clear up before we went into the mountains. I didn't sleep a lot that night.

We had breakfast the next morning with Chris, an Australian who was sorting out our flights to Pokhara and Lukla. He seemed well informed about the whole Himalayan situation and was very concerned about the impact of Western tourism on the cultures and ecology of the mountains. He had treks in Tibet at that moment, which he was having great problems with as the Chinese had closed Tibet down that morning because of the riots in Lhasa and he was finding it impossible to get any information from the authorities. His Tibetan wife, Sashi, was working on various government officials but it was still hard to get any news.

The journal:

A fat Australian choosing a postcard in the shop – to his wife, 'Get some mountains, any'll do, they're all the same to me. That'll do. Only get one. I've only got one friend.'

A team of middle-aged American motor cyclists has arrived here. Their slogan is 'motor cycles to the roof of the world'; their route was Delhi,

Nepal, Tibet, China. Only, now they've had it. Tibet is closed to foreigners as from today because of the riots.

Later that afternoon John returned with Pema Dorje who wanted to take us for a mystery treat. I was feeling terrible but I wasn't going to miss this. Pema led us down the back streets of Kathmandu to a Tibetan house that sold 'tungba', Pema's favourite drink. Basically it's fermented millet served up in wooden quart pots, looking a bit like caviar. Boiling water is poured over the millet and, after leaving it for five minutes, you drink it through a bamboo straw. It tastes like saki and is very strong.

The room was bare, except for a few chairs and tables. A handsome young Tibetan girl kept coming in and filling our pots with boiling water from a Thermos. Pema was flirting with her and making her laugh. In the opposite corner two men drank deeply and smiled. It was extremely heady but very pleasant to drink and after two pots of tungba I was in no pain at all. If I'd had another I'd have danced home.

That night, still reeling with the tungba, we went to see Bill Jones at the hotel he was staying at while on one of his infrequent incursions into the big city from Ghorapani, where he and his partner Josette run an Alternative Technology centre. He is a tall sandy-haired Australian, an ex-photographer and climber, a sound bloke with a lot of good ideas on stoves, vented toilets, composting closets and other things that local people can make for themselves very cheaply. Bill's basic premiss is that Western technology has largely failed in the East because of a basic lack of understanding. He believes, firstly, that the people have to be involved and that it really has to be something that will help and not exploit them and, secondly, it has to be cheap and, if possible made from materials to hand. Expensive imported machinery is out of the question because, when it breaks, spare parts are not available and take for ever to get hold of.

Bill was concentrating on simple, easy projects that would improve the health of the people, and lessen the deforestation of the valleys. He lives alongside the most trekked area in the Himalaya, the Pokhara-Jomsom trail. Water was a bit of a problem, even though Ghorapani means 'place for watering horses', because it was contaminated. Infant mortality caused by amoebic dysentery is as high as forty per cent in some of the villages. Bill had devised a system of self-aerating collecting tanks where the water flowed slowly over a reflective surface. The sun's ultra violet rays killed the bacteria and made the water safe. It sounded simple and easy to make. We were going to Ghorapani to film some of Bill's projects.

Next morning I left John and Pema to get on with the business of organising gear, flights, trucks and porters and dragged my problem and me off to the Bodhnath temple, through streets where gangs of lower-caste workers (men and women) were mending the roads, carrying baskets of broken stones and dumping them in the holes. There was not a wheelbarrow in sight. One wheelbarrow could have held ten basket-loads but it must still be cheaper to employ labourers than import wheelbarrows.

The stupa of the gompa is very impressive. Gold-covered, in a great square of houses, its eyes look to the four corners of the world. Great lines of prayer-flags flutter in the breeze and each evening at the time of puja, monks, old women, nuns with prayer-wheels and small children trail round the massive base of the stupa in procession spinning the wall-mounted prayer-wheels. In a small room by the stupa gateway a massive prayer-wheel was turned continuously by praying pilgrims, its brass surface covered with the words 'Om mani padme hum'. The stupa is worshipped mainly by Tibetan Buddhists and has an interesting history. Legend tells that the stupa was built by a woman called Kangnma. She was a supernatural being banished from Indra's heaven because she had stolen some flowers. She had four children in her life as a mortal and worked as a goose girl to

The magnificent stupa of the gompa at Bodhnath, its four pairs of eyes looking to the four corners of the world

support them. She eventually accumulated a fortune and asked the king for some land to build a stupa. Land was very scarce and valuable in the valley and the king told her she could have as much land as could be covered by a buffalo hide. Kangnma cut a buffalo hide into thin strips, and tied them together making a long rope that 'covered' the square that Bodhnath now stands on.

Around the stupa a complete town has grown up with shops and houses, a monastery, chapels, lodges and carpet factories. In the gateway, massive bells were tolled by hand as the devotees bent in prayer. An old man prostrated himself in ritual obedience, sliding forward with his hands on pieces of cardboard until he lay flat on the gentle curve below the yellow-spattered dome of the great stupa.

In the last rays of the sun, women were winnowing barley in the street, throwing the shining grain into the light and letting the evening breeze carry the chaff across the stones as the grain fell back on to matting. A Tibetan walked slowly by carrying a heavy load on a tumpline across his forehead, chanting 'Om mani padme hum'. The chant is not performed in an attempt to gain grace but to make holy the action being performed at the time. So in this way it is possible to dedicate your whole life to the search for the infinite.

A few days later we filmed the American 'Motor Cyclists to the Roof of the World' at Nagarkot just beyond Kathmandu, where tourists go to see the sunrise over the Everest range. We wanted to film the motor cyclists because we both agreed that this was a good example of people with the wrong attitude towards the hills.

I feel that there is an essential harmony between men and mountains that can only be felt by walking, trekking or climbing amongst them. It is to do with peace, with pace, with quietness, with solitude and with something, I believe, that lies deep within us and which modern civilisation sets out to destroy.

Westerners think that they can achieve mastery over Nature through the use of machinery and technology when all they will do ultimately is destroy it, and themselves in the process. The motor cyclists, rich, Western and in the main uncaring, seemed to epitomise this attitude. One man I spoke to, who had motor-cycled to Kathmandu from Delhi, had no knowledge at all of the people or the country he was travelling through, and was just annoyed that he couldn't get into Tibet and up to the Rongbuk glacier and the base camp used by expeditions attacking Everest from the Tibetan side. He was fairly representative of the bunch.

Unfortunately, at Nagarkot, Everest was hidden by end-of-monsoon clouds. The Americans dined al fresco, with tables and chairs, and were served a full fried breakfast with a team of Sherpas cooking chips, sausage, mushrooms and omelettes. They ate their breakfasts and bellyached about the weather.

'What with Tibet being closed and these clouds covering Everest I'm not sure we're getting our money's worth on this trip, honey.'

They mounted their massive Japanese motor cycles and, in the world-wide spirit of 'been there, seen it, done it, got the T-shirt', roared off down the hill back to Kathmandu, to the amusement of dozens of little children who waved and jumped up and down at the noise.

We drove from Nagarkot through beautiful terraced fields and dusty villages to Bhaktapur where we spent the whole day just wandering around amongst the most beautiful Hindu temples. There are three main cities in the Kathmandu Valley: Kathmandu itself, Patan and Bhaktapur and there is so much to see that the Kathmandu Valley alone would take years to explore.

The main square of Bhaktapur is dominated by two of the most beautiful temples in Nepal. The wide open space of the square gives a feeling of light and air that you just don't get in the more crowded Durbar Square in Kathmandu. Central to the square and rising above it in a succession of steps is the Nyatapola Temple dedicated to a mysterious and terrible Tantric goddess. Her image is so fearful that

The snow-covered Himalaya towers behind the main square at Bodhnath

The rice fields fall away down the hillside in ripples: near Nagarkot

only the brahmin priests may see it, and then only in the dark of night by lamplight. The main, steep stairway to the temple is flanked by two lines of stone guardians on plinths. Their power diminishes tenfold at each stage so that the stone image at the lowest level is ten times more powerful than the one above it.

Adjacent to the Nyatapola Temple is the Kasi Bishwanath Temple. Almost totally destroyed by earthquake in 1934 it was rebuilt in the same year. All round the rest of the square are the permanent market stalls where farmers sell kids, vegetables and grain and where the curio sellers display their prayer-wheels, kukris and thankas.

A short walk from the temples took us into Durbar Square (each of the three cities has a Durbar Square). On the top of a tall column was a golden, praying figure, while in the temple wall close by was a huge golden gate, the Sun Dhoka, according to the guide, 'the most precious masterpiece of art in the valley'. It was aflame and massive, burning in the afternoon sun.

At dinner that night we finalised the plans with Pema, this time without the mind-clouding tungba to make us silly and giggling. It was now Thursday. On Saturday we would fly to Pokhara and begin a nine-day trek to Jomsom in the Kali Gandaki Valley where we would film some of the worst of the deforestation. From Jomsom we would fly back to Pokhara and then on to Kathmandu. By then the Indian film crew should have arrived from Delhi and we would all fly out together to Lukla and then trek on up to Everest base camp. It all

The main temple at Bhaktapur

seemed straightforward enough.

Pema arrived early the following day to tell us that he had been detailed to lead another trek and that he wouldn't be able to come with us but that a friend of his would be our sirdar. I thought it a pity since we had got to know Pema quite well in just a few days and he seemed an ideal leader and companion. We went off to get the trekking permits from the immigration office, hooting and jerking through the bicycles, rickshaws, cars and all the crazy traffic of Kathmandu. When we arrived there at two o'clock, the office was closed. Apparently it opened between ten in the morning and noon only. The office was full of thwarted trekkers, red-faced, sweaty Westerners, in the main looking angry and ugly. The air was hot with bad temper and oaths. It was hard for them to understand that Western efficiency is not a quality sought after by all the nations of the world.

We decided that the only thing we could do was return the next day and left them to their muttering and banging.

I left John and Pema and went on foot to Pashupatinath Temple on the banks of the sacred River Bagmati that flows through the heart of Kathmandu. The afternoon light was turning golden when I arrived at the temple, one of the holiest of all Hindu shrines and a place of pilgrimage. Non-believers are not allowed to set foot inside the precincts, which is a shame because it is reputed to be very beautiful inside. But there is a great deal to see outside the temple, on the river banks and beyond.

Opposite, across the river, stands a line of eleven identical 'chaityas', open, stone shrines, each containing a stone 'lingam', or penis symbol. A set of steps lead away from the river with alternate lingams and 'yonis' (the female equivalent) and on the doors of many of the temples there are erotic carvings, symbols of life.

I was walking the bank opposite the temple when I saw, beneath a tree a sadhu, seated in the lotus position, a symbolic trident in his hand. He called out to me, 'Where you from?'

'England,' I answered.

'Oh, Englan! I bin Englan. I go Englan in Indian Army. Mountbatten good man. Leave Englan I go Holy man. Fifty years I bin Holy man.'

The temple has a golden roof, is home to two thousand monkeys and is the site of Royal and other cremations. There are two hospices where the dying go for their final hours, one is for the rich, one for the poor. They are taken down to the river for one last drink at a holy spring, then, after death, they are cremated on the burning ghats. While I was there, I saw one body being made ready for burning, that of a man in his middle forties. His eldest son and brother had shaved their heads and, wearing simple white loin cloths, were squatting quietly while one of the ghat attendants prepared the pyre. The little boy had a scalp lock of hair and during his year of mourning would wear white and would not eat salt or curds.

When the pyre was ready the body was carried down to the river to be washed in the holy waters. Then, wrapped in white muslin, it was

The sadhu outside the temple at Pashupatinath

placed gently on the pyre. A bunch of burning reeds was brought and the brother and son walked round the body three times carrying the flaming brand. The flames were held to the corpse's mouth to signify that the soul had left the husk of flesh behind and the pyre was then set alight. Across the river, through the heat haze of the pyre, I could see the shimmering images of young women bathing in the holy river and from beyond the bridge came the shouts of children swimming and splashing.

The body took a long time to burn. The muslin cloth burnt through, then the nose and lips disappeared and the face became little more than a mask. The family sat quietly watching, the little boy crying, his uncle squatting, slowly rocking backwards and forwards on the balls of his feet. As the tendons tightened in the heat, the dead man's forearm was raised as though in a final salute and then slowly sank down into the flames again. When all was consumed, the ashes were brushed into the holy river.

That evening back in Thamel we met our new sirdar, Ang Phurba. Slightly shorter than Pema Dorje and with a broader face, he seemed tough and wiry and set about organising us straight away. I half expected him to pull out a Filofax.

There would be no problem, we could get trekking permits at the government office in Pokhara tomorrow. The important thing was to get on the flight because there had been a lot of difficulties with flights to both Pokhara and Lukla. There was a SAARC (South Asia

The cremation at Pashupatinath

Association for Regional Cooperation) conference of Asian govern-ment ministers about to take place in Kathmandu and flights were being delayed and cancelled sometimes for days. It looked bad.

That night we dined with Karna Sakya and the Minister for Tourism. Karna, who runs the Kathmandu Guest House, probably the most famous hotel in Nepal, is a short rotund man; intelligent, perceptive and a great talker. He is also a trekker and the author of the only book ever written on the Dolpo region, the largely unexplored land beyond the Himalaya leading to Mustang and Tibet. Karna had met with great personal tragedy only a year before when his wife and young daughter had both died of cancer within weeks of each other. He had bravely fought through the grief and was now putting all his energy into raising funds for a cancer hospital. The Minister left after a few drinks and Karna treated us to a wonderful meal of mildly curried chicken and traditional Nepalese dishes. I wasn't sure that my ravaged system would stand it but decided it might be worth trying to burn it out.

Karna was a wonderful host and an extremely knowledgeable commentator on the problems facing Nepal. He talked at length on the difference between hard tourism – package tours and exploitation – and soft tourism – trekking, climbing and other activities. Hard tourism he saw as ultimately destructive of both the culture and the landscape. Soft tourism, where people interact with the culture they pass through, where there is no huge superstructure of roads and hotels and Western standards are not demanded, he saw as much less harmful.

'People will come and they should come. We have the most beautiful mountains and the most wonderful people in the world. But they must come in the right way.' The Tourism Minister said he was hoping for a million tourists by the year 2000 as against the current year's quarter of a million. How are the sewers of Kathmandu going to cope with that?

After the meal Karna kindly drove us through the dark night back to our hotel where we packed ready for the next day's flight.

2

In Search of the Fish Tail

'Anyone who leaves strange coolies to their own devices on the first march deserves all he gets.'
– H. W. Tilman

POKHARA IS ONLY a hundred and sixty miles from Kathmandu so we hardly seemed to have taken off before we were landing on the grass runway there and dragging our baggage off a trolley outside the little terminal building. Ang Phurba had taken us over completely and had a taxi sorted, a price agreed upon and our gear loaded in the time it would have taken us to ask where the taxis were. There aren't many taxis, by the way, since Pokhara, though it is growing, is still only a twentieth the size of Kathmandu. The few battered taxis turn up to watch the planes arrive then go away again, like cows coming to a field wall to watch someone walking past.

We wanted to stay at the Fish Tail Lodge on the Phewa Tal Lake, a magnificent stretch of water to the east of the town, but it was full of American motor cyclists still looking for the roof of the world so we were forced to stay in a small, side street hotel in town. It was clean and neat and with the added advantage of a flat rooftop from which it was said we would see the sunrise on Machhapuchhare, the Fish Tail mountain.

Machhapuchhare in the Annapurna range and Ama Dablam in the Everest area are my two most favourite mountains in the world. Ama Dablam, with its single peak surmounting two arm-like ridges, and Machhapuchhare, with its twin peaks looking like the end of a fish

tail, are, I feel, beautiful beyond description. We had missed out on the Fish Tail Lodge but we had sunrise over Machhapuchhare to look forward to.

We hired bicycles and in the warm afternoon pedalled off towards the lake. The streets seemed quiet after the row and rush of Kathmandu and we cycled past the stalls of Tibetan curio sellers and huddles of men listening to the news on transistor radios. Children were swimming and women bathing as we left the bikes and hired a boat and boatman to row us round the lake. The sky was cloudy but bright, the last of the monsoon still hanging in the valley. Pokhara gets the brunt of the monsoon in this region. It lies much lower than Kathmandu and has an average rainfall of 157 inches It is surrounded by rich, lush vegetation and by the lake the citrus and banana trees and fields of grain give way to forests where thousands of monkeys chatter and swing from branch to branch, dropping to the ground to run along the shore gibbering and rolling over.

The lake is six miles long and at its widest point two across. From its southernmost bank wooded hills rise up hundreds of feet while to the north are the Annapurnas, One and Two: Dhaulagiri and Machhapuchhare. The lake has a small island at its heart with a Hindu Temple, the Barahi Bhagvati, standing reflected in the waters. As we

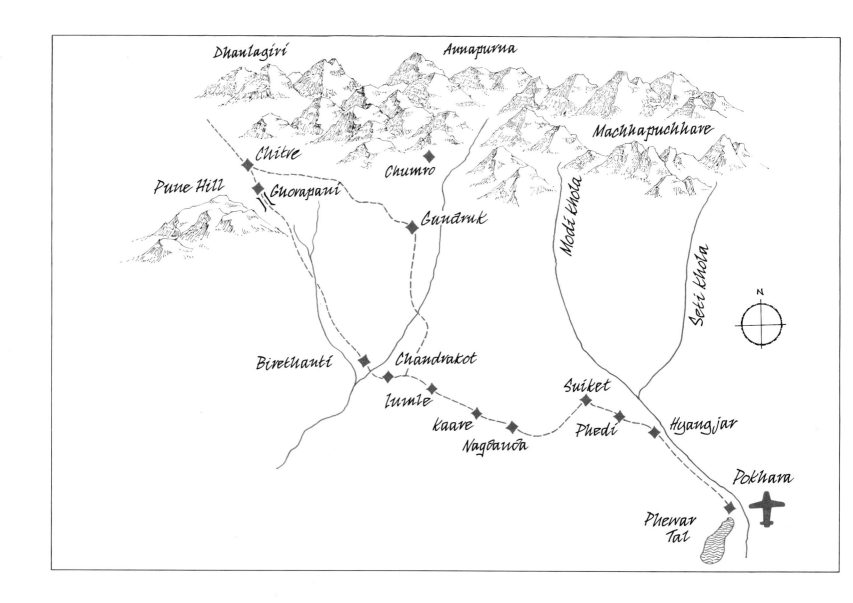

Phewa Tal lake, a magnificent stretch of water outside Pokhara

rowed round it, we saw the pilgrims in their boats going quietly out to the island, fish eagles swooping overhead then settling on the poles and stumps of trees on the bank. John, who lives much of the time in the Norfolk Broads, is a keen boatman so we gave him a paddle and let him row us back. With his straw solar topee and his wire-rimmed welder's glasses he looked like Lytton Strachey. I suggested to the boatman that John looked like Lytton Strachey and he agreed out of politeness, though it impressed John who thought the boatman was certainly well up on the Bloomsbury set.

As dusk rolled over the lake we took turns at rowing back, singing sea shanties, 'The Song of the Volga Boatmen' and the theme from 'Saunders of the River'. Our voices carried over the water and sent the monkeys scuttling from the trees. Egrets swooped low over the lake in the dusk, landing candle-white in the gathering shadows. A band of pilgrims rowing from the temple back to the shore waved and sang a song in Nepali as they crossed our wake. The evening air was warm as we cycled back to town.

John alias Lytton Strachey

Five o'clock the following morning found us sitting on the hotel roof with a cup of tea, waiting for the dawn. We waited a long time, the grey skies lightening to show a rose blush to the east where the rising sun was hidden by cloud. We did get the occasional glimpse of Annapurna peeping through the cloud but Machhapuchhare was well hidden in swirling grey.

After breakfast we cycled to the airport to try and book return flights from Jomsom. It proved impossible. We would have to do it when and if we got there. Jomsom is a small landing-strip close to the Annapurna Sanctuary that takes short take-off and landing aircraft, or STOLs as they are called. Although there are flights there on a regular basis, they are often delayed or cancelled and we had heard stories of people being marooned for up to ten days there, sleeping at the side of the airfield waiting for a speck in the sky over the mountains. We would have to be prepared to walk out.

We had no trouble with the trekking permits; the office opened an hour early and the official in charge smiled and wished us a pleasant trek. We packed, loaded a

That night we ate with Ang Phurba who had managed to find us two porters for the next day so the provisional running order for the schedule read in theory: airline tickets for the return flight from Jomsom; trekking permits; jeep out of Pokhara, then off.

taxi and set out for the pipal tree at the beginning of the trail. On the way I bought some Jeevan Jal (a salt replacement for dysentery) and some Tinibar. Tinibar is banned in Britain and the USA because, as yet, it hasn't been passed by the Food and Drugs Administration, but people had recommended it as a sure-fire cure for dysentery. I'd had a day's respite from the trots and, although I was hoping that this meant I was clear, I decided to take some Tinibar along for desperate remedies.

We pulled up under the shade of a huge tree, where already a dozen or so porters were waiting, squatting and sitting on the porters' wall beneath the huge trunk. Pipal trees are planted all over Nepal and are often found accompanied by a two-tier wall. The first tier stands about three foot from the ground, the normal height at which a porter can rest his loads. Sitting on the wall were our two porters. They were both thin, wiry little men with traditional Nepali caps on their heads, the smallest of the two, in shorts and a khaki shirt, had the widest grin I have ever seen. He was to keep that grin all the way and back. The other was a surly, taller man in bri-nylon slacks and a waistcoat. He proved to be trouble. The smiling porter was called Kharka Bhadur, the sullen one's name we never got to know. To save problems we called them Jim and Eric. Jim the happy one and Eric the miserable one. It sounds condescending, I know, but it wasn't meant to be. It was difficult pronouncing and remembering names at times.

There is a jeepable track north along much of the Pokhara Valley to the beginning of the trek and we bargained with a driver who ran a public jeep service to take us for twenty-five rupees each. A spiv with a much more modern-looking jeep shouted at us.

'His jeep very bad. I take you for four hundred rupees.'

'His jeep very cheap,' I shouted back.

'Too many people are getting on. Road is very bad. Jeep break down,' he answered.

The jeep did look very old and there did seem to be an alarming number of people standing round and loading stuff on it. But we were on a very tight budget and four hundred was just too much. We crammed ourselves into the jeep. The roof was piled high with kitbags, rucksacks and baskets and with men hanging off every finger

and toe hold. We groaned slowly away from the outside of Pokhara and along a rough track that got steadily rougher.

I sat in the front next to the driver; behind were John, Ang Phurba, Jim and Eric and two Dutch and English couples who were heading the same way, trekking to Jomsom. On the outside were eight Nepalis and a little boy who regularly jumped off and topped up the radiator from any streams we came across.

I noticed a polythene jerry can between my legs with a rubber pipe that led under the dashboard in the general direction of the motor. It didn't smell like water. The driver was chain-smoking as were Jim and Eric.

'Petrol?' I asked pointing between my legs.

The driver nodded.

'You smoking?' I shouted over the noise of him slamming through the gears as we crossed a rough river bed.

He offered me a cigarette.

'No!' I shouted. 'I mean it is dangerous to smoke when there is petrol very close.'

He grinned at me and lit up again, not having understood a word I said, puffing a great fog of smoke into the air as the petrol sloshed about, inches from my important bits.

The track became even worse as we climbed the valley and crossed and recrossed the river. Each time we forded the river the driver stopped to change down into low gear and I had to put my foot on the four-wheel drive gear shift to stop it leaping out of drive. With my legs wide apart inhaling rancid smoke and petrol sloshing all over the seat, I wasn't having the best of times.

When we got to the really big hills, the driver made the men clinging on the outside get off and I had to push extra hard on the gear shift. I worked out that there were nineteen of us travelling on that jeep. At one village a couple more jumped on and held on for several miles smiling at the driver as he shouted at them to get off.

The landscape levelled out after a few hours and we crossed a flooded part of the plain where hundreds of egrets were standing in a shallow pool tinged a pale shade of pink by the light reflected from the water.

A wheel fell off just before we reached our destination, so we all got out and stood round offering advice as the driver put another one on. Some of the hangers-on had got bored and had started to walk the last couple of miles to Phedi where the rough track ends and the trek begins. We hung on in there and rolled into the little collection of shacks and tea stalls only minutes ahead of them. The driver got out and started moaning at everybody. Ang Phurba told us he was blaming the passengers for the wheel coming off.

Jim and Eric loaded their 'dokos' (the baskets that are universal carriers to the porters of the Himalaya), John and I loaded up with camera gear and set off on the trek, leaving Phedi, which means 'bottom of hill', well below us as we climbed thousands of stone steps that led up on to the ridge.

It came as a great surprise to see how heavily populated this part of the trail is. We walked through tiny neat little villages, one house deep either side of the track, the trail paved with stone flags as it went through them. Porters constantly passed up and down carrying the heaviest of loads, their little thin legs pushing them ever on and up. At Nagdanda, the first village of any size on the trail, we stopped for dhal batt in a batti house. Jim grinned at us, Eric moped against the batti wall: he was not happy about something and it showed. We sat in the sun watching mule trains, porters and Tibetan merchants go by. Behind us, in the dark of the batti house, the tiniest and prettiest little girl was collecting empty bottles and putting them into crates; no more than three years old, she was already helping out with the chores. She giggled every time she went past me as I called out 'Namaste', the Nepalese equivalent of 'Julay', and meaning 'I salute the God within you'. We rested for a short time after lunch while Jim

and Eric, having consumed a mountain of rice each, raced off, puffing on their cigarettes. We wandered round the curio stalls run by Tibetan refugees, selling temple bells and knitted hats, socks and mittens. A Tibetan girl asked me if I was married and, when for a joke I said no, enquired whether I wanted to marry her sister, pointing at a handsome girl beside her. Then they both roared with laughter and started tickling each other. I didn't know quite what to make of it all.

At Nagdanda there is a police checkpoint to which all trekkers must report to have their documents checked. All my documents, including my trekking permit, were with Jim and Eric who by now were miles ahead. There was almost an international incident and it looked at one time as though we would have to wait at the police checkpoint while Ang Phurba raced along the trail to stop the porters who were going like lightning towards the village where we were staying for the night. We tried to look as honest as we could but it didn't seem to work. Then Ang Phurba sorted it out. We signed the register and I put my passport number down in the book, left ten rupees where the officer could see them and promised to bring my trekking permit on the way back.

He smiled us out of the checkpoint and we climbed on, the valleys opening out on either side, the terraced fields falling away beneath us, in the far distance the shining mirror that was Phewa Tal.

All along the way the harvest was being gathered. In one village we passed through an old lady was winnowing millet on the stone flags in front of her house; in another, a little boy was sitting beneath a corn store, built on stilts with straw skirts tied round to foil the rats, and in the porch of one house a baby was standing up in his cradle watching the world and Jim and Eric go by. As dusk was gathering we came to Kaare, our billet for the night, and Ang Phurba set off to find us some beds.

The sirdar's job is quite complex and doesn't easily break down into clearly definable roles. A young Sherpa boy will work as a porter,

Nagdanda, the first village of any size since Pokhara

perhaps even a high-altitude one, but his ultimate aim is always to be a sirdar. The sirdar leads the trek or expedition; he is responsible for route finding, for the well being of his sahibs and for hiring porters; cooks and yaks. On a trek like this Ang Phurba was responsible for all our dealings with porters, with batti house and hotel owners, as well, of course, as acting as a guide, advising on distances, places to film and the time it would take to travel between points. One thing sirdars never do is carry, which is a porter's job. There were times when Ang Phurba would take certain pieces of camera equipment but that was not lowering his status since he was involved in the technical work of filming, and he helped me tremendously with my gear, heavy and bulky as most of it was. The more we got to know Ang Phurba the more we liked him. He never made a fuss yet he seemed to be able to make things happen all the time. If he did get angry it was usually on our behalf and in the end he became as concerned as we were that the film should be a success.

Everything in the upper reaches of these Himalayan valleys gets there in one of two ways. It is either carried in by mule or on the backs of porters. The bottles of mineral water and Coca Cola that are available all along the trail as well as the toilet paper and the terrible sweet Indian biscuits are all taken in mainly by porters. From dawn to sunset and beyond the human chains endlessly tote their loads up the mountain trails. Mules are used for other goods, though it is said that they will carry less than a man: men are expendable, mules are not.

The Complete Guide to Nepal tells us:

A very interesting sight is a caravan of mules. Each mule is caparisoned with a yak-tail whisk of red colour and an embroidered triangular piece of cloth on its forehead. The owners of these mules are Thaks of Tibetan origin heavily dressed in their traditional ways. Generally these caravans come from Jomsom or Tukuche. The loads they bring consist of salt from the dry lakes of Tibet and raw yak wool. After staying for a few days, the caravans go back carrying with them either rice or wheat.

The indispensable four-legged porters

Even during the worst of the disturbances in Tibet the mule and yak trains continued their trade, seemingly crossing the border without any difficulty, although of course all Westerners were barred from entering either Tibet or the Mustang area of Nepal. The trail is virtually the M1 of this part of Nepal and the numerous hotels and batti houses along the way are evidence that, long before the advent of the trekker, the route was a lifeline through the mountains.

There is a particular smell along the trail that even now, seated at a keyboard in the Yorkshire Dales, I can sense so strongly that I feel I'm almost back there. Imagine if you can an October day with a bright sun warming you, while in the shadows there is a coolness that is almost chilling. There is little wind, below you terraces of fields fall away to infinity and as you enter a village with neat houses on either side of the trail, a woman is washing clothes, squatting by a water trough; a baby watches wide-eyed as you pass and through the street there comes an aroma compounded of cooking, curry, humans and horse sweat and dung. The whole is not overpowering or unpleasant, it's just raw and earthy.

We stayed that night at Kaare in a clean guest house. The beds were basically wooden laths hammered together and we slept fully clothed in our sleeping bags. Washing and teeth brushing were carried out at the village water supply and the only toilet was an old fashioned thunderbox.

All along the trail the batti houses and hotels offer an amazingly full menu running through Tibetan pancakes and dhal batt to omelettes and fried potatoes. Most of the cooking is done on wood fires. Ingenious clay ovens with the fire beneath and two cooking holes above are all the cooks have to work on and yet they seem to be able to serve twenty trekkers at very short notice.

Darkness comes early in the hills and that evening, by the light of an oil lamp, I found myself drinking chang with a group of Indian pilgrims *en route* to Muktinath, a holy Hindu shrine where natural gas seeping from the ground burns constantly in vents that come through rock and water. Earth, air, fire and water, the four things basic to all life are thus enshrined together in this most holy place. 'Muktinath is second most holy temple in all Nepal,' said one of the pilgrims. Then he laughed and pointed at one of his friends who was getting the beginnings of what I later came to call a 'chang-over'.

'He second most holy man in Nepal. He very holy sadhu! Drink much beer and then meditate, Sir!'

The journal for the next day begins:

> The sounds of a Himalayan village. At 4.30 a.m. a dog starts to howl under my window. This wakes a cock up. He decides to outdo the dog and starts crowing. This wakes another cock up at the other end of the village. These

Annapurna and Machhapuchhare from Chandrakot

> two cocks have been daggers drawn for some time now. The first cock insults the second cock's mother. The second cock has information concerning the first cock's wife that has not been heard before. In the end I got up and threw my boots at them.

I awoke while it was still dark and stood at the window watching the sunrise over the hills to the east. Broken cloud was set alight by the sun as it climbed and warmed the street below where, already, fires were being lit, children were getting ready for school and men were loading up their mules and sending them off down the trail.

After a breakfast of Tibetan bread with jam we dropped down from Kaare, through the village of Lumle, and on to Chandrakot where we stopped for tchai. The clouds that had formed broke for a while and, looking up the valley, we saw Annapurna through a hole in the clouds but Machhapuchhare still remained frustratingly hidden.

A long descent from Chandrakot, following thousands of well-made stone steps, brought us down to the river. The porters stopped to make batt at the trailside and we carried on across the left bank of the river to Birethanti, a pleasant little hamlet by a suspension bridge. The dysentery had returned with a vengeance and I was feeling fairly weak, but strangely enough, I was almost deliriously happy. Everything was so strange and so new that I hadn't really got time to feel sorry for myself. The wooded slopes we climbed down, the thousands of brightly-coloured butterflies fluttering in the sun, the yellow of the maize fields, the bronze of the millet in terraced steps descending one after the other, the water buffalo wallowing in pools, the roaring rivers and streams and all the people smiling and calling 'Namaste' as they passed were like an incredibly vivid dream. We dropped from 5,400 feet at Kaare to 3,400 feet at Birethanti where I made use of the foulest latrine I have ever seen at the back of which a filthy slide of excrement and toilet paper ran down into the river. It's easy to see how disease spreads in the water in the mountains. The water looked crystal clear but God alone knows what was in it.

From Birethanti we climbed gradually upwards, a long haul in the afternoon sunshine towards Hille (5,000 feet) and Tirkhedunge (5,125 feet) where we planned to stay the night. I was well ahead of John and Ang Phurba and was resting against a porter's wall looking at the river when a passing Nepali heading downhill with a sickle in his hand called out 'Namaste!' I waved and called back to him. Then he suddenly stopped and with a look of fear on his face said, 'No move!

Stay! Stay!' He held out his left hand palm towards me. I froze and slowly he reached out his sickle and flicked something away from the base of the wall between my feet. It was a snake, about eighteen inches long. Before I could stop him he had killed it with his sickle and slit it open. Inside was a full-size undigested rat. Ang Phurba came along just as the snake was being cut open.

'Oh, he shouldn't have killed it,' said John, who hadn't been nearly bitten.

'Yes, this is very bad snake,' said Ang Phurba. 'This is small cobra. This man say two people killed in Birethanti with these snakes.'

The man was obviously terrified of the snake, even when it was well and truly dead but I still don't know how deadly it was, if at all.

'Are there many snakes around here?' I asked Ang Phurba.

'I never see snakes before in my life,' he answered. But no more than two hundred yards further on at a very dusty part of the trail where sandy rocks were covered in sparse vegetation, a copper-bronze king cobra, four foot long and as thick as my arm, slid across the path and down towards the river. It was what Australians would call a 'brown trouser sort of day'.

The sun shone all that afternoon and the heat and humidity made walking tiring. We stopped many times in the shade under the pipal trees along the way to drink. Behind us came a string of porters carrying the heaviest loads. They too stopped and squatted on the plinths formed by the walls and the tree base, smoking and chatting. They seemed to smoke like chimneys and I wondered how they managed to smoke so much and yet still be able to carry such heavy loads. An average load is ninety pounds yet some of these men were carrying double loads. They mostly seemed to smoke pipes. Not pipes as we know them where the bowl is bent at right angles to the stem but pipes whose bowls continued from the stem like a tulip. They held it between the second and third fingers of a clenched fist and sucked the smoke through a hole at the thumb and forefinger end.

Porter smoking through his clenched fist

At Tirkhedunge Eric deserted. One minute he was there, the next he was gone, running down the hill, his day's wages in hand. Within minutes Ang Phurba had found another porter from the village, a boy in his late teens called Sheer Bhadur who was a distant relative of Kharka Bhadur and whom we christened Sid.

Tirkhedunge is a neat little hill village with a lodge and tea shops, one of which is run by a retired British Army Gurkha. The Gurkhas are not a caste but are drawn from a variety of the hill tribes of Nepal, though the greater part of them do come from this region. At the dinner table that night there were close on a dozen trekkers; the majority were Spanish, German or Dutch though alongside us at our table was an Irish couple from Dublin who were having trouble with

their porter. It had taken them longer to get here than it should have done because he was always getting drunk and losing his wages playing cards with other porters along the way. He had borrowed and lost his wages in advance as far ahead as Ghorapani.

Conversation at the table centred on bowels as it always does in the Himalaya. It's either that or altitude sickness. The thunderbox here was particularly gruesome: a double-header with two closets that were basically little sheds with a door and a hole in the floor through which everything dropped ten feet to the bank below and then slithered into the river. There was no back to the building and somebody said that a few days before a woman doctor from Yorkshire, already weak and sick with dysentery, had used it in the night and gone over backwards, fallen out and had not only been badly injured by the fall but had landed in the mess of years. The poor woman had had to be carried down the trail on a stretcher and had been hospitalised. We heard similar horror stories all along the trek.

That night I was woken by the Irish couple's porter banging on their door asking for more rupees. It was four o'clock in the morning and I'm afraid I strained international relations the next day when I threatened to rip his head off if he did it again. John did point out that the man was a Gurkha and was just as likely to use his kukri to similar effect on my skull.

The mornings were cool and a little misty. Smoke curled from the ovens outside the houses and as we waited for our breakfast, seated on the bench in the open air dressed in our fibrepile jackets, children wandered past singing on their way to school. And teams of mules fully laden, their bells jangling and their yak-tail plumes tossing, laboured along the trail ahead of their whistling and shouting drivers.

The days had rapidly fallen into a pattern. We woke-up around five-thirty and were washed, breakfasted and off by six-thirty or seven. Breakfast was usually tea and Tibetan bread, although John seemed to be able to get through a couple of omelettes and three

Porters moving through the thick sub-tropical rain forest

Fields and flowers near Banthanti

helpings of bread every morning. He ate meals that would have crippled a navvy and yet he was as thin as a lath. I was convinced he had a monster worm lurking somewhere inside him.

I visited the terrible thunderbox at Tirkhedunge too many times for comfort and after a hurried breakfast we set off, dropped down to the river, crossed two bridges, and began a climb that would take us all of the day and would see us climbing through six thousand feet into thick, sub-tropical rain forest of birch, oak, rhododendron and Himalayan holly. The rhododendrons here were anything up to sixty feet high. In the early summer the hillsides must be on fire with their blossom.

The signs of deforestation became more apparent the higher we climbed. As we rounded a bend breathless and woozy, the cloudy sky ahead suddenly broke and opened to show Annapurna standing above; the clouds then closed up again as though there was a door in the sky. We stopped at Banthanti for something to eat and then pushed on through thickening forest that grew very humid with a lot of post-monsoon cloud and mist about. At one point we were completely enclosed by dense Himalayan jungle and our world became a green tunnel through which we wandered with the sounds of bells and shouting muleteers hidden in the forest before and behind us.

The jungle thinned out as we climbed higher and the track became a succession of thousands of stone steps. Whereas the trail in Zanskar had been quite rough at times and, in fact, on the Shingo La had been difficult to follow, here there was no possibility of getting lost. We were walking on a motorway.

The afternoon grew cold and low cloud rolled in from the south, so low that at times we were walking through clammy, chill fog as we reached Ghorapani and stood on the pass looking down to where the Kali Gandak Gorge and the mountains Annapurna and Dhaulagiri lay hidden in the mist.

We found Bill Jones and Josette Wander in their house in the village and had tea with them. We were going to be here for a few days so Ang Phurba set about finding somewhere for us all to sleep. Jim and Sid looked particularly cold in their shorts and thin shirts and we managed to find some blankets that they wrapped round themselves like cloaks. They sat by the fire with mugs of tchai in their hands, grinning.

In The Himalaya View lodge, which was to become our favourite lodge, I met an Englishman from Ambleside who works for the British Trust for Conservation Volunteers. He was over in the Himalaya on a sort of busman's holiday, looking at conservation work. A year later I spent a day with him rebuilding footpaths in the Langdales in the Lake District – a small world indeed.

Gandhi's Revenge came back at four o'clock the next morning and I only just made it to the thunderbox in time. It was quite strange squatting there in the moonlight at nine thousand feet with Annapurna peering above the clouds. At dawn we climbed Pune Hill, which stands above Ghorapani at ten thousand feet, to watch the sun rise over Annapurna and Machhapuchhare, but thick clouds rolled in and the mountains disappeared. The Fish Tail was still something I had only seen in books.

After breakfast we spent a few hours filming Bill's work in the area and then suddenly it was John's turn to be ill. He collapsed, wiped out by a gastric bug. I said it was no wonder the amount of food he'd been throwing down his neck, his stomach was probably just worn out. He crashed out for the rest of the day.

Bill's work here has been really effective. He has built a series of dry, self-composting toilets that break down the faecal matter to produce a manure for the land and he has also built pit latrines where an easily dismantled toilet is built over a deep pit. When the pit is full it is earthed over and the toilet is moved somewhere else.

The other major problem, alongside sanitation and water, is the deforestation caused largely by the great numbers of trekkers that travel through this area. Ghorapani is probably the busiest village in the Himalaya, something like twenty-five thousand trekkers journey through here every season; if you add to that their porters and sirdars you come close to a figure of fifty thousand people passing through a village of no more than a dozen lodges. The Kali Gandaki Valley is now being called, only half jokingly, 'the Coca Cola Gandaki Valley'. The strain on the ecosystem is incredible. The forest all around is being cut down steadily, some of it for building but most of it for fuel. Where it has not already gone, the forest is dying because the branches have been ripped off for fodder and fuel, and the constant pollarding means that many of the trees will soon be dead. Kerosene is expensive because it has to be brought in from India and India charges heavily for everything that crosses its border. Wood is really the only fuel available to them.

The problem is not just that the trees are disappearing and that by the turn of the century there may be no trees at all in the Himalaya but that without tree roots to bind the soil it gets washed by the heavy monsoon rain down the steep slopes into the river. This constant erosion is believed to be largely responsible for the recurrent massive flooding in the Brahmaputra basin. But the forests serve another important function; it is from them that the people's herbal medicines come. When the forests go there will be no fuel, no wood for building, the hillsides and fields will slide down the mountains and into the sea and the natural store of medicines will be lost.

Bill is building heating stoves that are ten times as economical as any that currently exist in the mountains and cooking stoves that heat water on a simple system of pipes which means that the lodges get hot water for free and don't have to burn extra wood for the trekkers' showers. One of the problems is not that trekkers demand food but that they also ask for hot showers and hot water, little imagining the havoc they are wreaking on the environment. While Bill cannot halt

Deforestation at Ghorapani

the deforestation, he is doing a great job of slowing it down and in a small nursery below the village there is the beginning of a replanting scheme that could be the salvation of the area. All the technology Bill has introduced is simple, cheap and easily available and what is more important, the people are coming to Bill for help. The village 'panychat', or council, has worked with Bill all the way through. This is then no imposition of technology from outside, it is something growing from within. Bill is scornful of most foreign aid. What doesn't find its way into the pockets of corrupt politicians is often ineffectual. If the Chinese build a road in the hills, they leave behind bulldozers and earth-movers. When they break down there are no parts to repair them and no technicians to work on them, so millions of rupees' worth of equipment simply rusts.

In Bill's appropriate technology the only implements used are pipe benders and jointing tools. The pipe is cheap and comes from Pokhara on mules. Ang Phurba was greatly impressed and made detailed notes and drawings to take back to his own village in the Solo Khumbu.

John seemed to make a miraculous recovery when he smelt cooking from one of the neighbouring lodges and staggered over to eat an enormous meal of dhal batt and chocolate pudding. He claimed that the homeopathic remedy he'd been taking since arriving in Nepal had cured him. I'd been taking everything under the sun and still couldn't get rid of whatever it was that had me by the sphincter.

We ate that evening again in The Himalaya View. It was run by a young woman called Ang Bikka, a handsome dark-eyed lady who always seemed to be smiling and laughing. She was gentle and intelligent and she was also divorced. This is quite unusual in the hills and Ang Bikka, a fiercely independent lady, had had to pay a great sum of money to get rid of her former husband, who it appears, was a drunken sot. But she had done it and now she ran the lodge, kept more than twenty beds clean and neat, cooked from five in the morning until nine at night and provided hot showers for the sweaty and often rude trekkers that came through her doors.

I never ceased to be amazed and upset at the ignorance of Westerners in their relations with the Nepalese who ran the lodges. They shouted, haggled over one rupee, complained about prices when a good hot meal cost less than a cup of coffee in the West, accused the Nepalis of cheating and, worst of all, abused their culture and religion.

In a Nepali or Sherpa home, the hearth is sacred. You do not sit by the fire unless bidden to and once there you never throw anything in it or spit in it. One evening a group of Israeli trekkers barged in and pushed their way in front of the fire, shoving Ang Bikka's old father and mother out of the way. They took off their boots, sticking their steaming feet up to the fire and then proceeded to clear their throats and gob into it. They ignored Ang Bikka except when they ordered food in rough shouts and grunts. One of them went upstairs, dumped his stuff in the dormitory and came down again in a T-shirt and jockey shorts, half his wedding tackle hanging out of one side. He stood over Ang Bikka who was cooking on the fire and shouted 'Hot water!' several times, indicating that he wanted a shower. He wouldn't have walked up to the front desk of the Tel Aviv Hilton in his underwear shouting for hot water, so why was he doing it here? The league table for ignorance and insensitivity was headed by the Israelis, who won hands down. After them came the French and the Germans. Bottom of the league were the Dutch who were generally very polite and the English who, apart from the occasional Raj-type, were usually respectful. The Australians, while they tore each other to pieces and made a study of insulting any Poms they came across, were usually quite good with the local people. The most sympathetic of all were the Irish. Whether it has much to do with the strongly pastoral-religious base of both cultures I don't know, let an anthropologist spit the bones out of that lot.

We were woken early the next morning by the sounds of cocks crowing, children shouting and two women fighting over a girl. Bill said the fight was something to do with a daughter being too forward in her new mother-in-law's house and her mother had come along to back her up. There was a tremendous amount of shrieking and screaming, then the two women jumped at each other and started slapping and pulling hair. Their husbands stepped in and both got kicked for their troubles. The whole village came out and stood round watching and commenting. Eventually it seemed to sort itself out and everybody went about their business.

Josette plays a very delicate role in bringing suitable technology to the village. She talks to the women and, more importantly, listens to them. Because she speaks Nepali and lives in the community they have come to see her not as someone who interferes but as a friend. Infant mortality is very high in the hill villages, largely because of the

Dhaulagiri

Ang Bikka

said that it was like being in the middle of some sort of force field.

Some years ago a friend of mine had been trekking in this area and an Englishwoman in the party had simply disappeared off the track. She had wandered a little way off but when they came to look for her there was no trace. Sherpas and Nepalis searched the forests for days but she had gone. Nothing was found, no body, no bones or scraps of clothing, nothing.

We were leaving the next day, turning south and cutting through the forest to Gundruk, having abandoned the idea of getting to Jomsom in time to get a flight out to Pokhara. John was worried that the Indian film crew, who would be working on the most important part of the film, would be arriving in Kathmandu soon and we needed to be back and ready to begin working on the Everest trail.

At dawn we climbed Pune Hill again and this time the clouds largely stayed away and the whole of the Annapurna range was spread before us: Dhaulagiri, Annapurna One, Annapurna South and Hiunchuli.

Below lay the Kali Gandak Gorge running northwards to Tibet, the deepest gorge in the world. Half a day's walk north of Pune Hill at Tatopani (3,900 feet), Dhaulagiri (26,795 feet) and Annapurna (26,545 feet) are only twenty-two miles apart and they tower 22,000 feet above the village.

We stood for more than an hour, watching the light change on the mountains from deep golden-red to a pale-rose blush and then swirling mists rolling from the south stopped at the pass, and as the sun burnt off the vapour, choughs and ravens swooped and circled, calling above the lodges of Pune Hill where the breakfast fires were smoking in the cold morning air.

I looked for Machhapuchhare but couldn't see her distinct twin fins anywhere.

'Where is the Fish Tail, Ang Phurba?' I asked.

'Hidden behind Annapurna,' he grinned.

contaminated water. Babies get acute dysentery and die, often of dehydration. Josette tells the women that it is the bad water that is killing their babies. They in turn begin badgering their husbands until something gets done. In that way the whole village has worked on the water scheme. In twelve months' time Bill hoped that every lodge and house in the village would have pure drinking water from the stone cistern they had built up on the hill.

One night, around the table in Ang Bikka's lodge, Bill talked about the forests and the people of the hills. There are some areas of forest, he said, that were so old that they were seen as very holy places by both Buddhists and Hindus. Very powerful spirits were said to live there. In some parts this sense of raw power was so strong that nobody would go into the forests. Bill had been to one such place and

Annapurna One and Annapurna South, with Hiunchuli on the left

3

Electric Soup and the Last Boat Home

'Children and valleys should belong to those who care for them best.'
– Bertholt Brecht *The Caucasian Chalk Circle*

WE LEFT GHORAPANI far below us and climbed up the steep ridge towards Gundruk. A party of Japanese walkers in tweed jackets carrying rolled umbrellas, looking strangely out of place, overtook us as we stopped to take photographs. I began to wonder if I was hallucinating. Near the top of the ridge is the pass that leads to Gundruk with a tea house astride it. From there the views of the Annapurna – Dhaulagiri range and down the Kali Gandaki towards Tatopani are superb. From the tea house the track dropped down steeply through dense mountain jungle, past tumbling waterfalls and sheer cliff edges. Sometimes the tree cover would break and through maple leaves that were yellowing at the approach of winter, we could see Annapurna South and catch occasional half glimpses of Machhapuchhare dodging in and out of the clouds. In the jungle, maples and oaks, silver birch and creepers closed in around us blocking out the light. Bill had told us that the forests were the haunt of grey leopards and Himalayan bears though it was doubtful whether we'd see any since they were more frightened of us than we were of them.

Descending rapidly from one section of the forest, we hit upon a clearing with a batti house where a dozen porters were sitting in the sun, wearing their colourful knitted hats, taking a break. Three of them were playing drums and singing while all the others joined in.

They smiled and waved and sang louder as we passed them heading downhill.

Back in the forest again we found the pathway quite hairy with at one place a risky scramble over slimy rocks down the side of a steep waterfall. When we reached the bottom Ang Phurba had a nosebleed and, as he was trying to staunch it, he began to lose his footing on the rough track by the river. I grabbed hold of him and also lost my balance. He tried to stop me falling and started sliding towards the river himself, then I pulled him back hopping backwards as I did so. John just sat down and laughed himself silly saying it was the best bit of dancing he'd seen in years.

We sat Ang Phurba down with a cold, wet cloth on the back of his neck and I paddled up to the waterfall to take a photograph of a clump of purple flowers growing in the moist vegetation at the side of the waterfall. I took a couple of shots and turned away to paddle back to the bank, which I had just reached when a half-ton block of rock dislodged itself from the cliff and landed on the exact spot where my head had been just ten seconds earlier.

'It's a good job you moved or there would have been two of you with a nose bleed,' said John succinctly.

We walked through miles of thick forest, dropping downwards

Annapurna from Gundruk

Terraces of rice fields near Tatopani

following the banks of a deep gorge. Coming towards us through the trees we heard voices and saw a party of Nepalis heading uphill, on their way to a wedding and all dressed in their best clothes, singing and smiling as they went.

We stopped at a tea house in a tiny place called Banthanti which caused much confusion since there's another Banthanti on the other side of Ghorapani. Two Australians were convinced that they had gone miles out of their way and, being Poms, we failed to convince them otherwise. They wandered northwards staring at the map and shaking their heads.

The maps of this region, by the way, are pretty poor. Mandala Maps do a fairly detailed trekking map but it's on the sort of paper that blueprints are printed on and it doesn't last very long in your back pocket. The US Army Corps of Engineers map at 1:250,000 has hardly any of the village names on it. (What are the US Army doing mapping Nepal anyway? Another Sphere of Influence?)

After Banthanti we climbed slowly through more jungle. On either side of the trail there were thick mats of flowers and around them flickered flocks of bright yellow butterflies. There was a long tedious climb that seemed to go on for ever up towards the pass at Toudepani where I suddenly saw ahead of me, standing above the clouds, Machhapuchhare glowing in the afternoon sun, its twin peaks majestic and fierce. At long last I had seen the Fish Tail Mountain and it was beautiful beyond words.

According to Ang Phurba it is a sacred mountain and has never been climbed. When I asked why, he said that the god of the mountain was a particularly angry one and that anybody who had tried to climb the mountain had died.

At Toudepani there is a lodge run by yet another ex-British Army Gurkha and we sat drinking tea and watching the clouds rise up until they had blotted out the Fish Tail; but at least we had seen her. The light was beginning to fail as we left the pass and pushed hard downhill through wonderful country to Gundruk, arriving just as the oil lamps were being lit at the Snowland lodge where we were staying for the night. The thunderbox here was one of the better class ones and didn't have a forty-foot drop at the back of it, which was a relief to me as I was its most dedicated patron.

There was a wonderful little boy at the Snowland, about nine years

Machhapuchhare's twin peaks glowing in the afternoon sun

old, who seemed to be running the whole show. He took all the orders and ran to and from the kitchen serving and translating. He spoke English well but could also talk a little French and German. His name sounded like Am Ett but everybody called him Omelette.

We ate next morning at a table on the grass in front of the lodge, and across the valley Annapurna South and Machhapuchhare looked almost within touching distance. Round the table were a motley crew of trekkers. Frenchmen, Germans and a couple of Australians as well as us. The conversation at breakfast covered the usual topics, dysentery and altitude sickness with a minor diversion from the Australians, Neal and Dave, into the works of Myles Na Gopaleen, otherwise known as Flann O'Brien or Brian O'Nolan, probably the greatest comic writer that Ireland has ever produced. In his book *The Third Policeman* one of the characters has a theory that, since all things are composed of molecules, tiny pieces of matter whizzing through space, then people's backsides and bicycle

Terraced fields and flowers, with Annapurna in the distance

seats must exchange molecules on account of their being pounded together. He concluded that there were some people in his parish who were more than half bicycle and some bicycles that were more than half people.

There's always something of the unexpected in foreign travel and having a conversation about molecular theory as it applies to Irish

backsides and bicycle seats with two Australians under the shadow of Annapurna must rank as one of my more bizarre experiences.

We spent some of the morning at the project centre of The King Mehindra Trust For Nature Conservation. Like Bill Jones at Ghorapani, the Trust is introducing reforestation and sanitation schemes into the hill villages. Run by Nepalis, the Trust is making steady but slow progress in educating the local people about the problems faced by their ecosystem.

The track back towards Pokhara followed a well-made paved way and long stone-stairways dropping down to the valley of the Modi Khola. We were well above the river, but higher still were great waterfalls dropping down through the thick forest. At one bend in the trail an impressive fall tumbled down from a steep cliff-face while by the side of the bridge that spanned it was a shrine round which strips of cloth tied to the trees waved in the breeze. The cloth hanging from the trees was exactly like some of the shrines I had seen in Sligo, Ireland where a statue of the Virgin in a stone bower is obviously on the site of a much older sacred well or spring. I asked Ang Phurba what the shrine was for.

'A very angry god lives here,' he answered. 'Many people have been killed here and people make offerings to the gods.'

This spirit of place and the belief that certain springs or cliffs or waterfalls have their own demons or gods is common all over the Himalaya. On the bridge over the Barai Nala on the way to the Shingo La there was a shrine with prayer-flags devoted to whatever demon lurked in the chasm beneath. There was a time when I might have laughed at such beliefs or at least treated them with scepticism, but not any more. There is something about this whole area, in particular the river gorges, that made me feel a very strong presence. Whether it was a collective build-up of emotions in a place that was particularly holy or whether something bad had happened there I don't know. Certain areas of the forest had felt very old and very unfriendly and yet others not at all. I'm not going to try and explain it. It's just the way I felt.

Round the corner Jim and Sid had made a small fire in the sun and were cooking dhal batt. They carried with them all they needed for food for three or four days, cooking onions and vegetables in a little pan and boiling the rice separately; the cumin, coriander, salt and other seasonings are added to the butter early. All this is carried in a bundle or sack which goes in the doko. It made us a bit ashamed to think that we had carried our film equipment only while they had carried heavy loads with so little in the way of food and clothing for themselves.

The valley widened out and we walked amongst terraces of maize and rice. A small girl, hardly more than a baby, smiled from a garden wall as we passed and handed me a flower. It was a simple act of giving and I found it almost overwhelming.

Everywhere people were bringing in the rice harvest singing as they worked, a lone boy climbing through fields above us played a flute as he walked, the notes floating out around the valley. Watermills were grinding buckwheat by the side of the fast-flowing streams and on the veranda of a house a woman wove a rainbow-coloured strip of cloth. As we passed a house garden a young woman called to us and handed us an orange she had just picked from a tree. We bought a dozen of

Jim cooking dhal batt at the side of the trail

these fresh juicy green oranges and sucked them noisily all the way down the trail. At another garden we bought mangoes and sweet chestnuts and strolled through the golden afternoon eating them. I was still trying to convince myself that I was working.

We crossed the river at Bhichuk and worked our way up the opposite side of the valley, climbing towards Chandrakot. Now the way became steep and treacherous; a recent landslide had washed away hundreds of feet of terracing and we had to pick our way carefully across the slip, working our way up the hillside looking for the remains of the zigzag path. Eventually we found it and climbed into Chandrakot meeting a team of something like fifty mules going down towards Pokhara carrying bags of salt.

At the lodge we met a Dutch couple who shamed us by speaking excellent English. Over a bottle or two of the local dark rum, which I christened 'Electric Soup', because of its rapid and devastating effect, they told us how they had packed in their jobs, sold their house and were using the money to finance their trip round the world.

'We may only be able to do it once,' they said. 'Why should we tie ourselves down to a house and a car and all that rubbish. We can do that again when we come back. If we want to.'

This freebooting way of life appealed very strongly to both John and me and, the rum having given us Dutch courage, we contemplated telling the television company where they could put their camera but fortunately there was no phone handy as we might have regretted it in the morning. Their porter was so drunk he couldn't speak.

'I don't know how he's still standing,' said the girl. 'He has been drinking all day and he has drunk two bottles of rum since we came here. He has no clothes for cold weather and we are going very high.'

There is no system of registration of porters in Nepal. Anybody can hire him or herself out as a porter and one problem is that many of the porters have no cold weather gear. Porters have been known to freeze to death having been deserted by trekkers. The Dutch couple were heading north to Muktinath and were going to try and buy the porter some clothes on the way. He just sat and grinned at us all and opened yet another bottle of Electric Soup.

I awoke in darkness the next morning thinking that John, in the bed next to mine, was choking to death. In fact it was the noise of a buffalo snorting under the stairs and the Dutch couple's drunken porter asking the child of the house for water.

As we were breakfasting the first of the day's mule trains went through, their bells clanging. Anybody who wants to imagine what village life was like in Europe a hundred and fifty years ago should visit a Himalayan village. In eighteenth- and nineteenth-century Europe, goods were transported on pack animals like this and the noise as a mule train went through, bells jangling, must have been very much like this.

If you add to that the sound of cocks crowing, children shouting and a herd of goats and sheep bleating their way through the narrow street you begin to realise that the eighteenth century must have been a noisy time in which to live.

The journal:

> We heard at breakfast that the jeepable road from Phedi is now closed. The Chinese are busy moving some heavy equipment along it to begin work on a new stretch of road, so we'll either have to walk to Pokhara or walk down to the lake. Apparently they're going to build a road up here to this village. Goodbye Shangri-La, hello Disneyland.

From Chandrakot our path went back along the way we had come through Lumle and Kaare and by fields of people singing and harvesting to Nagdanda where the policeman stamped my trekking permit twice and where the Tibetan girl asked me again if I wanted to marry her sister and laughed twice as much. We dropped down a difficult and rambling path towards the lake, Sid and I racing each other. I was wearing a good pair of boots and was carrying only my camera gear. Sid was carrying a doko of kit and filming equipment and wearing only a cheap pair of rubber-thong sandals and he still beat me.

At the lakeside we walked through a sea of shoulder-high golden rice, crossing paddy fields knee-deep in water until we came at last to a lakeside village where we hired a boat and a boatman to row us the six miles to Pokhara. We sang and joked all the way, everybody taking turns to row, even Ang Phurba, who did very well considering that there aren't any lakes where the Sherpas come from. It's a bit like asking a fish to climb a mountain, if you see what I mean.

Egrets stood in the rushes and fish-eagles hunted in the shallows as the sun went down behind us and our boat drew up on the shore by the road to Pokhara. There we said goodbye to Jim and Sid. They had

Paddy fields: a sea of shoulder-high golden rice

John with Jim and Sid

carried our gear cheerfully all the way, had fetched us sweet chestnuts from the forest trees and apricots and green oranges from the orchards. They spoke no English and we no Nepali yet we had liked each other and we had formed a tremendous respect for them. They walked into the night turning many times to call Namaste, their hands together and heads bowing until they were out of sight.

From my journal:

> Two things remain burned in my mind from today's trek. One is the little girl handing me the flower from the wall of her house, the other is the look on the face of a young girl I saw climbing from the lakeside with a doko full of potatoes. The look of utter exhaustion on her face was so powerful it filled me with a confusing mixture of emotions ranging from guilt and sorrow to understanding. She seemed to represent the hard life of the mountains, perhaps the hard lives of peasant people everywhere. She was all griefs, all sufferings. No man is an island. She was my sister and there was nothing I could do.

SLEEPING COOLIE

On his back a fifty pound load,
spine bent double
six miles straight up in the January snow,
naked bones,
two rupees worth of life in his body
to challenge the mountain.
Cloth cap black with sweat
and worn to shreds,
body swarming with lice and fleas,
mind dulled.
It's like sulphur, but how tough
this human frame.

The bird of his heart panting,
sweat and breath.
On the cliff his hut, kids trembling:
hungry griefs!
No greens to eat: his wife combs the woods
for weeds and nettles.

Beneath the snow peak
of this more than human hero's mountain,
conquering nature, with a hoard of pearls –
The sweat on his forehead –
and above only the lid of night
bright with stars:
in this night he is rich with sleep.

– Laxmiprasad Devkota, Nepali poet (1909–59)

4

Kathmandu No Can Do

'And the wildest dreams of Kew are the facts of Kathmandu'
– Rudyard Kipling

WE HAD MADE the trek to Ghorapani for two reasons: the first was to film Bill Jones and the work he was doing; the second was to get fit for the trek to base camp. But it was now October 19th and the film crew was due to fly in from Delhi at any time. Naresh Bedhi the cameraman and Nandu Kumar his sound recordist are probably the finest wildlife film-makers in India and are certainly amongst the top of that profession in the world. Naresh had made two prize-winning films on the Bengal tiger and was busy working on a film about the Indian elephant, which he was delaying to work on our film. Both he and Nandu were on a tight schedule and had to be back in India early in November.

A monsoon storm had raged all night and looking out of the windows of our Pokhara hotel the next morning we could see that the garden was under a foot of water. Rain was still bucketing down and a high wind was buffeting the trees, sending the rain sideways across the land.

The news at breakfast was that the airport was unsure whether any planes would be flying in or out that day. John was becoming a bit desperate. Never very happy when he's away from the phone for any length of time, he now set about trying to discover whether the film crew had arrived in Kathmandu. There was no news of them there and the lines to Delhi had all gone down so that it was impossible to discover whether they'd left or not. Then John discovered that the film stock, which was travelling overland from Jiri to Namche Bazar in the keeping of a Canadian yeti-seeker called Robert Hutchinson, had only just left Kathmandu. Allowing for a nine-day walk, this meant that we could be in Namche for three or four days without film. John sat down and began ripping his hair out. I helped him.

We went to the airport hoping that the gods would smile on us, the rain would stop and that the sun would come out. They didn't.

So now we sit in the airport lounge looking out at the rain, the mountains totally hidden in mist and low cloud. We settle down into that mélange of speculation, myth, rumour and fantasy that is the only recourse of besieged Westerners marooned in Eastern airports. Asians seem to have the ability to wait patiently for whatever changes Fate and Time may bring. We peer expectantly into the mist and pray for miracles.

A Finnish film crew here to make a film on Nepalese culture are staring glumly into the murk. Nothing happens. Then nothing happens again. I talk to one of the Finns about Finland and filming and we get on quite well until I mention Chernobyl and ask about the plight of the Lapps whose way of life may be threatened because their reindeer are so badly contaminated they are having to be slaughtered. He suddenly becomes mute and stares out at the rain again and doesn't even say much when I change the subject to football hooligans. I don't think I look like a KGB man but I suppose you never can tell.

I drink a Japanese lady's tea by mistake, thinking John has bought it.

Her friend says, 'May I take for glass?' I think she's clearing up for some reason and say,

'I haven't finished it yet.' She retires in confusion. Then, Mrs Sakiyoto, the interpreter, comes and explains that the lady bought the tea for herself and put it by my chair while she went for some sugar. John buys everybody another cup of tea. Smiles all round. Bows all round. No ploblem.

Ang Phurba is a treasure. John mentions that he would like a biscuit if there were any to be had and Ang Phurba sprints through the rain returning with a packet that John wolfs, only giving Ang Phurba and me one each. Mean bugger. And still we wait.

Eventually, towards noon, we were told that there would be no flights that day and we were faced with a choice of staying another night at Pokhara and trying for a flight the next day or hiring a car to take us to Kathmandu. It was not certain that we would fly the next day. If the monsoon persisted we could be stranded at the airport for days. It certainly didn't look as though it would lift. The rain was still belting down from a black sky. We decided that eight or ten hours by road would at least get us into Kathmandu that night, so Ang Phurba set out to look for a car.

We took the least wrecked looking car he had seen and we agreed a price with the driver, who looked about twelve years old, and his assistant, who looked about six, and we started out on a car ride that I shall not forget as long as I live. We left the airport marginally ahead of the other passengers who were clamouring for taxis and, after filling up with petrol, sped out of town and over a bridge. The driver wound his window down and threw a handful of small coins into the river as we crossed. This was for luck, to appease the gods of the river and to make sure our journey was successful. The wretched things must have been counterfeit.

The rain lashed down and mist turned the trees and the fields into the delicate brushmarks of a Chinese water-colour landscape. People stood patiently waiting for buses by the roadside in the rain, holding newspapers over themselves. A little boy pedalled his bicycle through the puddles, an up-turned bucket on his head. We watched the landscape roll slowly by as the car lurched towards Kathmandu. For three hours we ploughed through the rain. For an hour we were stopped altogether as a team of hundreds of Chinese manoeuvred a massive piece of earth-moving equipment across the road. The Chinese are building a huge hydro-electric scheme here and have drilled a tunnel through a mountain to do it. I suppose that's just what Nepal needs, plenty of electricity; not a flushing toilet for miles, but as much electricity as you like. An hour or so later, as night was falling, we trundled into a place called Muling where the road from India joins the Pokhara–Kathmandu highway. Apart from Darwin in Australia, it was the closest I've been to a Wild West town. Lorries, cars and buses were parked everywhere and on each side of the road batti houses were doing a great deal of business with the wild-eyed Punjabi drivers and their assistants.

While our driver was changing the tyre that had punctured just as we were pulling into town, John, Ang Phurba and I went into the nearest batti house. Loud music was crashing out of a ghetto-blaster in the back of the shop where a cook was working at a mud stove. We ordered dhal batt and tchai and sat and waited, trying to talk to each other over the noise of lorries changing gear and somebody on the radio singing one of those Indian love songs that goes on for hours and sounds as though the singer is trying seriously to injure himself, while a regiment of violinists slide swirling down a modal scale as though they are on a fairground helter-skelter. It was very dark and we were very wet and not very happy. Gandhi's Revenge, or the Green Apple Quickstep, had now become a way of life and I began to wonder what I had ever done without it.

There was a lot of coming and going in this particular batti house and there seemed to be a large number of what I took to be waitresses in smart dresses and leggings with make-up on. Make-up is quite unusual in Nepal. There also seemed to be a constant stream of rugged men and leather-jacketed youths going to the back of the shop and reappearing ten or twenty minutes later – smiling.

'They all seem to be getting served before us,' muttered John, who hadn't eaten for at least an hour. It dawned on me that what we were in was basically a whorehouse-cum-café, and that the reason it took a long time to serve us was obvious.

Yet another puncture: Ang Phurba in charge

'No good Kathmandu tonight. Road is closed.'

Apparently a landslip twenty miles ahead had completely blocked the road leaving hundreds of cars, lorries and buses stranded on either side. We looked for beds in the town but only one could be found. It was a smelly, rag-covered plank in a cupboard above a kerosene store and they wanted one hundred rupees for it.

'Where is the toilet?' I asked and a hand wave indicated anywhere and everywhere. This town had the biggest toilets in the world. One bed between four of us and a toilet that stretched for miles didn't sound a good idea. The driver said we could

After the meal I asked for the toilet and a hand pointed me out to the back. The 'toilet' was a mud-filled open yard with a sad, broken down Chinese lorry stranded in it. Squatting there in the rain I couldn't avoid seeing the hookers through the open windows of the little rooms in front of me going about their business with the Indian lorry drivers and leather boys of the town by the light of one dim, bare, fly-specked bulb. It made a change from reading *Peanuts* in the bog.

Back at the table we chain-drank cups of tchai and watched the rain bounce off the mud outside. Then our driver came in smiling and we knew it was bad news. In Nepal everybody smiles. They are the happiest and most pleasant people I have ever come across. But there are different sorts of smiles and this was a 'there's not a lot we can do about it, isn't Life a bitch and at least we've got our health thank God' kind of smile. He sat down and lit a cigarette. We waited for it.

all sleep in the car but I didn't fancy spending the night bent up in a clapped-out old banger in a Wild West town full of lorry drivers and knocking shops. We could probably return to Pokhara in four or five hours, then try to get through to Kathmandu in the morning.

There were floods and fog all the way back. Chinese lorries loomed out of the dark, blinding us with their lights and covering us with mud. At one o'clock we arrived at the Hotel Crystal, Pokhara. It was empty but they couldn't give us any rooms because they were waiting for a busload of tourists from Kathmandu.

'But the road is blocked,' we told them. 'Nobody can possibly arrive until tomorrow.'

'We are still full,' they said.

'Suppose they don't come? You will be empty all night and we have nowhere to sleep.'

'If they don't come we will be empty but we will still be full of bookings. But they will come and then we will be full of Germans.'

In the face of such superior logic we retired beaten. We phoned the Fish Tail Lodge and they said they would have us. So the driver went off after arranging to come back early in the morning and we ferried across the lake to the Fish Tail Lodge under a sky that had suddenly cleared and was heavy with stars.

I spent a poor night dancing the Green Apple Quickstep on my own, trying not to wake John up and shaking him occasionally to stop him snoring. John doesn't snore so much as grumble in his sleep. I have spent the night with far worse snorers. I once shared a room with the King of all snorers, a Geordie who worked for a record company I was once involved with. His snores weren't so much snores as sound effects. He did a milk-float going across cobbles on a frosty morning, bottles rattling and engine whining. He did a Dornier bomber flying low in fog over the Lincolnshire coast and a bus with a faulty exhaust driving over a ploughed field. He did a pig being run over by a steam train and a Volkswagen Beetle being push-started underwater. His *pièce de résistance* was a suit of armour falling downstairs on to a teddy bear in a bath of custard. I was more amazed at his virtuosity than annoyed at my loss of sleep.

The star bejewelled sky turned into a miserable grey dawn. We debated whether to try flying out yet again but it didn't look as though there was any chance. In the breakfast room of the lodge I found a week-old copy of *Rising Nepal*, the national daily paper. An article on health problems told me that the sewers of Kathmandu and the drinking water supply are virtually interchangeable. That half glass of water I drank on October 1st must have been a new cocktail called 'The Dysenteric's Delight'!

Our driver arrived at eight o'clock and we set off again for Kathmandu.

'Should only take about five hours,' said Ang Phurba. 'Should be in Kathmandu maybe by two o'clock.'

We had three punctures in fairly quick succession. After the first we all got out to unload the boot so that the driver's assistant could get the spare tyre. It was as shiny as a patent leather shoe with not the slightest memory of a tread on it and had two deep gashes in the side where two neat bubbles of innertube were peeping through. The punctured tyre was little better.

We drove along until we got to a wayside garage that was simply a hut with some tyres piled against one wall where a man was hitting a Chinese lorry with a massive spanner in an attempt to make it say it was sorry for breaking down.

He levered off the tyre, threw the innertube in a tub of water and watched as bubbles came up. An iron was heated on a fire and a patch hot-vulcanised on to the innertube, adding a deep-red lozenge to the already tartan surface of this Joseph's innertube of many colours. He put it back in the tyre and blew it up. There was little to choose between this tyre and the spare save that this had only one gash in it. Ten miles further on, on a bend above the river, there was a bang and we stopped. We changed the tyre and rolled into another truck stop where another man was hitting another Chinese lorry with another spanner. We repaired the tyre and changed it over yet again and John had a row with the driver about the roadworthiness of his car and how much all this was costing us. The driver shrugged, his little assistant shrugged, and we all got back in the car and set off once more. We passed though Muling where the girls were leaning against the open front of the batti house looking at the traffic growling past, obviously hoping for another landslide.

Beyond Muling we came to the landslip. It had been cleared enough to allow single-file traffic and people were directing cars and lorries through the thick glutinous morass of mud that still covered the road. We crawled through, wheels spinning, spraying everyone around with yellow slime and a hundred yards later the tyre went again.

There is a village called Galchi Bazar, where the Trisuli River crosses the Pokhara-Kathmandu road. We stopped there to fix puncture number three and to buy more cigarettes for the boy assistant who was determined to stunt his growth. The village was full of people who had come in for the market and Tamangs, Newhars and Gurongs mingled in the streets. A woman suckled her baby at the roadside and an old lady wearing a head-scarf and a large gold nose-ring squatted before a spread of chilli peppers smoking a large hand-rolled cigarette. At the roadside people were busy at the tchai stalls, the smoke from the cooking fires spiralling through the soft afternoon sunlight.

A Gurong woman

It was by now four o'clock. There is a mathematical puzzle that explores the relationship between Achilles and a tortoise. Achilles begins running after the tortoise when they are a hundred yards apart. In ten seconds Achilles can run a hundred yards and the tortoise one yard. By the time Achilles has got to the tortoise's starting point the tortoise has moved on a yard. By the time Achilles has run that further yard the tortoise has moved on a few inches, by the time Achilles has run those few inches, the tortoise has moved on fractions of an inch and so on and so on. The result is that, though the gap between Achilles and the tortoise gets smaller and smaller, it never quite

disappears, and therefore Achilles never catches the tortoise. QED. Kathmandu was our tortoise.

We left Galchi Bazar and headed out towards our final obstacle, the pass through the high hills above Kathmandu. The road was clear. The sun was shining and we had only twelve miles or so to go. The fields of the valley shone brass bright in the sun and people were working in the fields. A group of workmen were busy on the roof of a house and at a roadside tea stall a woman and her three children waved to us as we passed. Then we saw just ahead of us a queue of lorries, buses, cars, jeeps and vans that ran along the valley as far as the eye could see towards the range of mountains that blocked the fertile Naubise Valley. At a rough guess the tail-back was six or seven miles long. We joined the queue and switched off the engine. Gradually more cars and lorries rumbled to a halt behind us.

We waited and nothing happened. The sun rolled over the mountains and still nothing happened. Long shadows swept up the valley and drivers got out of their lorries and began cooking their evening meal at the side of the road. Still nothing happened.

Then a lorry came in the opposite direction; to repeated questions all along the queue the driver threw out the same answer. 'No landslide – police checkpoint on pass – SAARC conference.'

The police, worried about the heads of state who had flown into

A tea stall in the market at Galchi Bazar

Nepal for the conference, were checking every vehicle going over into Kathmandu. We could be there all night.

In fits and starts the queue of vehicles shuffled laboriously towards the foot of the pass, engines overheated, people shunted into each other, somebody lay down to have a baby and the rumour was that somebody died. In two and a half hours we had covered five miles and reached the foot of the pass. Ahead of us was a line of vehicles, mainly Indian lorries spewing out black fumes. It was six o'clock and pitch dark. We'd been on the road ten hours. We looked at the taillights and headlights of a series of lorries stretching away up the hair-pin bends of the pass as far as what looked like the summit. Nothing moved up and nothing came down.

We had a letter with us from the King Mehindra Trust, printed on official notepaper, asking whomever read it to give all possible assistance to the people named on the letter who were making a film on Nepal. I told the driver to go up the outside lane to the checkpoint.

He looked at me as though I was mad. I was.

I told Ang Phurba to translate what I'd said into Nepali just in case he hadn't understood the first time. Ang Phurba translated.

The driver still didn't want to do it.

I told him I'd drive the bloody car myself if he didn't do as I asked.

Reluctantly he set off. Drivers shouted and waved their fists at us as we overtook them, the sheer drop falling away below our bubbly-tyred wheels. Nothing came the other way and we wound round the bends towards the col. Every time the driver pulled in front of a lorry and stopped, saying he wasn't going any further, I waved the letter under his nose and used bad language. It wasn't the driver's fault and I could understand how worried he was – we were jumping a tail-back towards a police checkpoint on the wrong side of the road on a dangerous mountain pass – but I'd had enough. All the frustrations of Dras and the Leh-Srinagar road and the landslides and whorehouses of the Pokhara-Kathmandu highway had been too much and I'm afraid I hassled him all the way to the end.

At the summit checkpoint, a policeman blew his whistle and waved us into the side of the road. He said something in Nepali that was the equivalent of 'Hello, hello, hello, playing silly buggers are we? Where's the fire then? Who do you think you are, Nicki Lauda? Do you know you could lose your licence/get locked up for ever/be stoned to death for what you just done?'

I shoved the letter under his nose and, getting out of the car, told him in my best backstreet Manchester English for a full five minutes what I thought of his road block, the SAARC conference, Nepalese roads, Nepalese airports and policemen in general. I used every swearword I knew and made up a few for good measure. He didn't understand a word I said but he knew he was dealing with a madman. We were blocking the road and I was giving him earache. He gave me the letter back, waved us on and we dropped over the pass and rounded a bend. We saw the lights of Kathmandu blinking in the valley far below us.

'Mike very angry,' said Ang Phurba to John.

'Mike very nearly arrested,' said John who had tried to pretend he wasn't with me.

5

To Namche Bazar

'We never achieve mastery over the mountains; the mountains are never conquered; they will always remain and sometimes they will take away our friends if not ourselves.'

–Joe Tasker, *Everest the Cruel Way*

AT KATHMANDU WE WERE able to get our kit laundered and to rush through the last of the formalities before we left for the Everest region. The film crew had arrived and John went off to meet them after sending a radio signal to Namche Bazar instructing a messenger to contact Ang Phurba's father. He was to send a runner down the trail towards Jiri in search of Robert Hutchinson, who had last been seen vanishing into the sunset with our film. Robert Hutchinson is an old Himalayan hand who has spent years looking for the yeti. A Canadian by birth, he now lives in Switzerland and was in Nepal mounting a major expedition in search of the yeti at the head of the Khumbu Glacier. He was going to spend the whole of the winter above sixteen thousand feet exploring the high passes and snowfields where the yeti had been most often sighted.

John was to lend him a video camera and tapes and the small Bolex hand-cranked 16mm camera that we had used on the trek to Ghorapani. He was also going to give him whatever was left of our film stock when we had finished our project, in the hope that ECO might be able to use any footage of the yeti that came back. In return, Robert was portering all our film stock and our tent to Namche.

I left John at it, happy with phones, telexes and fax machines as all television producers seem to be, and sat down and had a serious think about my position. I had been up all night with dysentery yet again, which meant that I had had the disease for twenty-one days now in either mild or severe form. All the symptoms indicated that it was amoebic dysentery and I can only put the fact that I was not laid out by it down to my being very fit after the trek in Zanskar and Ladakh. If I was going to make it to base camp I'd have to get myself well and quickly too. I don't normally take any medication, even for headaches; I think the more chemicals you pump into your body, the more harm you do to your own natural immune and recuperative systems. But for three weeks I had tried starving the bug out by fasting, burning it out with curry and coaxing it out with homeopathic medicine and nothing had happened. I decided to bomb it out with Tinibar. Tinibar has unfortunate side effects. You feel nauseous for two to four days while taking it and you also suffer from the most acute indigestion that results in wind at both ends and makes you unsociable and unlovable.

I went to the Thamel to change my reading books at the bookshop and to do some last-minute bits of shopping. After the quiet of the mountains, the noise and shouting of Kathmandu took a lot of getting used to. I nearly got run over twice and felt like a country bumpkin.

Back at the hotel I met the film crew. Naresh Bedhi is a tall, thin man full of nervous energy and eager to get on with things. Nandu Kumar, dark-eyed and handsome with a thick black beard, is more solid and deliberate in everything he does. He had been on two Indian expeditions to Everest and had climbed to twenty-five thousand feet. He knew the Khumbu Valley well and had Sherpa friends there whom he was looking forward to meeting again, Ang Phurba's uncle amongst them. We had tea together and talked about the film, our approach to it and to the people we would be working with. Later, John and the crew went to customs, where the film equipment had been impounded, to try and clear it, while Ang Phurba went to the immigration authorities to arrange our trekking permits.

I stayed at the hotel writing postcards and talking to trekkers. Rumours were multiplying at a logarithmic rate. The monsoon that had hit Pokhara had hit Lukla Airport and washed it out. Hundreds of trekkers were stranded and, since the people who were supposed to clear the runway also ran the batti houses and were making a fortune serving meals to the stranded trekkers, nothing was being done. People with flight connections back to Australia and Europe had all missed their flights. The SAARC conference was also causing problems as flights everywhere were being cancelled or delayed. Hundreds of people at Lukla were said to be going crazy.

We planned to fly to Lukla and walk to Namche in a day, film at Namche and acclimatise for three or four days there, while Ang Phurba hired porters, yaks and a cook for our trek to base camp. His home village of Thami was only a few miles above Namche and his family had a large herd of yaks to choose from. His family also seemed to be composed largely of porters and cooks, many of whom would be willing to come with us.

The following Saturday was market day in Namche Bazar and we needed to be there by then to stock up with fresh vegetables and food

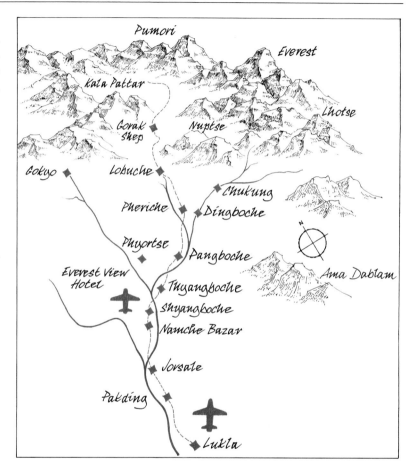

for our trek. Whereas we had used lodges and tea houses on the Ghorapani trek, we would have to be totally self-sufficient in the Everest region. There are lodges at places like Thyangboche and even as high as Lobuche, but they are small and were likely to be full. It was better too that we were flexible and able to stop wherever necessary since we planned to spend the mornings filming and the afternoons trekking. That would mean a hard push to make it to base camp and back in the time allowed, but we were going to try. The biggest problem was getting out of Kathmandu.

John went to the airport to see if we could either get on a scheduled flight or charter a plane. My job was to man the phones and to relay any information to Naresh and Nandu. It very soon began to look as though everything was falling apart. There was another festival on in the valley, the second of the end of summer, Diwali. And whereas Badh Dashain had been the festival of ritual slaughter, this was the festival of lights and the beginning of the Nepali New Year. Many of the pilots who would have been flying were on holiday because Diwali is a time when everybody tries to be with their family. Ang Phurba advised that we try for a flight regardless; there wasn't much else we could do.

We loaded a mountain of gear into two big cars and drove to the airport. As well as all our personal belongings we now had several aluminium flight cases of camera and recording equipment. We piled them up in the airport in a line like a terminal moraine, with other people's gear, drums full of supplies for climbing parties and a small hill of trekker's kit bags all printed with the name of the trekking company. We got some cups of tea and waited.

And guess what? – nothing happens. Rumour follows myth in ever decreasing circles round the airport. Chance of a charter. No chance of a charter. A group of French people who bought tickets 4 months ago have still had to buy a charter.

At 3 p.m. we hear, 'All cancelled, no flights today.' John spends another hour trying to fix a charter, seeing everybody up to a director of Royal Nepal Airlines, but there is still no joy. We pile in cabs and trundle back to hotel.

There were lights burning everywhere for Diwali. As evening came, children roamed the streets in gangs singing and banging drums, groups danced in the streets and tiny clay, oil-filled lamps burnt before every door and were strung out along the walls and window-sills. We learned that because of the festival all government and airline offices would be closed for the next three days. Ordinarily we would have rolled with the punch and settled back to enjoy the festival, but now we had a film to make and a hill to climb and we really needed to be at Namche within the next twenty-four hours.

At the airport next morning we piled our equipment near the check-in desk and waited in hope. There were rumours of five flights to Lukla that day, then seven, then nine. Then it went back down to five and then none. Someone said the airport was closed because the Queen was going to Delhi on her plane to go shopping, then somebody else said the SAARC people were all flying in. Another person said they were all flying out. Nothing happened and the clock hands moved round towards midday. After midday it is often impossible to fly to Lukla because low clouds roll up the valley and cover the airfield in mist. We sat and waited.

I worked out in my head that the cost of keeping the film crew in Kathmandu for another day, plus the cost of them having to walk in another full day, was not much less that the expense of hiring a chopper to take us to Namche. We couldn't all get in the chopper, but if I left with Naresh and Nandu and as much of the equipment as the chopper's payload would allow we could at least get to Namche and begin filming while John and Ang Phurba brought up the rest of the equipment. I don't often have sensible ideas but this was one of them.

John found a helicopter and a pilot and paid over the money and leaving Ang Phurba and John to follow when they could, we climbed in the chopper and set off. It all seemed ridiculously simple. That day was my birthday and I remember thanking John and Central Television for one of the best birthday presents I've ever had as we

Trekkers looking at Everest from Namche Bazar: a jet-stream cloud banners from the summit

swooped out of the airport and flew low over the fields and villages towards the Khumbu Valley and Everest.

It was a little cloudy in the Kathmandu Valley when we left but the clouds cleared as we flew in over the ridges that the trail follows from Jiri to Lukla. We landed at Lukla to drop off some equipment that was needed at the airfield and hundreds of marooned trekkers stared mournfully at the helicopter. There was nothing we could do. John and Ang Phurba were still in Kathmandu chasing a flight out. We lifted off a second time, swooping low over the end of the grass runway that ends in a cliff and fifteen thousand feet high hill. There's not a lot of room for pilot error.

Twenty minutes later we landed at Namche on the flat helipad in front of the National Park Headquarters, half a mile above the village. We jumped out, running, bent double, towards a group of people standing on the edge of the field. An agitated young man ran towards us.

'Have you come about our accident?' he asked. He was English and there were three or four other men with him. They looked as though they were a party and he was the leader.

'No,' I replied. 'We've chartered this chopper to bring us and some equipment up here. What's your problem?'

'My wife and best friend have just been killed in an avalanche,' he answered. 'We're an RAF team climbing Island Peak. An avalanche wiped out some of our tents. We've lost four people, two Nepalis and my wife and best friend.'

It had all happened on the afternoon of the day before. They had only managed to dig out the two Europeans and had buried them in a shallow grave. Somebody would try and give them a proper mountain burial when the snows melted. Looking at him, it was obvious that he was in a state of shock. The others looked stunned and totally exhausted.

The young man asked if it would be possible for him to fly back in the chopper to Kathmandu where he would have to report the deaths. I took the chopper pilot to one side and explained the circumstances. He didn't seem in the least bit concerned and laconically said he supposed there was room. I think he was annoyed because he was hoping to pick up some passengers from the horde of desperate trekkers at Lukla.

The man ran down to Namche for his passport and his papers and returned breathless and pale. There was nothing more I could do but say how sorry I was and wish him luck. He got in the chopper, we stepped back and it fired up and whirled off down the valley. I asked one of the others in the team what had happened and he said there had been a freak snowstorm that had raged for nearly two days. There had been thirty-six hours of continuous snow and four to five feet had fallen in the open, drifting even deeper in parts. They had been awake for all that time digging the snow from the tents to prevent them collapsing. Exhausted by their efforts the young man's wife and friend had tried to get some sleep. One of the Nepalis was asleep in his tent, the other was in the cook tent.

Island Peak is often called a trekker's peak because it is easy to climb and is normally considered safe. The base camp they were using was the same one that had been used for years. It was not known to be prone to avalanche. It had been a freak tragedy.

The surviving members of the party had walked out from base camp after burying the bodies and notifying the trekkers' aid post at Pheriche. They had had to break the trail all the way back to above Thyangboche and had lent their duvets, fibrepiles and boots to their low-altitude 'coolies' from Jiri, who clad only in shorts, slacks and canvas shoes, had been freezing to death.

We learned later that a total of fourteen people had died in the snowstorms in the Khumbu Valley. Four Spaniards died on the Lhotse Nuptse face, four died at Island Peak, an Englishwoman and her guide died above Gokyo and four locals had died in blizzards that

The stone enclosures above Namche Bazar are evidence of attempts at re-forestation

Prayer-flags in Namche; Thamserku is in the background

had caught them unawares and miles from shelter. The Sherpa who ran the tea house at Gorak Shep below Kala Pattar had been frozen to death seated upright by the trail between Lobuche and there.

We walked down the trail to Namche. It was cool even in the afternoon sun and we soon noticed the altitude. We were at twelve thousand feet and, even though I'd climbed well beyond that in Zanskar, the thinness of the air was marked. Dropping below the shoulder of the hill we saw Namche nestled beneath us in a natural amphitheatre in the hills. Tiers of stone-built lodges with carved wooden windows ranged in a semicircle facing south and from every chimney smoke curled.

The people of Namche are, with few exceptions, Sherpas, for this is their country and it is from the villages of Khumbu, Namche, Thami, Khumjung and Khunde that most of the high-altitude Sherpas, the 'Tigers of the Snows' are drawn. Ang Phurba came from Thame and Pema Dorje from Khumjung.

Sherpas were originally from Tibet and in fact speak a Tibetan dialect. They came into the Khumbu Valley three or four hundred years ago as traders moving over the Nang Pa La. It was along this pass that Ang Phurba travelled with his father as a boy bringing salt and yak-skin boots in from Tibet and carrying grain and yak skins back.

We booked in at a lodge that Nandu remembered from his last Everest expedition, dumped what stuff we had brought with us and went for a walk. A thick mist swirled up the valley in less than an hour blotting out the late afternoon sun and turning the day damp and very, very cold. This was to happen every day during our stay at Namche. In the village children stared in innocent wonder as an American trekker sat on the ground to put lip-salve on her chapped lips. An old granny shuffled down the street past a huge boulder carved with the lotus mantra, the letters picked out in bright-painted colours; we were now in a wholly Buddhist area.

That evening there was a commotion as the low-altitude Hindu porters, who had carried their loads up this far and had dumped them to be carried further by yak or high-altitude porters, celebrated Diwali by banging drums, singing and dancing round the houses only going away when they were given drink, food or a few coins. The Sherpas accepted all this and laughed and joked along with the Hindus. It made me look at Northern Ireland in a different light.

We ate in the lodge that night with a handful of other trekkers. My dysentery seemed to have cleared up. I decided to treat myself to a birthday tea of yak steak and chips. The steak was different from anything I had ever tasted, dark and gamey, a little like the meat of Highland cattle. I didn't like it all that much but I'm stupid enough to try anything once. While I was eating my first full meal in more than three weeks, the daughter of the lodge-owner switched on a portable cassette player. A forkful of yak steak and chips stopped halfway to my mouth. The first track I heard was 'Streets of London' sung by Ralph McTell. Ralph has been a mate of mine for years and to think that I was sitting at twelve thousand feet on my birthday eating yak steak and listening to him was too much and I started laughing like a fool. The young Sherpa girl smiled. Sherpas like people to be happy.

'Your friend is very happy,' she said to Naresh.

'Our friend is slightly crazy,' answered Naresh, not far wrong.

When I could control myself enough I finished the meal and a friendly American guy who heard it was my birthday whispered something in Nepali to the young Sherpa. She came in with a big slice of chocolate cake with a household candle stuck on top. The American had bought it for me. I was so happy I bought a bottle of rum and shared it round. We toasted each other's health and while the glasses were raised and the Electric Soup was being downed, the door opened and who walked in but John. He was drenched in sweat and he had with him, carrying his pack, a young Sherpa who looked totally destroyed. John had managed to get the last remaining seat on one of the few planes that had flown that day, had landed at Lukla with most of the kit and had left it there at a lodge belonging to one of Ang Phurba's many relatives. Ang Phurba, who was still trying for a flight, would pick up the rest of the kit whenever he arrived and porter it up to Namche. John had landed at two o'clock and run from Lukla to Namche in five and a half hours, most of it in the dark by the light of a head-torch. I was impressed. So was the young Sherpa who looked as though he had been run over by a yak. We bought the boy a meal and some tea and he went off to stay with his sister who lived in Namche. We noticed that everybody seemed to be related to everybody else in Khumbu – it reminded me a little of the Yorkshire Dales where they're so interrelated in some villages that they have a saying, 'Kick one and they all limp.'

I gave John a glass of rum and he bought himself three meals, one after the other. Naresh and Nandu watched in wonder: they had never seen such a thin man eat so much food before.

'Lytton Strachey meets Jaws,' I laughed – a joke that was lost on everybody else in the room which was not surprising since, apart from Naresh and Nandu, the only other people there were the American guy, a Yugoslav woman who looked like Stalin with pigtails, a French couple who looked on the verge of divorce and an Israeli suffering from altitude sickness who'd left his boots on a wall to dry and had had them stolen. That night we all slept in one huge dormitory.

My journal for the next day reads:

Yesterday was my birthday. I got a helicopter ride, a slice of cake, and passed my first semi-solid stool in twenty-three days.

After spending the night with a lot of snoring, farting and whistling Yugoslavs, French and Ozzies I got up and watched the dawn over Namche. Dogs were barking on the hillside and two yaks were cropping the few frosted blades of grass at their feet as the first light caught the snowy peaks above the village.

Crows were calling, looping out over the valley and back again; prayer-flags flapping in the wind; smoke from the first fires of the day spiralling out of the roofs.

I hear American voices as the first trekkers of the day surface from their tents.

'Where you from?'

'Texas. Where you from?'

'Texas. Where's your friend from?'

'I'm from Texas too.'

One of them calls good morning to me and I hello back. He asks me where I'm from. I nearly say Texas but decide to say England. One of them inquires whether I've heard any news. They've trekked here from Jiri and haven't heard any for more than a week.

I tell them that just before leaving Kathmandu, I heard on the phone from England that the Wall Street Stock Market had collapsed and that the London Stock Exchange had followed suit. They were calling it Black Monday. 'Worst crash since the thirties,' I added.

One of them sat down and put his head in his hands. 'Is there a telex machine in Namche?' he asked.

'Yes,' I said. 'It's just around the corner behind the Jacuzzi and the Sauna, right by that little Bistro and the shop that sells the hand-made chocolates. Telex machine! There's only one link with the outside world and that's a radio at the National Park centre. It's allowed airtime for about an hour each morning and that's mainly for medical use. You can't radio your broker in Dallas from here.'

There was weeping and wailing and gnashing of dentures as pictures of JR impaling himself on a barbecue skewer flashed through his mind. I left him to it.

It was market day in Namche and the village was thronged with people from outlying villages. Tibetan traders were selling bits and pieces of jewellery, knitted caps and gloves, salt, fresh vegetables, sugar, live chickens clucking in baskets, eggs, rice, soap and oranges. Lentils and rice had come up from the lowland areas on the backs of Newhars and Tamangs while, at the far end of the market, spread out on sacking, were ragged lumps of meat piled in a revolting-looking heap, the butchers standing ready to hack you some off. Although the Sherpas are Buddhists they are not vegetarians. They will eat meat,

Market day in Namche when the village is filled with people from outlying villages and Tibetan traders

but not from small animals, and they seem to leave the killing and butchering to the lower-caste people from down the valley.

On a massive rock slightly below street level at the market's end the porters sat in the sun, men and girls, smoking and laughing, while beside them were cakes of yak dung drying in the sun, to be used later as fuel.

Ang Phurba's father came to the lodge with the uncle that had been on the Everest expedition with Nandu and set about buying supplies for our trek. The market began to fade away after lunch and the mist and cloud rolled up the valley as the porters loaded their dokos and set off back down the way they came. Namche became a cold whiteness through which moved figures bearing loads. A raven with a bell on its neck sat on the end of a fence staring at me; a little girl staggered past carrying a big, cut-down, polythene jerry can full of dung cakes and a grumpy yak snorted and huffed fiercely at me from a small stone enclosure. Yaks have a reputation for being a bit wild and I looked at this one from the safety of the wall.

I spent the rest of the day wandering around in the mist taking photographs. By dusk the mist had lifted slightly and, courtesy of an American-funded micro-hydro-electric scheme, the lights of Namche

The young boy with his home-made aeroplane

came on one by one, shimmering in the dark bowl of hills. Next morning I got up at 5 a.m. The dysentery had completely cleared up now though I was still feeling a bit weak and was having to push myself painfully up hills that I would have run up back home. I left the village by a back lane and, passing through courtyards and houses with finely carved doors, climbed part of the way along the track that led to Ang Phurba's village.

Slightly above Namche stands the village gompa and as I approached a monk staggered out, swaddled against the cold in his maroon cloak, chanting the lotus mantra, his breath steaming in the frosty air. Without pausing in his chanting he stopped to pee against a wall then carried on up the track, smiling as he went. At a small house by the track a girl looked over a wall and not a yard away was another raven with a bell round its neck. I decided that they must be pets. They certainly seem to be very bright birds.

After breakfast I rambled round the village taking more pictures and watching the day unfold. All the water for the lodges has to come from a spring at the lower end of the village and a chain of Sherpas trekked up and down all day carrying polythene jerry cans of water through the streets. A little boy had made a propeller from some cardboard and stuck it on a stick with a pin. He held it into the wind, the propeller turned and, for a few seconds, the boy was a plane flying through the air. An old granny wiped a toddler's nose on her pinny and cuddled him to her; another old lady stood at her door, watching the world go by and telling her prayer-beads through her fingers as she stood framed in the doorway. In a courtyard an aged lady wearing pebble glasses sat in the sun, her grandchild by her side.

I walked through the village to the rock where the porters sat on market day and there a man was spreading out yak turds to dry. I was standing on the rock looking towards Namche and the hills when somebody called my name. I looked down and saw below me Ang Phurba. I jumped down and put my arms round him. It was good to see him for many reasons, not least that behind him was

The grandmother in her mended pebble glasses

the cavalry in the shape of a porter carrying my rucksack with all my clean clothes. I had been in these for four days and certain items had become magnetic.

'Any news flim?' Ang Phurba asked.

I shook my head.

'The radio message about the runner wasn't passed on so nobody has gone down the trail. This morning one of your sisters set off at half past seven towards Jiri. We don't know how long we'll have to wait.'

Ang Phurba shook his head. 'This is very bad. What we do if flim not come?'

I didn't dare to think. Both John and I were doing this film for nothing. The budget was minute and getting smaller every day.

I took Ang Phurba for some soup and tea and we spent the afternoon trying to work out a schedule.

Every afternoon at 3.30 mist and low cloud crawls up the valley and shrouds the village. It becomes very cold and the trekkers huddle in the lodges swapping stories and talking about the snowbound track towards Kala Pattar. In the lodge tonight were a group of French trekkers and climbers looking totally exhausted. They had been at Pumori when the snows struck. One had summited. The rest had to pull off. Rumours are that all the major expeditions this year have failed. The Yorkshire and Lancashire lads have pulled off Ama Dablam. The Burgess twins and Pema Dorje's brother have pulled off Lhotse climb all safe; it was the Spaniards on the ridge who were killed and whose deaths we had heard about in Kathmandu. The Poles, the hardest of the lot, have pulled off Everest.

We heard on the World Service tonight that Big Ben has stopped. Is this the end of Western Civilisation as we know it?

We spent almost a week at Namche waiting for the 'flim' to arrive.

The tempers of Naresh and Nandu shortened as the days rolled past. We had brought a limited amount of stock with us, basically the few rolls left over from the Annapurna trip, and they had been used up filming the market and the people carrying the wood and water to the lodges.

My journal for one day of that week reads:

We are now convinced that John is definitely unhinged. Only somebody affected by the moon would entrust £1,000 worth of film stock into the hands of a man called Robert Hutchinson who is going to spend four months in the snow in search of the yeti. Nandu, Naresh and I are beginning to doubt in the existence of this man and the sanity of John.

Climbed up to the National Park office after breakfast to send yet another message to Kathmandu. It's so frustrating being stuck here unable to work. I wouldn't mind so much if we were able to move or do something but we daren't move in case the film arrives.

Three meals a day and all the frustration you can handle. Prison at 11,000 feet.

I'm reading *Hard Times* and renting *The Penguin Thurber*. There is a little shop here which, as well as selling hardly-used expensive mountaineering gear left behind by climbing expeditions for next to nothing, also rents books. They are too rare to sell and the Tibetan lady who runs the store hires them out. There is the usual rubbish, *Zen and the Art of Motor-cycle Maintenance*, one of the most pretentious books ever written, *Valley of the Dolls* about which I've nothing to say except that there are no dolls in this valley, and a lot of books about spies and war. The crows here are very friendly, and follow me around. They must be expecting me to die.

There are two main kinds of trekkers in the Khumbu: the sort who treks alone or with friends, staying at lodges and often carrying all his or her own kit; and those who trek in big organised groups. They arrive with a team of Sherpas who put up the tents and cook their meals for them. The big treks are sounder ecologically in that they bring all their own kerosene and food but most of the money paid by these trekkers goes to organisations outside Nepal, in America, Europe and Australia.

The lodge trekkers, particularly those using Sherpas, contribute quite a lot to the local economy but they have inadvertently forced up the price of food at the market and, since the lodges almost all cook on wood stoves, and yak turds, there is of course a heavy demand on the little remaining wood.

At one time, according to some of the older people, traders were often late setting out over the Nang Pa La because they couldn't find their yaks in the thick forests between Namche and Shyangboche. Now the forests have gone and the National Park authority's attempts to enforce the laws against cutting wood in the park are often ignored. All the way along the trail to Thyangboche we heard the sounds of wood being chopped and limbs being torn from the trunks of trees. Before the National Park came, each village appointed a guardian of the forest who kept an eye on the trees and regulated the demand of the villagers. The forests were able to replenish themselves. When the Sherpas heard of the coming of the National Park and its forestry laws, they went out on an orgy of felling, taking and storing as much wood as they could before the laws were enforced. It's said that they did more damage in those few days than trekkers have ever done since.

The trekkers who passed through Namche while I was there were a motley crew. Lean stringy youths, alone and solemn, plodded along the trail with massive backpacks, shunning the porters because they felt that to employ a porter is to degrade him. They sadly missed the point that it is not degrading here since portering and guiding is one of the only ways of making a living. There were Australian hard men, Crocodile Dundee clones, leading treks into Gokyo and beyond who looked and sounded like old Himalaya hands. There were overweight Germans in droves, mostly in their fifties, following their porters, sweating and out of breath, propelling themselves along with a pair of ski sticks looking like a chain of dry-land skiers. There were Americans from San Francisco dressed in the brightest and best mountain gear and stylish French groups outdoing them all. The English

Chorten near Namche, Thamserku in the distance

plodded through from time to time looking dowdy and unsure of themselves as the English always do abroad. They seemed to be either ordering little brown people about or slinking along self-consciously as though they'd walked into the wrong room.

Through it all went the climbers, either looking fit and healthy on their way to various mountains or looking wrecked and emaciated on their way back, shaggily bearded with cracked lips and peeling noses and panda-eyed where their snow goggles had stopped the sun from burning their skin.

The trekkers were all ages too. The youngest we saw was a boy of eight or nine, who'd gone down with the Kathmandu Quickstep while travelling with his parents and was being carried down the trail in a doko by a porter. The oldest I saw was an Englishman in his early seventies built like a whippet. He was shaving in a small bowl of warm water stripped to the waist, around him the freezing cold morning mists of Namche.

There were a lot of trekkers too who obviously shouldn't have been there. One afternoon an overweight American lady in her late fifties pulled into the lodge panting and groaning. It had taken her party and herself two days to cover John's half-day run from Lukla to Namche and she was completely finished with water on the knees and mild altitude sickness. The rest of her party was going on to Gokyo and perhaps to Kala Pattar. She and a couple the same age had pulled off the trek and booked into the lodge leaving the trekkers and their tents to travel on. I felt very sorry for her.

'I paid good money to get here, one thousand seven hundred and fifty dollars. I couldn't keep up. I've a bad cold, my knees are bothering me. I'm too fat and I'm not fit.'

She talked incessantly of her situation and obviously felt isolated and culturally adrift.

'I was always two hours behind the others. They were always in such a hurry.

'I might go to Thyangboche. There's a festival on there. I believe that's quite something.'

The trek leader had left a young Sherpa behind to look after her. He was pleasant and helpful but she couldn't understand why he wasn't more of a servant and less of a Sherpa.

'He doesn't understand English all that well and I don't speak Nepali.'

She sat glumly in the lodge, eating and drinking all day and every day telling everybody her troubles and debating her predicament with whoever would listen. Should she try and go on gently to Thyangboche, an easy day's walk away? Trek up to some of the villages like Thami and Khumjung? Or should she go back to Lukla and try to fly back to Kathmandu?

'At least there are shops there and things. I could do some shopping. I'd have things to look at.'

There was still no news of the film. We radioed each morning to see if there was any information but there was nothing. We questioned every trekker as they arrived panting under the arched chorten on the southernmost edge of the village. No they hadn't seen Robert Hutchinson; and there were no big parties of porters carrying tons of equipment anywhere along the trail.

One afternoon I went with Naresh and Nandu to Shyangboche to see one of the craziest follies in the world. We climbed the path behind the gompa and followed the trail up past a chorten, the beautiful snow-draped peak of Thamserku ahead of us. Below we could see the Dudh Kosi, the 'River of Milk' carrying waters from the Khumbu Glacier. Its milkiness, like that of the rivers of Zanskar and Ladakh, comes from the crushed stone dust held in suspension by the swirling waters. Yaks were grazing in some pastures on a bluff ahead of us.

Naresh put his hand on my arm to stop me, put his finger to his lips and pointed ahead. To the right of the track was a group of what I took to be large goats.

Thamserku with a cloud plume

'Tahr,' he whispered.

We crept slowly forwards and, hiding in some undergrowth, were able to watch the tahr for a while before they sensed our presence and scooted away down the steep hillside.

Tahr, according to one guidebook I read, are neither sheep nor goats, nor are they any kind of cross between the two. The official guide to the Mount Everest National Park, however, says that they are a species of wild goat and can interbreed with the domestic variety.

We climbed a small mound and in front of us was an airfield, where yaks grazed peacefully on a rough grass runway that headed straight out a thousand feet above the Dudh Kosi towards the sheer flanks of Thamserku.

At the western end of the airfield a windsock flapped noisily while, before us, the ruined control tower and abandoned earth-movers were witness to the folly of some men's attitude to the mountains. We left the deserted airfield and followed a well defined track through some junipers.

Rounding a bend we saw the reason for the airfield's construction. In the most amazing position, fronted by a well-made stone staircase, stands what is either a crazy folly or the beginning of the end for

A tahr, a wild mountain goat

Khumbu, The Hotel Everest View.

The main reason for the construction of the hotel was greed. A consortium of Japanese entrepreneurs built it in 1971, rightly thinking that in an age of instant everything, a bit of instant Everest would appeal to the rich and stupid whose idea of travel is a video of themselves standing in front of St Peter's Rome, the Taj Mahal, the Tower of London and now Mount Everest. The faster and more effortless you can make the travels of these immediate culture vultures the better. They don't really want to meet or try and understand the people they are amongst, they just want them to be funny and strange so they can photograph them. It is ultimately a total consumer experience. They come not to discover but to buy.

With this in mind and knowing they could charge two hundred dollars a night, the businessmen cleared more forest than has been lost in Khumbu in the last thirty years and built a mini-Hilton with running water, central heating, electricity and the best views in the world. While sitting on the toilet you can slide back the window and look out at Everest, Nuptse, Lhotse and Ama Dablam, truly a loo with a view. Water had to be carried round the clock from its source an hour away and wood had to be brought in from outside the

National Park. Fuel for the electricity generator and all the Western food, drink, carpets, saucepans, cutlery, crockery and toilet paper had to be flown in.

At first they came in mobs, all the journalists and travel writers on their 'freebies', and they came prepared to write favourably about 'the highest hotel in the world'. Naresh had been at the grand opening with an Indian television news crew. The weather closed in, and journalists from all over the world were stranded there for days because, of course, no planes could land. And these were busy men, not used to being away from phones and telex machines for more than a few minutes. They didn't like it.

There was another aspect of life in the Khumbu the developers had overlooked. Ascending gradually to fourteen thousand feet is often demanding and uncomfortable enough, but coming directly to that height is madness. People were flown from Kathmandu to the airstrip, loaded on to yaks and brought to the hotel. Oxygen had to be provided in all the rooms and people often became so ill they had to be evacuated. One Japanese woman died on the doorstep. Word spread and soon nobody was prepared to pay two hundred dollars to see Everest and die.

> In the chill, damp, deserted dining room that advertised 'Oxygen available in all rooms. Please ask management', we drank tea from china cups and ate pancakes, shivering in the cold room while the caretaker and his assistant played cards in the sunlit front lobby. From our table a wonderful view of Ama Dablam and the Lhotse Everest group.

In the lodge that night the poor American woman, who now had diarrhoea as well as a head cold and a touch of altitude sickness, was telling her story to an Irish couple who had just trekked up from Jiri.

She finished her story and then asked, 'You guys heard any world news? World War Three started yet?'

'India got beat by Pakistan at cricket.'

'What's cricket?'

The Hotel Everest View, a mini-Hilton which went wrong

A group of Englishmen in our lodge was involved in an Everest Marathon. Some runners were apparently going to trek in to base camp and run out again to Lukla. They were measuring the track as far as base camp. One of their helpers, an artist called Jan, had been bitten that day by a village dog. Rabies is one of the biggest killers in Nepal. Every year hundreds of Nepalis and a few trekkers die of bites from rabid dogs. Jan had been to the hospital at Khunde and the doctor had told him he had two chances.

'Either the dog wasn't rabid in which case you should be fine or it was rabid in which case you're going to die, unless you get to Kathmandu where they can treat you.'

He was walking to Lukla and going to try and fly out the next day. A sad end to his trip.

Breakfast at the Hotel Everest View with Ama Dablam on the right and Everest on the left

That afternoon, returning from the airstrip, I had walked off on my own along one of the narrow trails above Namche. Schoolchildren overtook me laughing and singing, holding hands and shouting Namaste as they ran past. Every morning the children in our lodge got up, had a wash, helped to cook breakfast and serve a lot of hungry trekkers, then climbed the two miles to the Hillary school in Khumjung. Every afternoon they came home, did their homework then helped serve another group of hungry and thirsty trekkers. I looked at the exercise book belonging to one of the young Sherpa girls at our lodge. She was studying trigonometry in Nepali, the state language, as well as English and world geography. As far as my memory of mathematics could tell me she was at about the same standard as children of her own age in a normal secondary school in Britain.

As I was following the shouting children down the mountainside I met a European climbing up towards me; he was lightly laden with a small rucksack and obviously not a trekker. We stopped to talk. He was a New Zealander, the doctor at the hospital at Kunde. His wife, also a doctor, looked after the midwifery and he covered everything else. I asked him what kind of cases he mostly dealt with.

'If you discount the trekkers with their altitude sickness and Delhi Belly, then I suppose it's usually dysentery, alcohol problems and yak gorings.'

A young Sherpani of Namche

The dysentery I could understand, as all over Nepal the dysenteric cycle affects local people as much as it does trekkers, but alcohol and yak gorings?

'The Sherpas drink a lot. Drink is part of many of their social and religious ceremonies. Some of them get sick with it, a few get violent from time to time. You get the occasional wife beating, but many of these Sherpani are as strong as the men so you get the occasional husband thumping too. The yak gorings? Well yaks are vicious animals. They only really put up with what we do to them under sufferance. The Sherpas know their yaks and treat them very carefully. But accidents do happen. Last week I had to sew a bloke's thigh muscle back on. A yak swung at him when he wasn't taking care and ripped through his leg. Those horns are bloody sharp you know. Couple of months back I had to operate on one bloke. A yak had had a go at him and nearly disembowelled him.

I climbed down to Namche with a whole new perspective on those fluffy lovable-looking animals.

In the lodge that night we drank chang with some Americans who had been wiped out at Everest. Nobody had died but three of them had been pinned down by a blizzard and raging winds at twenty-six thousand feet. Exhausted, they had had to pull off. While we were sitting there another American came in, bearded and looking haggard and hot. He had trekked all the way up from Jiri, ten days away.

Yaks, fluffy, lovable-looking animals, but capable of inflicting serious injury

'You guys the English film crew.' We said yes.

'Robert Hutchinson will be here tomorrow. I passed him on the trail. He should be here after lunch.'

I almost kissed him, beard and all.

The next day's journal reads:

A miserable grey misty morning until the sun burnt it away. Spent an hour washing smalls and then sat in the sun reading, watching the crows watching me, and waiting for the film to arrive. It arrived 3 p m. The fog arrived 3.10 p.m. Nandu and Naresh are much happier working.

Ang Phurba's sister and a little boy arrived just ahead of Robert Hutchinson. He'd been delayed four days with porter trouble, 20 porters = 20 times the trouble. The Diwali festival caused a lot of problems but there always are difficulties with low-altitude porters. His team decided they were taking New Year off and went on strike for four days. He managed to get them together and got here as fast as he could. Nobody was really to blame. It was just one of those cock-ups that are endemic to the Himalaya. The biggest mistake we all make is expecting a third world country to function like a first world one.

That evening was our last in Namche. Next morning we were off for base camp. I walked round the village before dinner. Ang Phurba had brought the yaks down from his village and was feeding them and getting them ready for the trip.

I climbed through the fields that stood in front of some of the higher lodges. I was looking for Pema Dorje, the Sherpa who had introduced us to Ang Phurba. Word was that he had just arrived with an American group and was camped somewhere in one of the fields. I found him grinning and giving orders and we had a few minutes together, promising to try and meet up again in Kathmandu at the end of our respective treks.

On my way back down the street I saw a Sherpa paying off some low-altitude porters. They were shivering in the cold, bare-legged in shorts, shirts and little waistcoats. From here on their loads would be carried by Sherpas or yaks. The sirdar who paid them off was wearing an expensive watch and working out his accounts on a pocket calculator.

6

Chinese Sing Song

'Bring only yourselves, take only photographs, leave only your footsteps.'
– Motto of the Sagarmattha National Park

WE SPENT OUR last morning in Namche filming round the village and at the headquarters of the National Park. After a quick lunch we climbed up to the airfield, which we were going to film on our way to the Hotel Everest View.

True to form the clouds rolled in the minute we started working and stayed there, rolling round the airport in a thick fog. We finished filming and 'wrapped' for the day, walking along towards the hotel, the yak bells clanging ahead of us in the mist.

Our retinue had now swollen to four 'sahibs', six Sherpas and one sirdar. We had almost as many yaks as Sherpas. The food, tents, personal kit and film stock were carried on yaks but Naresh and Nandu didn't trust the yaks with their camera and tape recorder so that was being carried by two young Sherpas and a Sherpani with a very pretty smile. Ang Phurba's father was coming to lead some of the yaks back when we had finished with them, a close neighbour was coming as cook and another of Ang Phurba's sisters was coming as cook's assistant.

When we got to the Hotel Everest View, they unloaded the yaks and set them free to graze while we loaded our gear into the bedrooms. We were staying here for one night and filming the hotel in the morning before setting off for Thyangboche. The Sherpas carried the kitchen equipment into the empty kitchens of the Everest View and started preparing the evening meal while the sahibs sat round a fire that had been lit in the lounge. We were not alone, the dining-room-cum-lounge was full of Taiwanese also on their way to base camp. After our meal we all sat together round the roaring log fire: two Englishmen, two Indians, a dozen or so Sherpas, ten Chinese and the caretaker-manager and his friends. Outside clouds and mist enveloped the hotel, chill and bleak. Inside there was candlelight, firelight and warmth.

The Chinese began singing, treating us to 'Greensleeves' sung beautifully by the girls in their high voices. John and I sang 'The Wild Rover'. The Hindu Nepalis sang a song about love and somebody threw another log on the fire. Sparks drifted up the chimney as we passed round a bottle of Electric Soup and the Taiwanese gave us dried meat to chew that tasted like American 'Jerky' and sweet, dried fruits which were delicious. My journal reads:

Mr Sherma, the caretaker, told us that the Japanese are going to enlarge the runway and spend one and a half million dollars on the place. If they do so it's the end of the Khumbu Valley.

I hope the whole place vanishes in one huge explosion of dry rot but a part of me couldn't help enjoying sitting there, eating sweet, dried

Everest peeping over the Lhotse Ridge, seen from the Hotel Everest View

mangoes with a Taiwanese geology professor who sang Hank Williams' 'Your Cheating Heart' with a Chinese accent. A cross between a luxury hotel and Miss Haversham's wedding breakfast. It was an evening of Instant Everest with dry rot.

Towards the end of the evening the mist and clouds cleared, and through the windows we watched the moon rising over Everest and Ama Dablam. The Taiwanese sang a soft gentle song that went on for a very, very long time; it seemed to have hundreds of verses. When it finished I asked one of the English-speakers what it was about, expecting that it was an epic ballad of war and bravery or at least a song of impassioned love. 'It is about a chrysanthemum,' I was told. A chrysanthemum! I had expected at least twelve murders!

John and I made a poor showing I'm afraid. We taught them to sing 'Ilkley Moor Baht 'At'. I'll never forget the firelight, the moon shining through the window and a host of Chinese voices singing:

'On Eekey moo battat
On Eekey moo battat
On Eekey moo battat'.

Later I stood alone on the balcony and looked at a moonlit Everest, Ama Dablam and Lhotse standing in a wall at the head of the valley. In the forest below a dog howled, above there was a wilderness of stars.

The next morning dawned clear and sunny with a liquid crystal light. Everest and the Lhotse Nuptse ridge, lit by the rising sun, were crisp and sharp and a way ahead of us on a spur jutting into the Khumbu Valley was Thyangboche and the monastery, looking a lot more than merely two thousand feet below.

By the time we had finished filming the Chinese had vanished northwards. We loaded the yaks and the film gear and set off on the trail. From Shyangboche we trekked down through the remains of the old forest towards the col below Khumjung where we turned north, dropping through a beautiful wooded gorge. Himalayan pheasants were calling out, making human-sounding screams. Along the trail, near Trashingo, we met Pema Dorje who was climbing towards us returning from Dingboche. His party of Americans had cancelled the trek, there was too much snow and it was far too cold they said. They didn't look very happy. Pema wasn't happy either: though their return meant that he would probably have less work to do, Sherpas take great pride in seeing that things go well.

Near Phungi Tenga there is a suspension bridge across the Dudh Kosi. When we arrived there I hung back to take some photographs of the bridge and the river while the rest of the party crossed to the other side and went on to a tchai house a few hundred yards further along. A yak driver with four heavily laden yaks came down through the forest and I waited to take their picture before following them across the bridge. We weren't very high above the water but it was a long bridge and it began to shake with the movement of the animals. The yaks panicked and began to shuffle back towards the driver, his wife and me. The bridge started to swing violently. The yak driver kicked the last yak up the backside trying to force it across but it wasn't very happy with that arrangement and neither were the others. They somehow managed to chase us off the bridge and into the trees on the river bank. The yak driver and his wife, who had been shouting and screaming while all this was going on, threw stones at the yaks to drive them out of the woods and on to the bridge again. This time two of the yaks crossed to the other bank but the last two turned completely round on the bridge and chased us off yet again. The yak driver looked as frightened as I was, which wasn't very reassuring. On the far bank John, Ang Phurba and the film crew were rolling about laughing. Two young monks came along the path and, while the yak driver and his wife were stoning the yaks back out of the woods, the three of us sprinted across the bridge. I watched as the yak driver eventually coaxed his charges over the water.

We had lunch at the tchai house and afterwards sat in the sun on a

Yaks crossing a suspension bridge near Thyangboche

Namche Bazar. They had obviously been at the chang all day and were what is known in medical circles as 'blitzed'. They stopped every few yards to hold on to one another and gibber beerily into each other's face and, though I don't speak a word of Sherpa, I knew exactly what they were saying. They were pledging undying love and comradeship to each other, they were damning everybody who didn't like them and calling each other the finest of very fine fellows that ever lived. It could have been Oldham on a Saturday night.

The clouds advanced up the valley as we climbed, covering Shyangboche and creeping towards us, turning the world a thick cold, grey. All along the path below Thyangboche were fresh turds and clumps of pink toilet paper; we were now well on the Kleenex Trail. We came at length to the gateway chorten of the village and for a brief few minutes the clouds parted and I saw Ama Dablam, my other favourite mountain, washed in the golden glow of the afternoon sun. Then the clouds closed up again and she was gone. We put up the tent and dumped our stuff. It was getting very cold, far colder than it had been at Namche, and we were glad when Ang Phurba told us to follow him and that there was some tea to drink.

We ducked under a low door into a dark room where firelight provided the only illumination. The cook and the others were off in some other corner of the building making dhal batt and we were shown to a wooden bench near the fire. Along the wall on a rough pallet lay an old Tibetan with long white hair tied in a pigtail and a leathery, crevassed face. His lips moved silently as his fingers passed over his rosary beads. It was his house we were using as our dining-room. As we shared our dinner with him, smoke curled upwards from the fire making its way out through holes in the roof.

That evening we went to the gompa, the religious centre not just of Thyangboche but of the whole of this area of the Khumbu Valley from Namche northwards. There are important gompas at both Thami and Pangboche but they are not as large, as rich or as

low stone wall. Above us, a line of water-driven prayer-wheels clanged and groaned in a series of little huts along the roadside. We loaded up again and walked past them and up into the forest to begin the long climb up to Thyangboche. Ahead, a group of Sherpani were talking ten to the dozen carrying immense loads and hardly pausing for breath while I was already sensing the lack of oxygen and had to stop to let my heart resume its normal rhythm every few minutes. Two drunks in front of us were making their unsteady way back from

The gompa at Thyangboche

important as Thyangboche, for Thyangboche has a 'Rimpoche', a living reincarnation of the previous head lama. We would be visiting the lama later on, but first we were going to see Brot Coburn, a young American who had built the micro-hydro-electric scheme at Namche, and who lives in one of the many buildings attached to the gompa. He was working here on a new hydro-electric scheme.

We met Brot in the gompa lodge where a great number of monks and small boys cooked, sang and ran about serving people. We sat with Brot drinking rakshi and talking. We had heard of him back in England from various sources. He was described as an old Himalaya hand who spoke Nepali fluently and had a good grasp of what was really going on in the mountains. We had met him in Namche when he had drunk a glass or two of chang with us on his way back up to Thyangboche and we were anxious to meet him again and film him.

We were trying to include something about Nepal's foreign aid situation in our film because it is the subject of many varied and often conflicting opinions: whether any of it actually goes to where it is supposed to go; whether it has encouraged bribery and corruption; whether or not it is appropriate; and ultimately whether it doesn't degrade and destroy rather than uplift and sustain. There were too many questions to get through in one night and the rakshi took hold very quickly. I think it was because of the altitude. We somehow or other found ourselves talking about the sexual lives of the Sherpas. In Ladakh I had learnt that Ladakhis still look on polyandry as quite normal. As I mentioned earlier, it is the only way of sustaining a population where the high altitude and the increased exposure to ultra-violet radiation lowers the fertility of the people. There is a yearly festival in Ladakh where everybody drinks a lot of chang and rakshi and all sexual mores are abandoned. Any children born as a result of this festival are regarded as children of the marital father and no questions are asked. Brot said that, though the Sherpas didn't go in for 'carnival' in the same way, they nevertheless had a very relaxed attitude towards sex

A mani wall, Ama Dablam in the background

Brot did say that there was one problem in Sherpa sexual relations. Apparently a Sherpani's idea of foreplay is a prolonged and fearfully energetic bout of wrestling in which there are no holds barred and no quarter given. It is not a feigned fight in which the Sherpani is secretly pretending to resist while all the time wishing to submit. Brot said it can take anything up to a couple of hours and involves arm locks, leg holds and full Nelsons. I asked Brot if this happened just the first time a Sherpa and a Sherpani got together, thinking that it was perhaps some sort of ritual whereby a couple found out how well suited they were, and he said no, it happened every time, even after marriage. If you bear in mind that Sherpanis wear several layers of clothing, most of them thick and long, and that all these have to be removed during the course of the struggle, it makes you first wonder how there are so many children in Sherpa villages and second admire the endurance of these 'snow tigers' who still manage to perform after a two-hour wrestling bout. It also helps to explain many Sherpas' fascination with Western

and sexuality. It was common for a young couple who were engaged to sleep together, often in the same room as the parents, and that while Sherpas were not particularly promiscuous, they were not prudish either and there was no stigma attached to any child who was born out of wedlock.

women, particularly Australian ones, who are said to give in without any struggle whatsoever. John and I staggered to our tent that night, our minds reeling with all the information and mine in particular boggled by the thought of a two-hour pre-coital wrestling match and thanking the Lord that the custom hasn't yet reached England.

Detail of the gompa at Thyangboche

I lay for a while looking out of the tent door. Clouds had cleared from Ama Dablam and she was shining stately and serene in the moonlight. Another few days and the moon would be full and with luck we would be back at Thyangboche.

During the night our sleep was disturbed by yak bells clanking just outside the walls of our tent as the yaks tore up the grass and muttered between our tent pegs. One yak started mooing. It sounded like a tug blowing its fog horn across the Mersey Bar. I woke John up and told him to go and shut it up but he said something about sex and travel

and huddled in his sleeping bag like a bespectacled wireworm in a cocoon.

The next day dawned bright and sunny and we were busy packing the tent away when an English voice shouted out 'They let anybody here nowadays!' I looked up and saw Bill O'Connor who, along with Galen Rowell, ranks as one of the world's best mountain photographers. He had been leading an expedition to climb Ama Dablam but his group had been forced to withdraw by the freak weather and was now on its way back down to Namche and Kathmandu. The last time I had seen Bill, who lives not far from me, was in Buxton at a British Mountaineering Council conference. 'I'll see you back in Yorkshire,' he said walking off down the track as though he was just going for a bus.

We were spending the morning in Thyangboche to film a special ceremony at which the Rimpoche would bless the site of the hydro-electric scheme. We sat waiting in the sun. Crows looped above us and the wind shook the prayer-flags on the gold-domed chorten by the path.

Then, in an almost random, casual way, monks wandered out in ones and twos from the monastery, their maroon and yellow robes flapping in the gusts of wind. Two boy monks carrying armfuls of wood ran ahead along the path climbing up into the gorge where the hydro-electric scheme was to be built. There on a solitary rock they built a fire of juniper branches and threw incense into the flames as the smoke writhed up to where the wind took it. As though they knew there was to be a feast, the crows circled in from the crags, cawing and warning each other off.

By the side of the narrow trail above the gorge, the monks placed mats and thin mattresses for the musicians and the Rimpoche who were now coming along the path, the musicians with their drums and bells and horns, the lama dressed in his golden-yellow robes, his little

The blessing of the hydro scheme at Thyangboche

Sunset over Everest from Thyangboche

dark eyes like shining beads beneath his closely cropped grey hair. It was a fine sight.

He squatted on the mat and the horn players began sounding their horns, their bulbous cheeks pushing the low farting noises down the long tubes and out, echoing across the valley. The Rimpoche, gently shaking a handbell, began chanting and then, as the monks took up the chant, beating drums and cymbals. Above, the crows spun and flapped, twisting and sliding into the upcurrents like knives. The Rimpoche took a handful of rice and threw it into the gorge. The crows tumbled from the sky like shaken leaves falling on the food, squabbling noisily amongst themselves. The calling horns and the chanting of the monks echoed with the crows' harsh cries and over it all loomed Ama Dablam and Khumbila, the Sherpas' sacred mountain. The chanting and music continued for more than an hour, then food was carried on trays to the onlookers; sweet, yellow rice mixed with chopped nuts and sultanas and cups of Tibetan tea, the first I'd had in Nepal. It reminded me of Muni Gompa and the evening puja we had spent there. Almost as suddenly as it had begun the ceremony ended and, as the last echoes were dying along the gorge, the monks were already walking back to the monastery, the mats rolled up under their arms and their instruments over their shoulders.

After the ceremony, I went with Brot to meet the Rimpoche. I took a white scarf or 'khada' to present to him and Brot showed me how to hand it over while saying 'tushi delek', hands clasped as though in prayer, the scarf held between the thumbs. Through Brot I talked with him about the changes taking place in Khumbu and when I asked him what difference he thought the coming of the hydro-electric scheme would make to Thyangboche, he said it meant that it would save fuel and his many monks would be able to cook and to read their books of sutras by electric light. I suspect that the Rimpoche already sees the way things are going in Nepal and feels that if change is going to come then it is better that the people have some say in it rather than

Everest: the pinprick of light is from a trekkers' lodge

lying back waiting for the government to come in and force it upon them.

We left Thyangboche following our yaks along the path through the forests to Deboche but we had left too late in the day for our trek to Pheriche to be anything but a slog. The cloud rolled up the valley, dead on time, and as we crossed the Imja Khola by a high rope-bridge the afternoon turned dull and grey. John felt fine but after a while I began to suffer from mountain sickness and felt weak, feverish and nauseous. We stopped for tchai at a small hut beyond Pangboche but I

The Khumbu Valley near Pheriche

couldn't drink anything. The light went completely and as we climbed steadily upwards, we hit the first of the snow. It was deep, but a trail had been broken across and we followed it through the gloom. Because of the darkness we missed the point in the track where it turns off to the north for Pheriche. We floundered along lost. The yaks had gone on and with them Ang Phurba and Nandu. Normally there was no way we could have gone wrong, but in the dark, with the snow covering any landmarks, we walked for nearly an hour until we met a German who was even more lost than we were. However, he had a more detailed map than us and we checked our position on it.

We backtracked until we found the place where we had gone wrong and cast around in the darkness until we picked up the trail again and through deep snow scrambled up what seemed a never-ending ridge. John had his head torch to guide us down it and I followed numbly in his footsteps. We all fell once or twice, but it wasn't especially dangerous and we just got wet and a bit more grumpy. When we hit the level again, the moon broke through the mist and we saw ahead of us the three or four lodges that make up Pheriche. I was too knackered to cheer out loud but something inside me weakly whispered 'hurray!' We went into a tea house to get warm and I drank several mugs of lemon tea. The Sherpas were serving dinner in the cook tent but I couldn't stomach it and, wrapping myself in everything possible, I crawled into my sleeping bag and crashed out. It was only six-thirty, yet it felt and looked like midnight.

I woke next morning feeling great. The banging head and nausea had gone and all round me was a world of white. We were now on the north side of Ama Dablam, which had assumed a totally different shape. Ahead of us at the head of the valley was Awi and beyond that Lobuche Peak. We did some filming before breakfast and then afterwards Naresh and Nandu turned back with one of the young Sherpas and Ang Phurba's father and two of the yaks. They had

simply run out of time, both of them had films to finish in India and England and it was very doubtful whether they'd return on time. There was nothing they could do. They had to leave. John and I would go to base camp and film there on our own.

We watched them moving down the trail in the sunshine before we loaded up our own yaks and moved on.

That morning it was Ang Phurba who felt sick. He seemed to be coming down with some kind of flu. He stopped to throw up once or twice and we felt very concerned about him, but he insisted that he was fine. We climbed from Pheriche towards the col at Dughla through thick snow and jumbled moraine. In places the snow was four feet or more deep and we followed the yaks along the narrow broken trail. Across the valley a glacier shone in the sun and ahead of us a stone-slab bridge led across a raging stream to the herders' hut at Dughla where we stopped for a mug of tchai. It was warm in the sun but we could see mist creeping up the valley. We set off and climbed quickly towards the col. The view behind was incredible; in the light that slanted between the mountains wisps and blocks of cloud were shimmering and rolling between the summits like a vast waterfall.

Ang Phurba and John were falling behind a little but for once I was feeling good. It was a hard pull from Dughla to the col and we were climbing from 15,000 to 16,175 feet in a very short time. I seemed to find some sort of second wind once I had got over the pass above Dughla. Along the edge of the col, looking down the valley, is a line of chortens erected to commemorate Sherpas who have died in climbing expeditions. In his book Stephen Bezrushka says that when he first came here there were no chortens, now there are many. Around them the crows swoop and call and the wind blows along the valley shaking the prayer-flags on the chortens which face Khumbila, the sacred mountain of the Sherpas. Ahead of me was a vast snowfield cupped by the walls of the valley, at the far end a massive wall that was the boundary of Nepal. Beyond was Tibet.

Alpenglow at the head of the Khumbu Valley

Lobuche was a frozen snowfield, a handful of tents and two small huts crammed full with trekkers. I had a lemon tea while I waited for the others to arrive. It was bitterly cold. We huddled by the fire in the lodge; twenty or so trekkers all staring into the flames.

John and the others arrived and set up camp. We ate in the cook tent and by keeping the doors closed it was just possible to feel some warmth. The little Sherpa and Sherpani watched us eat and smiled when we said it was good. They looked very cold. I asked Ang Phurba whether they would be warm enough. He said yes they had sleeping bags.

We stepped out to go to our tent for the night and saw on Mehra and Pokalde the red blush of the alpenglow as the dying sunlight was reflected off the upper atmosphere on to the mountains. Then, as we were watching, the moon rose from behind the peak. It was beautiful beyond words.

The next day we were going to try for Kala Pattar, an eighteen thousand feet hill opposite Everest. Base camp was covered in six feet of snow so there was apparently nothing to see. We would finish the film instead on Kala Pattar. It was so cold that night that I dressed in every item of clothing I could find and still only just managed to get to sleep.

The last entry in my journal records in very shaky writing:

Incredible views but too cold to write.

7

Turn left for Shangri-La

'Whereof one cannot speak one must be silent.'
– Wittgenstein

'Human language is a cracked kettle on which we beat out tunes for bears to dance to, when all the time we wish to move the stars to pity.'

– Gustave Flaubert

I woke feeling lousy with a typical altitude sickness headache coupled with lethargy and nausea. Strange light, high clouds are dusted across the sky, not thick enough to look threatening but almost lurking in a menacing way as though they presage some change for the worse in the weather. Ang Phurba is doubtful. The last time he saw clouds like this was just before the big snows that wiped everybody out. The frost lies thick inside the tent. Every time you move showers of snow and ice fall on you, down your neck, in your sleeping bag, everywhere. John has been coughing and snoring all night. I've hardly slept with this bloody headache.

Eventually we got up round about seven o'clock when Ang Phurba's sister woke us with black tea. Ang Phurba was worried that the high cloud over Lobuche Peak meant that more snow was on the way. With fourteen people already dead in the Khumbu Valley I didn't want to add to the number. Sherpas are excellent judges of weather and it is insanity not to listen to them. I was happy to call it a rest day but Ang Phurba felt that if we didn't climb Kala Pattar that day we would have no chance tomorrow. With the yaks finding it hard to get food he was also getting worried about them. And since yaks are a

Sherpa's sole investment and are incredibly expensive, he wanted to get them back down the trail as soon as possible.

It was a difficult decision. I was feeling pretty rotten and John didn't look too well. We had a hill to climb and a film to finish and neither of us felt much like doing either. I was reluctant to go, John was a bit more keen but not much. John, Ang Phurba, the little boy Sherpa, Ang Nurba, and I all agreed that we would go on as long as it felt safe. If anybody felt ill, they were to turn back and the others would carry on. We needed some film of Everest from Kala Pattar but if necessary we could do without it. I was climbing the hill for another reason. It would be the highest I had ever been and it would also be the realisation of a dream. I doubt that I'll ever get to climb Everest but I wanted to do the next best thing which was to climb Kala Pattar on the shoulder of Pumori and see Everest across the Khumbu Glacier. The views we'd had of Everest so far had been teasing; she'd peeped over the shoulder of Nuptse and Lhotse looking smaller than either of those peaks, a black fang with the banner of the jet stream flying from

Trekkers coming down from Kala Pattar

Hard going in the deep snow

back. Then, in the middle of a snowfield, I looked up at the sheer beauty of the Khumbu Glacier with Pumori and Nuptse before me and I was overcome with a strange but certain knowledge that everything was going to be all right.

It was as though I'd walked through a door into some other sort of being or awareness and I felt incredibly happy. It was a totally spiritual experience, as if I'd walked out of that miserable prison cell of the self and into something bigger. It didn't matter too much whether I got to the top of the Kala Pattar, for something more important had happened. The infinite majesty of the mountains had opened the way for me into a very special valley and I was shot through with a feeling of intense elation, of total perhaps mystical happiness. It is a feeling that even now, given time and peace and quiet, I can recall. In this way did the mountains change me.

From Gorak Shep, Kala Pattar, 'hill of black stones', can be seen rising above the glacier. Today, the black hill was a white cone shining above a great snowfield with the looming presence of Pumori behind. I crossed the snowfield and began following a broken trail through waist-high snow. Then the climb began. At seventeen thousand feet the air has less than half the oxygen of that at sea level. Gentle slopes become steep climbs and steep climbs are like climbing a wall with your boots full of lead. Above fifteen thousand feet the body tissues begin to degenerate, fat burns away completely and the body begins to eat up muscle. After weeks at high altitude even the fittest climbers often have to pull off a hill because they are becoming progressively weaker.

We were unacclimatised and not very fit and, though Kala Pattar is only a little over eighteen thousand feet, it's still a tough climb. One foot went before the other through the deep snow, slowly pushing up the last thousand feet towards the summit. Three weeks of dysentery and dehydration had done a pretty good job on me, but I pushed on. Five steps forward then a halt while I counted to fifty, then another

her summit. Now we couldn't see her at all, and wouldn't until we climbed Kala Pattar for she was hidden by the mountains before us.

The going was very tough, a roughly-worn track across the glacial moraine, through thick snow with massive boulders and sheets of ice. Normally the trail is fairly clear and easy, but covered by the deep snow it was a nightmare. I ploughed on, stumbling along like an automaton. Then halfway to Gorak Shep something happened that I'm going to find hard to explain.

I was way ahead of the others, pushing myself hard, perhaps too hard. I was feeling very weak and almost beginning to wonder if I could carry on, climbing through a snow-covered boulder field that seemed to go on for ever. I thought more and more about turning

Lhotse, from where there was a continuous thundering sound of avalanches

The black summit of Everest looking lower than its flanking neighbour, Lhotse: the Khumbu Glacier in front

Ama Dablam, one of my favourite mountains, on the right; the Everest range on the left

On the summit of Kala Pattar

steadily towards the summit were the tiny flecks that were John, Ang Phurba and the little Sherpa. Across the glacier were Nuptse and Lhotse, massive and white and above them all, Chomolongma, Sagarmatha – the Goddess Mother of the Universe, looking far too grand to be called after a prosaic English surveyor, Sir George Everest. Below I could see the icefall, ravens circling above it, and further off still the orange tents that were the remains of the Poles' base camp. In the far distance I could see Ama Dablam and way, way below, the tiny, dark scratch of a yak train on the Khumbu Glacier making its way by the frozen teardrop of a lake towards Everest base camp. From Lhotse there came the constant thunder of avalanches as white waves rolled one after another down its west face.

On the Khumbu Glacier

five steps and another count. Each time I rested on my ice axe, bent double, counted to that magic number of fifty, by which time my heartbeat had returned almost to normal. If this was climbing to Kala Pattar, God knows what Everest was like!

I scrambled the last few feet to the top and looked round me. It was of course far more wonderful that I'd ever imagined. Flaubert and his cracked kettles sprang immediately to mind.

The whole Khumbu Glacier was spread out below me. Climbing

We filmed for a little while, then just sat looking at the mountains. They were beautiful beyond words. We had brought some biscuits with us and while we were sitting there, a raven, tamer than I have ever seen, perched on a rock and ate from Ang Nurba's hand.

The history of the climbing of Everest has been well documented, from Mallory and Irvine's attempts from Tibet in the nineteen-twenties, to the successful climb from the Nepal side in 1953, to the tragic deaths of Tasker and Boardman on the unclimbed ridge, and to Reinhold Meisner's incredible solo climb without oxygen. But in my humble opinion the most interesting attempt on Everest was made in 1934 by a Yorkshireman, Maurice Wilson. He claimed that Everest was only a hill like any other and that anybody who was reasonably fit

A raven feeding from Ang Nurba's hand on the summit of Kala Pattar

Sherpani on a small bridge below Dughla

The others finally got to the top and sat down panting. I put my arms round Ang Phurba and gave him a hug. He said he felt a little better but that at one time he thought he might not make it. It was his first time at this height too, and had a headache from the altitude. We had ascended too quickly from Thyangboche. All the books recommend at least a day's acclimatisation at Pheriche and, if the Sherpas were feeling it, then we had done something wrong. At 18,450 feet we were more than three thousand feet higher than Mont Blanc.

should be able to walk up it. He had had no climbing experience whatever and further astounded the world by declaring that he was going to climb the mountain single-handed.

He planned to fly to Tibet and crash-land on the Rongbuk Glacier below Everest. He taught himself to fly, bought a Gypsy Moth (which he rechristened 'Ever Wrest') and flew it firstly to Cairo, then on to Darjeeling in India. There the authorities impounded his plane so he sold it, hired three porters and trekked, without permission, into Tibet and up to the Rongbuk Valley, where the glacier leads to the north face of Everest, by mid-April 1934.

With his porters he got to the base of the north col on his second attempt. Leaving them he began the steep ascent of the north col snow climb. He spent four days and nights climbing the north face, sleeping on various ledges and porches. His porters, meanwhile, had deserted him.

He died in a snowstorm in early June at the bottom of the ice chimney, his body being found two years later and buried by Shipton's expedition. I always think that only a Yorkshireman would have got that far at all.

It took almost three hours to get back to Lobuche; John cheated and slid down the hill on his backside using his ice-axe as a brake, his waterproof trousers and jacket turning him into a human sledge. I was loaded with cameras and didn't particularly want to fill them with snow. Once on the glacier we retraced our steps to Gorak Shep where there are a couple of low huts, one of which sells tea and drinks during the season. Outside were piles of aluminium ladders dumped by some expedition. They are used to negotiate the ice-fall below Everest. I made John buy me a Coca Cola just so that I could say I'd had a Coke three miles from base camp. Some poor yak or Sherpa had carried that bottle all the way from Kathmandu. How long will it be before McDonald's open a branch on Kala Pattar?

Again I seemed to get a second wind and I moved quickly over the snow-covered moraine. The afternoon mist and cloud arrived just before Lobuche and the sun made phantom shapes in the writhing vapours above the white waste of the glacier. As we reached our camp the cook and sherpas ran out to meet us, grinning.

That night there was a beautiful ripening moon and an alpenglow on the mountains before us. The last entry in my journal for that day reads:

> The majesty, the overpowering majesty of the mountains, no photograph, no words can ever convey.
> They say explorers don't get homesick but I am a bit. One thing I learnt on the glacier, you don't need to turn left for Shangri-La. If you only look inside yourself you'll find you're already there.

The next day got off to a cold and woozy start; grey clouds and threatening snow made us pack in a hurry after drying our sleeping bags out as best as we could. The yaks had been driven down to Dughla while we were climbing Kala Pattar because there was fodder for sale there and they returned just as we were breaking camp to carry our gear back down the trail. Ang Phurba's sister drove them along laughing and calling to us and, if possible, I'd say that the yaks looked happier too. Yaks are strange animals. They are only really content above twelve thousand feet and if they go very much lower they get sick and die. Their massive fur coats protect them from the most bitter cold and they seem to be able to find food almost anywhere and to survive on very little. We loaded up these tugs of the snows and set off from the cold, frozen wastes of Lobuche towards Pheriche and Pangboche.

The clouds lifted a little and became wispier and fragmented. The track cut down through snowfields falling gradually by the side of a stream until we came again to the col above Dughla. The mountains ranged all round, massive and breathtakingly beautiful. Chains of

Evening light in the Khumbu Valley

A yak team climbing through the shadows of Dughla

The mountain in the middle distance is Ama Dablam seen from the other side

yaks went by constantly on their way to Everest base camp to bring back gear from this season's expeditions, their bells jingling across the snow. Below the col we stopped again at the tea house for a drink. An old Tibetan wandered away over the snow telling his beads. A man drove a yak across the snowfield and smoke filtered through the slates of the lodge roof.

Then the glacial valley spread out before us as we dropped lower towards Pheriche, a dark smudge in the snow below the lateral moraine and the massive bulk of Ama Dablam. We made good time on the descent, feeling increasingly strong and fit.

From Pheriche the track dropped to a rushing snow-melt stream and then rose again to the skyline with a magical range of mountains visible to the south: Khumbila, Thamserku and the flanks of Ama Dablam.

> A short hard pull and I was over the spur and dropping down into the valley of the Imja Kosi again. So much of my previous journey had been made in mist or darkness it was hard to remember the way back as the stumbling, wet, fogbound misery of a few nights ago.
> Now, cloud came and went across Ama Dablam, low cloud a thousand feet below the summits of the peaks.

Our cook and little Sherpani in the yak herder's house

The track along the Imja Khola is one of the greatest footpaths in the world. Ama Dablam ever on your left and the river below, roaring in its gorge, a sense of light, space, immense beauty and power surrounds you as you walk. Porters carrying huge mind-numbing loads stomp purposefully on, breathlessly calling out Namaste as they pass. Yaks, downward-bound, lumber past grinding and crunching their teeth together, and trekkers of all shapes and sizes come and go in their colourful Day-Glo gear.

Far below in the gorge, lammergeyer sailed, their massive wings barely moving in the updraught while below them the river chattered and muttered on its way to the Ganges.

We stayed that night in a yak herder's paddock above Pangboche.

Now, at 12,800 feet, all signs of altitude sickness had gone and even Ang Phurba's flu and sore throat seemed much better. As we arrived at our camp the setting sun fell behind a chorten, glowing through the prayer-flags, and Ang Phurba took us into the yak herder's house for some chang.

The downstairs section of the house was where the animals were kept in winter, the family's quarters were upstairs. We followed Ang Phurba up a wooden ladder into a long, low, dark room where four women and two little boys were seated around a fire. They beckoned us over and Ang Phurba laughed and joked with them as they poured out three glasses of chang.

While we were being served I noticed, at the far end of the room, a monk sitting cross-legged on a table chanting from a book of scriptures before him. Wire-framed glasses were perched on the end of his nose and he had in his hands a bell and the lightning sceptre which he shook to punctuate his chanting. A yellow window light fell over his shoulder through the dust and smoke.

He was a lama from the Pangboche monastery, Ang Phurba told us, and he'd come to call for a special blessing to bring good luck on the house. The women round the fire took no notice at all of what was going on, which I thought a bit unusual. That I suppose was only because in the Catholic household that I was brought up in everyone froze when the priest arrived. We all had to be quiet. If we talked at all it was in a whisper. Here the women sat round a fire of yak turds and wood, cooking the evening meal, joking, laughing and filling our glasses with chang as though the lama was a television repair man. I suppose that's a healthy attitude. His job is to bless the house – let him get on with it. It's nothing to do with us.

The journal:

Outside the house the moon rose behind Ama Dablam, softened by cloud, back lighting it. Below, rock falls rang and thundered across the valley and the river sang eternally on its way down from the mountain's roots.

8

Sherpa Beer and Lama Pee

'Oh! Queen of the hills, victory to you for ever!'
– The prayer of Mani Rimdu

AFTER BREAKFAST THE next morning we trekked up to Pangboche gompa by mani walls shimmering in the sun, to see the hand and scalp of the yeti which are preserved in an upstairs room above the chapel. The yeti, or 'abominable snowman' as the Sunday papers in England used to call it, has, like the Loch Ness monster and Bigfoot, become part of the mythology of monsters and demons that our technological society either refuses to believe in or embraces with a religious fervour. People seem either to discount them completely or, like 'Flat Earthers' and the people who claim that UFOs knocked out their fillings or aliens made them pregnant, they force you into corners at parties and with glassy eyes start to tell you how Stonehenge was really a landing site for our extra-terrestrial ancestors and that the pyramids were built to keep the Pharaohs' razor blades sharp.

The yeti, though, is somewhat different. When hardened mountaineers, who are used to spending months at high altitude, tell you they have heard and seen things, I for one tend to believe them. Jurek Kudelsky, a Polish climber and film-maker I met at a conference in France, told me that while he was at base camp on the successful 1980 Polish Everest expedition he had woken in the night to hear strange noises. Something outside was scuffling round knocking things over.

In the morning they found two sets of footprints, one inside the other, as though a smaller animal had been walking in the trail of one much larger. The footprints came from the moraine near Lhotse and went over the Lo La into Tibet. The English climbers, Pema Dorje's friends, said that while at base camp below Ama Dablam they had all heard something large moving round their tents in the night and had been too scared to go out. In the morning there were huge footprints everywhere.

Legends of the yeti have been part of the folklore of Tibet and Nepal for hundreds of years. They were dismissed as nothing but folk tales by many of the early mountaineers and explorers.

Then, in 1899, Major L. A. Waddell, an authority on the Buddhism of the Himalaya, discovered footprints and described them as 'the trail of the hairy wild men who are believed to live amongst the eternal snows.' In 1921, Colonel C. K. Howard-Bury, the leader of a party making a reconnaissance of the north side of Everest from Tibet, saw mysterious dark figures moving across the snow and later came upon enormous semi-human footprints.

In 1950, W. H. Tilman trekked to Kala Pattar looking for a way up the south-west ridge of Everest. One cold night they camped below Lobuche . . .

As we sat in the secure circle of the fire, our backs to the stone wall of the hut, the talk turned naturally to the abominable snowman. As one might expect, they are to be found in these parts in numbers, especially round Namche Bazar in the cold of winter when the cold drives them lower. Danu affirmed that the previous year a friend of his named Lakhpa Tensing had had his face so badly mauled by one, on the Nangpa La, that he died.

The following year Eric Shipton, surveying Everest again, found a clear trail of human-looking footprints high up in the snows of the Melungtse Glacier. Together with his Sherpa, Sen Tensing, he followed the trail for about a mile until it disappeared. Shipton took clear photographs of the footprints. Chris Bonington is convinced that there is something out there in the snows, although reports that he has mounted a special 'yeti search' are incorrect.

'Yeti' comes from the Tibetan *yeh-teh* meaning 'man of the high places' and the Sherpas believe that there are three kinds. There is a small yeti that most experts believe is an Assam gibbon that has strayed into the snows from some far-off valley. There is the large yeti, or 'juti', that stands about eight feet tall and is said to tear yaks literally limb from limb. Yaks have been found with their heads ripped from their shoulders and the marrow sucked out of their bones. Scientists reckon that this is probably the Tibetan blue bear which does grow to this size and is a meat-eater. The 'miti' is described as man-sized and covered all over in shaggy red hair. It is this animal which is probably the yeti of the Sherpas and which is most often found painted into murals and religious paintings.

In 1974 a girl was mauled by a yeti and Ang Phurba said that, only months before we arrived in Khumbu, a Sherpani had been attacked by a yeti while herding her yaks.

At the gompa an old lady took us into an upstairs room where butter-oil lamps burned before a statue of the Buddha; she took out a box with the yellowed skeleton of a hand in it and a large, hard, skin dome, shaped like a bullet and covered in coarse, rust-coloured hair.

The gompa at Pangboche

The scalp seemed to be all of a piece with no semblance of a join or stitching anywhere. I didn't and still don't know what to make of it. A similar scalp from Thami monastery was taken to Europe to be examined and scientists said it was made from the skin of a mountain goat. This one has never been examined as far as I know, although in his book *Himalayan Memoirs* Navnit Parekh makes a very strange confession. He had tried to buy the yeti scalp from the lama of Pangboche who had refused saying ill would befall the village if they sold the scalp:

> Now a brainwave struck me and I committed a 'theft'. While holding this piece of hide in my hands, I carefully pulled out a band of hair from the

scalp beyond the sight of the lama's unsuspecting eyes. I placed the hair carefully in my pocket to be brought to Bombay.

I sincerely and profusely thanked the lama in any case and presented him with a Khada (scarf) and a tin of Nescafé. Back home in Bombay I met the world renowned ornithologist Dr Salim Ali who was head of the Bombay Natural History Society. I handed over to him the precious band of hair which I had stolen from the yeti's scalp. Dr Salim Ali forwarded it to Dr Hausmann in Boston who, after thorough investigation, concluded that it could not be identified with any known species.
(Parekh Sangam Books, London 1986)

Ang Phurba told us a story about the yeti as we were walking down from Pangboche towards the Dudh Kosi. At one time there had been many yetis which had caused much trouble in the Khumbu Valley killing yaks and people. Then one day, the Sherpas discovered that the yetis were copying them, trying to dress and walk like Sherpas and they hit upon a plan.

They had a party one night which the yetis watched from the mountains above. The Sherpas made believe that they were getting drunk, dancing and laughing and singing. Then they pretended to fall out and fight, drawing knives and swords and making as if to kill each other, lying down upon the ground as though dead only to jump up again. The Sherpas left, leaving behind them the chang and rakshi, the swords and knives. They hid and watched what happened next. The yetis came from the hills and drank the liquor, becoming very drunk. They danced round for a while then they picked up the swords and stuck them in each other as they had seen the men do, killing all but two of their kind. The last of the yetis crept away to the hills where they bred again but never reached as great a number as there had been before. And that is why you don't see many yetis in Khumbu today.

We had a wonderful walk down the valley of the Imja Khola. We had seen the sunrise on Ama Dablam and the day that followed was warm and cloudless.

Ang Phurba was really excited that we had made it to Kala Pattar

The scalp and hand of the yeti at Pangboche

and back in such a short time, for it meant that we would be at Thyangboche in time for Mani Rimdu, the most important Buddhist festival in this part of Khumbu. The festival takes place every year at the first full moon in November, although of course Buddhists don't measure the year as we do but use the Tibetan calendar instead. Mani Rimdu is spread over three days and today was the first. We would be in Thyangboche not long after the start of the celebrations. I was looking forward to it because, back in England, I had seen some of the slides that Bill O'Connor had taken at a previous Mani Rimdu and it looked fantastic.

We walked past white-painted chortens and long mani walls down

An old old woman, bent double like a fishhook, makes her way to the Mani Rimdu celebrations

The Rimpoche seated on a richly-canopied dais

with flour to make a putty-like paste). I had seen the monks at Manali Gompa in Kulu making the very same cones and balls. The cones are said to represent specific deities and demons. A line of monks was crashing cymbals and blowing wooden horns bound with silver in the bright sun, while Sherpas were gathering from all over Khumbu, dressed in their finest clothes; Tibetan traders who had set up a small market on the edge of the field, nuns from the convent at Deboche and groups of Westerners, trekkers and aid workers.

From what I could find out, the festival of Mani Rimdu celebrates many things, including the triumph of the new Buddhist religion over the older animistic religion of Bon. Many of the dances we were to see the next day depicted the struggles and eventual victory of Padmasambhava, a powerful 'Bodhisattva', over the demons of the world. It also celebrates the forces of Life itself, and in particular enables anyone who watches the ceremonies and dances with a pure heart to increase his own personal store of Karma.

The lama of Thyangboche is, as I said before, a Rimpoche, the living reincarnation of the previous lama. When the last lama died the head monks of the monastery fasted, prayed and meditated until they received signs that they would find the lama's reincarnation in a nearby village. They went to that village and looked for certain signs in the little boys there; long ear-lobes are said to be one indication of holiness while another is a studious and quiet nature with an especially keen interest in things spiritual. They usually take a number of likely candidates into a room where some objects are placed, a few personal belongings of the dead lama amongst them. They watch the children carefully. The elect child will go straight to the dead lama's things and play with them and no others. By this and other signs the child is chosen. He is then taken to the monastery where the monks bring him up and train him in the ways of the faith. The Rimpoche of Thyangboche is also a Bodhisattva, one who having acquired all the qualifications to achieve Buddhahood voluntarily foregoes his own

to a swing bridge with the river boiling and fuming beneath, then up through beautiful woods where Sherpa families were hurrying towards the village to celebrate Mani Rimdu, singing amongst the trees. One old lady on two sticks, bent like a fishhook, was tapping her way slowly onwards and upwards.

We arrived at Thyangboche shortly after midday and the inaugural ceremony had already begun. On a flat field to the north of the gompa in the shadow of Khumbila, the Rimpoche was seated on a richly-canopied dais with attendant monks by his side. The Rimpoche was in rich, yellow ceremonial robes and was chanting, holding a small double drum in one hand and the lightning sceptre in the other. On a table before him were spread cones and balls of 'torma' (butter mixed

The Mani Rimdu procession

salvation until he has helped other fellow men to achieve liberation from 'Samsara' – the endless cycle of death and re-birth.

The Mani Rimdu festival of Thyangboche has another function special to the Khumbu Valley. Buddhists believe that all mountains have souls. Mount Everest is also called Sagarmatha (the Goddess Mother of the Universe), while Khumbila is the mountain whose soul guards the land of the Sherpa. Each year, for one or two days round the last full moon before winter, the demons of the earth attempt to steal or destroy the soul of the mountain. If that were to happen then all the people of Khumbu would almost certainly die. The festival of Mani Rimdu diverts and exorcises the demons.

For all these reasons it was easy to see why the Sherpas had come so far to be at Thyangboche that day, some of them walking many days from distant valleys, although, as Ang Phurba whispered, 'This Mani Rimdu not so good as the one in my village. Thami more holy.'

We had joined a queue of supplicants round the field waiting to present themselves to the Rimpoche. Ang Phurba had produced from somewhere white cotton scarfs for us and we stood behind a hundred or so Sherpas who were waiting to present similar scarfs to the lama, together with a small gift of money for the upkeep of the monastery. We waited in line, the Abbess from the convent at Deboche in front of us, shuffling slowly forward towards the Rimpoche, as the horns blew, the cymbals rang and the monks chanted.

The abbess from the convent at Deboche

Each of us, when we reached him, walked forward and presented the scarf and money to an attendant. We were given a small portion of red rice, some balls of torma and a few little hard pills. The Rimpoche next poured a pale, straw-coloured liquid into our hands. I watched what Ang Phurba did. First he tasted it, then he poured the remainder on to his head, rubbing it into his hair. We followed suit. We ate the tiny portions of rice and the paste and pills which had a herby, sweet taste. I asked Ang Phurba what the liquid was.

'It is holy water. It is from the lama.'

'I know it's from the lama because he gave it to me. But what is it?'

'It is from the lama,' insisted Ang Phurba a little embarrassed.

'What do you mean it's from the lama?'

'It's from his body.'

'You mean I've just drunk Lama pee!' and Ang Phurba laughed and nodded.

'It's very holy water, very big honour.'

'What were the pills?' I asked, now getting rather suspicious.

'They are for long life.'

I didn't dare ask what was in them.

That night we were invited by the Rimpoche to a meal in the gompa. I got off to a bad start by drinking too much chang with Brot Coburn who told me an incredible horror story which he swore was true. While sitting in a tea house one day he had asked for a glass of water. A little boy brought it to him and as Brot raised it to his mouth something flickered just on the edge of his vision. The boy ran away screaming. This troubled Brot. For some time he had had a blocked nose that no amount of blowing could clear. He raised the glass to his mouth again, and again something moved just out of sight. Later that day he asked a friend to watch what happened when he drank. The friend nearly fainted in horror. Every time he raised the glass to his mouth a leech flicked out of his nostril, only to shoot back in again. Eventually, after many tribulations and visits to doctors who were either too perplexed or too terrified to do anything, Brot held a glass of water under his nose and the leech simply dropped into the water and he could breathe again.

Anybody who goes to Nepal in the monsoon season will know that the forests are infested with leeches. What had happened to Brot was very simple and happens all the time to yaks. As he had bent down to drink in a mountain stream, submerging his face, a minute leech had swum up his nostril and fixed itself there. It had stayed as it would have done in a yak's nostril, growing bigger and bigger until the time came for it to drop off. With a yak this would happen when the beast pushed its snout into a stream to drink. With Brot it was every time he brought a glass of water near his nose.

He didn't seem any the worse for his adventure and it certainly hadn't affected his appetite for chang. Al Burgess, one of the legendary Burgess brothers, drank with us that night. Al and his identical twin Ade are slim blond giants with broad Yorkshire accents who live for climbing. They are rated amongst the greatest climbers in the world and they are great fun to be with. They are so tall they had to have special-length sleeping bags made for them. 'The ordinary ones made us look as though we were in a bloody sack race.' They had been on Lhotse when the avalanche hit the Spanish team and they had buried the bodies. Al had realised that their own route was ready to avalanche at any time but to change it he had to go back to Namche and radio Kathmandu for permission. While he was away an avalanche swept through the twins' base camp burying Al's tent. Just as

an academic exercise Ade tried to dig out the tent to see how long it would have taken him to rescue his brother had he been in it. After forty-five minutes he still hadn't freed it.

'Ah tell you what. You were dead, ar' kid.'

Al was waiting until the weather settled before he moved back up Khumbu to have a crack at another peak. Al believes that there is a yeti-like creature in the mountains although he thinks that it comes over into the Khumbu from the Hinku Valley to the east of Ama Dablam.

My memories of that night are of necessity dim and fuzzy, viewed, as St Paul might have said, 'Through a glass of chang, darkly.' I remember eating dhal batt in the gompa with a lot of other people, including a beautiful Sherpani, one of a new breed of climbing sirdars drawn from the women of Khumbu. Al said she was one of the best climbers he had ever seen. I remember the meal but don't remember showing the Sherpas an Irish step-dance which Ang Phurba tells me I did. I have vague memories of dancing with a great many Sherpas in the moonlight before staggering off to sleep on the floor of one of the guest rooms in the gompa, with Al Burgess and John having a snoring competition in the dark, smoky room.

I do remember two things vividly, though: one was earlier in the evening, before the chang and rakshi hit me, when the full moon rose behind Ama Dablam while the whole mass of Nuptse and Lhotse was lit by the alpenglow; the second was late that night when, alone, I stood on the balcony of the monastery watching a long line of perhaps a hundred Sherpas dancing in the moonlight, singing and chanting, moving in perfect step in a line dance that went on for hours, their voices ringing out in the icy night.

Up early on a magical sunny morning, monks blowing long, deep horns from the gompa, the low barking thunderous noise echoing across the mountains.

*

Ama Dablam, with prayer-flags in the foreground

The Mani Rimdu dance began early that morning in the gompa courtyard where Sherpas and trekkers filled every space and boy monks hung from the gallery watching open-mouthed. Even though the sun was burning down from a clear sky, it was cold in the shade.

Two horn-blowers sounded a solemn long note then various figures entered. First, monks banging cymbals and drums heralded the beginning of the dances. They spiralled round the courtyard in long ceremonial robes, turning and swinging out their legs as the Rimpoche, hidden from the crowd in the curtained gallery, chanted into some sort of amplifying tube so that his voice sounded harsh, metallic and eerie. His opening mantra was in praise of the mountains, first of all to Cholmo Lungma; 'Oh! Queen of the hills, victory to you for ever.' The other mountains in the prayer are Kanchenjunga, Gauri Shanker and Melungtse. The prayers then go on to deal with the monastery and its monks and finish with the beauty of the Khumbu Valley and the surrounding peaks. They finish: 'May the drum of religion never cease to beat for the good fortune of Khumbu Valley, nestled in the shining mountains under the sun and the moon.'

The drums are the drums of truth beating out over the world.

Next came four dancers wearing heavy, coloured masks; red, green, blue and white. They represent the four kings and protectors of the four cardinal points and are also the governors of many different demons and forces. The white king is the king of the east and controller of many demons, as is the green king of the south. The red king is the king of the west and ruler of all serpents, while the blue north king has sway over all those demons that carry disease.

A single dancer then entered. Ang Phurba told me he was 'very important god'. This was Padmasambhava. With a fierce dark face and a plume of yak-tail he lunged round the courtyard, scaring away the demons, just as centuries ago he had brought Buddhism to Tibet and Nepal and chased out the demons of blood and human sacrifice that were part of the older Bon religion.

Eager spectators at Mani Rimdu

He was followed by two skeletons who dragged a rag doll to represent a dead baby on a rope around the yard. Like the previous figure, this was seen as a very serious affair by the Sherpas, particularly the children. It was the Dance of Death; Death in Life – 'We give birth astride the grave.'

Following the skeleton dancers an old man clown-figure staggered down the steps and dragged a little boy out of the crowd whom he made help him to walk. But the 'old man' kept falling over on purpose, landing on the boy and rolling about in the dust. Then he picked on a trekker and pushed him up a ladder to the balcony, that is 'Heaven', where the Rimpoche was sitting. The crowd roared with laughter.

I wrote later in the journal:

The red king and the white king

Padmasambhava who chases away demons and bad spirits

The clown and little boy

The children in particular loved it. It reminded me very much of the mummers' plays we see occasionally in England when St George vanquishes the Turkish Champion. Just as the mummers' play has a clown who runs round amusing the crowd in the middle of the most primitive and dramatic scenes, or as *Macbeth* has the porter's scene, which functions as comic relief and underlines the serious intent of the drama at the same time, so this play has the old man clown. The universal need to explain the infinite mystery of life.

We left after Mani Rimdu for Shyangboche, trekking down through the forests in the warm afternoon sunshine on the last leg of our journey home. A plane was chartered for early the next morning to fly us and the film equipment and stock from Shyangboche airstrip back to Kathmandu. Brot Coburn had made radio contact while we were walking up the trail. Naresh and Nandu had left in the same way four days before. In the late afternoon we walked down to the Dudh Kosi and up through dense forest to Khumjung. Along the trail, by a yak herder's hut, some Tibetan traders had set up a stall selling prayer-wheels and jewellery. Bare-bottomed little children danced in the dust and a woman on a wall suckled her infant in the sun. I liked the look of a brass yak bell on a woven neck-halter. It had a full clear sound. I bargained for it with one of the women and for a bit of fun hung it round my neck and walked off up the trail making yak noises. The Tibetans fell about laughing as John drove me up the trail with a stick.

Cloud rolled in as we reached the chorten below Khumjung village and we somehow lost the path, wandering through misty spinneys along a sloping hillside, until we saw the Hotel Everest View ahead of us through the fog.

It was to be our last night in the Khumbu.

Note Just as this book was going to press, I heard from Bill O'Connor that a fire – caused it is said by the new electricity scheme – had burned down Thyangboche monastery together with its priceless books and paintings. It is unutterably sad.

9

The Bearded Man in My Room

'Home is the sailor home from the sea
And the hunter home from the hill.'
– Robert Louis Stevenson

MY JOURNAL FOR THE next few days is disjointed and full of disasters and sketchy impressions. Winding up any trip is a sad affair but in the mountains it is made sadder by the fact that relationships founded on absolute trust have to be broken when the parties split up. Our minds were already moving towards another dimension – home and our families and the journey ahead of us; while the Sherpas were thinking of their village and families and the next trek ahead of them.

When John and I arrived at the hotel that night, we found Naresh and Nandu still there, angry and miserable. The charter hadn't arrived. For four days they had sat by the side of the airstrip only returning to the Everest View to sleep. They blamed John but it was nobody's fault and I thought it was unfair of them. It was just Nepal and the way things are there, and had they been honest they should have admitted that India was no better.

We managed to get out on a flight the next morning but the light plane could take only three of us. John and Ang Phurba later trekked back to Lukla and John chartered a Puma helicopter that just happened to be there, covering most of the cost by selling seats to fourteen of the hundreds of trekkers still stranded. So we were eventually reunited in Kathmandu before parting once again for the journey home. But I think the journal, rough as it is, tells it better than any re-writing would do.

6 a.m. After porridge and hot chocolate round the revived fire of the deserted ghost hotel Everest View we set off for the airport, walking quickly so as to get into the warmth of the sun that was just appearing over the crown of Thamserku.

7 a.m. At the airstrip we sat and dozed dismally in a hot sun that was cooled by a mountain breeze.

The yaks and porters trailed over the hill and disappeared towards Thami and Namche Bazar. Saying goodbye to them after all this time together was a strange affair. In the mountains you get to know people very quickly. Your life depends upon them and sometimes theirs on you so there develops a relationship that doesn't need language to sustain it. When they walked over the crest of the hill and down towards the valley it felt as though four friends were walking out of my life.

9.30 a.m. A message came back via our young Sherpa that the police couldn't understand John's handwritten note of last night asking them to radio for an emergency helicopter evacuation of the film crew.

10 a.m. John re-drafted a letter and set off with Ang Phurba for the police station and the National Park office to radio Kathmandu again.

11 a.m. Nothing happened.

The plane landing at Shyangboche to take us back to Kathmandu; Thamserku in the background

11.30 a.m. Nothing happened again.

12 o'clock. Two little boys arrived and we threw stones at a discarded film spool.

1 p.m. There was a noise, a low rumbling sound over the river's constant moan.

'Plane coming,' said one of the boys, and it was.

Piloted, as we soon discovered, by the legendary A. K. Singh and carrying in equipment and an engineer for the Namche hydro-electric scheme, the Pilatus Porter circled twice. Nandu chased a yak off the runway and the plane landed.

The engineer gave me a note from Chris, our contact in Kathmandu, to say that conditions were chaotic and almost impossible. Because of the conference and the Queen's birthday there were massive backlogs of people. Some of them had been waiting twelve days.

We loaded what equipment we could on to the plane. I looked down the runway but John was nowhere in sight and though I asked him to wait, A. K. Singh said it was better that we left right away. The weather was changing and if the cloud came in we wouldn't get out.

I wrote a note on the back of the letter for John explaining that Chris in Kathmandu was trying to organise a charter for the next day and got in the plane.

We strapped ourselves in and the plane rolled down the grass runway. Ahead of us the sheer walls of Thamserku. The plane had to take off towards them and bank sharply before heading down the Dudh Kosi. It gathered speed and we rose into the air at the very moment that John and Ang Phurba appeared on the end of the runway. We soared over their heads.

I'll never forget the look on John's face as I waved helplessly at him from the window.

I felt a mixture of relief and guilt but at least with one of us in Kathmandu messages could be sent home telling people we were still alive.

Weather conditions were perfect for flying. To the east a range of mountains stood out sharp, white-flaked and massive. Below, ribbons of terraced fields edged the hills.

The Kathmandu Valley was full of tiny, coloured dots: brightly-dressed Nepalis working in the fields bringing the last of the harvest home.

Moving hayricks with legs walked along field boundaries in the hot sun.

We landed and Naresh and Nandu left immediately for Delhi. I tried to get A. K. Singh to return for John and Ang Phurba but he said that he was finished for the day. There was nothing I could do. I went to the hotel and checked in. I had my cameras and some of my kit with me and I'd left some of my clothes in store. I went up to my room and for the first time in six weeks caught sight of myself in the mirror. There was a strange thin man in my room with a matted beard, greasy hair and a sunburnt face. I washed and showered him and took him downstairs for a cup of cappuccino. It was the best cup of coffee either of us have ever had.

A day later . . .

Fog in the Kathmandu Valley. Chris phoned to tell me that John had two alternatives.

1. Wait and we can get him out in 2 or 3 days.

2. Walk to Lukla and it will be 5 to 7 days before we can get him out because of the congestion and because it's the Queen's birthday – everywhere's shut.

Went to Hotel Annapurna where there is a barber's shop. Got my hair cut and beard trimmed. Sorted my laundry out and sent it off – a pretty sordid mess it was too! Socks walking round the bedroom muttering etc.

Went for a walk this afternoon to the Jumla area of Kathmandu, smells of food mingled with the smells of dust and animals. Sacred cows wandering the streets, eating rubbish. One with its head stuck in a cardboard box. Cars and bicycles wheeled carefully past them.

The soft mud-bricks of the houses glowed in the sun, beautiful children stared from alleyways and dark entrances.

To Bhodnath Temple again this evening. That place holds a great fascination for me. I heard the noise of puja and went into the gompa. There is a lovely Buddha, massive and golden. Beneath it sat the monks in prayer. Outside in the evening sun hundreds of the faithful walked around the base of the gompa turning the prayer-wheels and telling their beads.

Yellow afternoon light filtered through the trees and buildings as I rode through the streets and by fields of burning brass where the last of the rice was being brought in.

Pema Dorje came to the hotel tonight and we had a drink together. It was great to see him again. We now feel that John and Ang Phurba will be on their way, walking to Lukla. Pema also thinks that a Pilatus Porter could have taken us all, which makes me feel more guilty though what I could have done to stop the pilot leaving beyond hijacking the plane with my Swiss army knife, I don't know.

The temple at Swayambunath, prayer-flags streaming from the stupa

The temple at Pashupatinath

Another day passed:

7 a.m. Got up and went to the Swyambunath temple to watch the sunrise through the mist. People were already up and about and schoolchildren appeared and disappeared in the pale fog in their neat school clothes, their schoolbags carried on straps round their foreheads. Just like little porters.

Monkeys were leaping everywhere fighting, scratching, picking things out of each other's fur. People walked round the stupa and brought flowers and rice to the various statues, chanting and scattering the offerings before them.

To Pashupatinath after lunch. The ashes and ends of a cremation were being scattered in the river. A few yards away, children played and splashed life in death, death in life.

I got back to the hotel to find a note telling me that John and Ang Phurba had arrived at the airport in a Puma! They walked through the door as I was reading it. So now we are all together once more.

Monkeys at the Swayambunath temple

On our last night in Kathmandu we went to Ang Phurba's sister's house in Kathmandu (how many sisters, I asked myself, did Ang Phurba have?) for tungba and dahl batt with Ade Burgess and Pema Dorje. We had a great night laughing and getting very happy on the tungba. I was leaving early the next day for New Delhi and home, so it was the last time we would all be together. We got merry and sad and then merry again as the tungba flowed and, as they say in Ireland, 'the crack was mighty!'

Home through the empty, moonlit Kathmandu streets with John and I very drunk on a rickety old tricycle rickshaw, pedalled by a strong, wiry, silent little man. Not a breath stirred the warm air as we wobbled slowly homeward through the dark, still, peopleless, squeaky-wheeled night.

The next morning Ang Phurba and Pema Dorje came to see me off at the hotel. We drank tea together, talked and were silent in turns, conscious of the parting to come. As I stood to go to the car that was taking me to the airport they tied white scarfs about my neck and wished a pleasant journey and a speedy return to Nepal.

Landing at Manchester a day later I walked straight past Pat who didn't recognise me. I had a thick salt-and-pepper beard, had lost two stone in weight and was dressed in a baggy, loose-fitting, Indian shirt and a thick woven Tibetan jacket. I looked like a short-sighted Afghan mountain fighter. She did eventually recognise me, and as we drove through the familiar streets, it was hard to believe that I was truly 'home from the hill'.

Peaks and clouds seen from Kaare

Epilogue

Far in the north HIMÁLAYA *lifting high*
His towery summits till they cleave the sky,
Spans the wide land from east to western sea,
Lord of the Hills, instinct with Deity.
            – Kalidasa

THERE ARE SO MANY things missing from this book, things I have tried to convey but that I know I have missed; the silence of those mornings in the mountains when we woke in a crystal dawn with not a breath of wind moving and not a sound except the noise of our own breathing; the smells of woodsmoke and cooking and the songs of children in the villages as we toiled up towards Ghorapani and through the sheer mind-numbing beauty of the Zanskar Valley.

There were times when I thought I would go mad with frustration but then I learned to accept and to stay calm. There were times when I was close to crying at the beauty before me and times when I laughed out loud at the joy or the fun of it all. I spent almost three months in the mountains and I can remember every minute of it. All my senses and perceptions were sharpened and everything round me took on a colour and a significance I hadn't thought possible.

I did also see a great deal of deforestation and enough pollution to make me fear for the future of the Himalaya, particularly the copper-rich Zanskar Valley, but I was deeply moved by the infinite grandeur of the mountains and by the people who live in them. It is a stunning and a fragile world. The West, if it goes there at all, should go on foot.

I know I will return. I have already written to Ang Phurba to see if we can organise a journey over the Indian Himalaya from Ladakh through some of the unexplored valleys into Padum and south by the Phuktal Gompa and Shingo La. After that I want to trek with him again in Nepal, perhaps into the Dolpo and Mustang or into Khumbu over one of the western passes.

Images of landscapes and villages are burnt on my mind for ever. But so are the faces of the people I travelled amongst and the friends I made in the high mountains. They were the warmest, friendliest and most spiritual people I have ever met.

Ang Phurba with the sherpas

To:
Ang Phurba
Pema Dorje
Ang Chota, our cook in Khumbu
Mingma Lhamu, our little Sherpani
Tsei Time, Ang Phurba's sister
Ang Nurba, our camera porter
Dorje, who left us at Pheriche to go south with Nandu and Naresh

Sultana, our cook in Zanskar
Mr Tickoo
The Lama of Muni Gompa
Tsering Norbu, the Copper Pot Man
The monks of Spitok Gompa
Tsering Dorje of Phuktal Gompa
Karna Sakya and
Jam Yang Hnoyz, the little boy monk at Manali Gompa.

To all of you I say,
'Julay' and 'Namaste'.

Appendix

A note for the gear freaks . . .

Almost everything we wore on our trek came from Mountain Equipment of Stalybridge, Lancashire. They seem to have kitted out more expeditions to Everest and beyond than any other known firm. Our basic kit comprised thermal underwear, slacks and shirts, fibre-pile jackets and duvet jackets. The fibrepiles were great during the day and at night time the duvet jackets kept out the worst of the cold. The sleeping bags were Mountain Equipment four-season duck-down ones and they were absolutely necessary.

Our boots were made by Zamberlan; mine were Alpine-Lites while Pat wore Trek-Lites. They are light and comfortable but able to cope with rough tracks and, in my case, heavy snow, without any problem. Too heavy a boot and you end up tired from simply lifting your feet up, too light and they don't give enough support. After years of trying all sorts of boots I've found Zamberlan simply the best. Neither of us blistered.

CAMERAS

I took a Nikon FE2 as my standard camera and an FM2 for low light shots because of its LED metering. I used both the meter on the FE2 and a Weston Euromaster with an invercone because the light is extremely strong at high altitude and meters are easily fooled; the light desert soil of Zanskar registered almost as high as the snows of Khumbu. When in doubt I bracketed my exposures half a stop over and one stop under.

I took a variety of lenses with me; 20 mm f2.8, 24 mm f2, 28–50 mm f2.8 zoom, 55 mm macro and 80-200 mm f3.5 zoom. They seemed to cover most of my needs although there were times when I would have loved a longer lens. Carrying one was just not practical.

For static shots and architecture I carried a Hasselblad 200 cm with three lenses, an 80 mm, 50 mm and 150 mm. I used it a lot but obviously not as much as the Nikons, which are less bulky and ideal for shooting on the trek.

I also carried a Widelux panorama camera that delivers a 62 x 28 mm transparency. The panoramic shots in this book were all taken on that camera.

The film stock was all Fujichrome Professional. I used 50 ASA for the landscapes and 400 ASA for some of the gompa interiors and the Mani Rimdu dances.

I used a Benbo tripod and a Manfroto monopod that also doubled as a walking-stick. I had a small flash unit but I hardly ever used it. I much prefer natural light. A small folding reflector was very handy for lighting faces from below. One problem with being so high is that shadows appear intensely black and you really need something to fill them in with. I used very little filtration.

On the trek I carried everything in two Tenba bags, slung pannier-fashion. It distributes the weight more evenly so that you don't end up throwing yourself to one side as you do carrying one big bag. It also meant that I could get at everything very quickly.

I also carried a Sony Walkman Pro tape recorder, microphone and earphones and used TDK tapes to record the pujas in the gompas and the dances of Mani Rimdu to use at audio-visual presentations once I returned home.

Acknowledgements

I would like to thank Bill Norman and Mandip Singh for helping to arrange our travels in Zanskar and Ladakh and when things went wrong it was never their fault, it was just the way things are in the Himalaya.

The text was looked at very closely by two people who saved me from making all kinds of stupid mistakes. Bill O'Connor read the manuscript and helped with place names and mountaineering facts and figures and Joyce Armstrong, a Buddhist friend from Cumbria, gave invaluable help with the finer points of Buddhist doctrine and ritual. The maps were drawn by Steve Morris of Dent.

The old and the new: an aeroplane takes off from behind the Spitok gompa

Index

Folios in *italic* indicate illustrations

altitude sickness, 3 27 28 42–3 44 141 197 202
    204 209
Ama Dablam, 131 177 182–3 190 191 194 197
    199 208 214 215 216 218 223; *184 193 207
    213 224*
Annapurna, 131 134 140 144 147 150 154; *xi
    139 149 151 154*
Awi, 199

Bagmati River, 128
Banthanti (first), 144; *143 (second), 152*
Barai Nala River, 30 32 36–7 155; *33 34*
Bedhi, Naresh, 159 167–8 173–4 178 180 183
    187 188 199 227 228 230
Bhadur, Kharka (Jim), 135–6 141 144 155
    156; *155 158*
Bhadur, Sheer (Sid), 141 144 155 156; *155
    158*
Bhaktapur, 125 128; *128*
Bhichuk, 155
Bikka, Ang, 146 148; *148*
Birethanti, 140
Boardman, Peter, x 209
Bodhkharbu, 84
Bodhnath, 123 125 230; *124 126*

Bonington, Chris, x 122 217
Buddhist religion and ceremonies, 23 33 38
    40 42 47 59–63 69 72 74 93–4 96 98 109 121
    123 148 194 197 218 220–2 225 227; *195
    200 221 225 226 227*
Burdun, 71–2 74 95; *73*
Burgess, Ade, 122 177 223 233
Burgess, Al, 122 177 223

cameras, 237
Carr, Biddy, xii
Chandrakot, 140 155 156
chortens, 32–3 47 49 199; *49 51*
Chota, Ang, 188
Coburn, Brot, 192–3 197 222–3 227
commercialisation, effects of, xii 22 31 47
    122 125 131 145 182–3

Dal Lake, 5 105 107 109; *104 106*
Darsha, 5 27 28 30; *31*
Deboche, 197 220
deforestation, effects of, xii 17 128 144–5 178
    182 235; *xi 4 145*
Delhi, 5 6–9 115 233
Dhaulagiri, 131 144 148 150; *147*

Dorje, Pema, 121–3 128 129 173 187 190 216
    230 233
Dras, 93 101–3 115 165; *102*
Dudh Kosi, 121 180 182 190 218 227 230
Dughla, 199 210; *209 212*
dysentery, 120 122 134 144 160 162 166 185
    204

Everest (Sagarmatha/Chomolongma), ix–x
    125 128 170 177 182–3 185 190 201 202 204
    208–9 216–17 222; *169 189 196 197 206 207*
Everest View Hotel, 182–3 188 190 228; *183
    184 189*

food, 30 46 139 173 178
Fotu La 78 86–7 101; *85 87*

Galchi Bazar, 163; *164*
Ghorapani, 123 141 144–5 150 154 159 166–7
    235; *145*
Gokyo, 170 178 180
gompas, 23–4 59–63 69 72 94–5 96 121 123
    223; *70 73 192 194*
Gorak Shep, 173 204 210
Gumburanjon, 46 47; *48*

Gundruk, 148 150 152

Harding, Pat, xii 3ff 27ff 112 233; *45 50 57*
Hille, 140
Himachal Pradesh, 15; *16*
Hinduism and ceremonies, 21 74 119 121
   128–9 148 168 173
Hiunchuli, 148; *149*
Hutchinson, Robert, 159 166 178 180 187

Imja Khola, 213 218
Island Peak, 170
Itchar, 63 66; *67*

Jalabi Bends, 87; *89*
Jiri, 166 170 185
Jomson, 123 128 134 135 138 148
Jones, Bill, 123 144–6 148 150 154 159

Kaare, 136 139 140 156; *234*
Kala Pattar, 177 180 201 202 204 208–9 210
   218; *203 208 209*
Kali Gandak Gorge, 144 148
Kali Gandak Valley, 128 145 150
Kargia, 32 47 49–50 62; *vi 49*
Kargil, 5 72 76 79 81 83–4 100–1; *83*
Kathmandu, 6 115–20 122–3 125 128–30 131
   159–63 165 166 168 228 233; *117 118 120*
Kathmandu Valley, 125 170 230
Khumbila, 197 199 214 220 222
Khumbu, 173 223
Khumbu Glacier, 166 180 202 204; *206 208*

Khumbu Valley, xii xiii 74 122 170 178
   182–3 188 190–1 197 202 208 218 220 222
   225 227; *198 199 200 211*
Khumjung, 173 180 185 190 227
Khunde, 173 183
King Mehindra Trust, 154 165
Kulu, 11
Kulu Valley, 5 13 15 17 22 25 31; *4 16*
Kumar, Nandu, 159 167–8 173–4 176 178
   180 187 188 197 199 227 228 230
Kun, 81
Kuru, 51
Kyelang, 27

Ladakh, xii 13 50 71 72 74 76 86 90 98 116
   180 193
Lahoul Valley, 11 25 35 43
Lamayuru, 86; *88*
Leh, 5 78 86 87 93 95–6 99–100 109 165; *91 92
   101*
Lhamu, Mingma, 188
Lhotse, 122 177 182–3 190 202 208 216 223;
   189 205 206
Lobuche, 168 201 210 217
Lobuche Peak, 199 202 216
Lukla, 128 129 167–8 170 183 228 230
Lumle, 140 156

Machhapuchhare, 131 134 140 144 148 150
   152 154; *139 153*
Manali, 11–12 13 15 17–18 23 25 220; *14 18
   19 20 24*

Manasbal Lake, 109; *108 110*
mani stones and walls, 42 51; *193 199*
maps, trekking, 152
medical advice, 3 120 134–5; *see also* altitude
   sickness, dysentery
Mehra, 201
Modi Khola, 154
Mulbekh, 84
Muling, 160 162
Muni, 68–9 71 72 93 95 197; *68 70*

Nagar, 18 21
Nagarkot, 125; *127*
Nagdanda, 136 156; *137*
Namche Bazar, 122 159 166–8 170 173–4
   176–8 185 187 188 192 217; *169 171 172
   174 179*
Namika La, 84 101
Nang Pa La, 173 178
Norman, Bill, xii 8–9 238
Nun, 81
Nuptse, 182 190 202 204 208 223
Nurba, Ang, 188 201 202 208–9; *209*

O'Connor, Bill, 194 218 227n 238
offence caused by some trekkers, 66 77 125 146

Padum, 5 72 76 79; *75*
Pahalgum, 112; *111*
Pakarchik, 81
Pangboche, 191 197 210 214 215 216 218; *217
   218*

Pashupatinath Temple, 128–9 233; *129 130 232*

Pensi La, 81

Pensi La Glacier, 81; *80*

Phedi, 136 156

Pheriche, 170 197 199 209 210 214; *215*

Phewa Tal lake, 131 136; *133*

Phuktal gompa, 55 57 59 60–1 63 65 235; *58 59 60*

Phurba, Ang, 129ff 235; *161*

Phungi Tenga, 190

Phyang, 93–5; *94*

Pokalde, 201

Pokhara, 123 219 131 135 146 148 154 156 159–62 165 167

Pokhara Valley, 135

ponies, 3 30 35 37 46 138 141 156; *138*

porters, 3 135 136 140 150 155–6 173 187; *141 142*

prayer-flags, 23 33 65; *12 33*

prayer-wheels, 23 72 123

Pumori, 177 202 204

Pune Hill, 144 148

Purne, 51 55 63 65; *52 53*

Ramjak, 37–8

Rangdum gompa, 5 79 81; *82*

Reru, 66 68 71

Rohtang Pass, 5 23 25 37 74; *26*

Sakya, Karna, 130

Sherpas, 121 136 174 176 178 185 187 188 191 193 202

Shey, 98; *98*

Shingo La, 5 13 31 36 37–8 41 65 74 77 96 107 144 235; *38 41*

Shingo River, 44 65; *45 64*

Shyangboche, 178 180 190 191 227 230; *229*

Singh, A. K., 230

Singh, Mandip, 7–9 238

sirdars, 136 138 187

Sonamarg, 86 102 105

Spitok, 94–5 96; *95 97 239*

Srinagar, 5 86 105 107 109 112 121 165

Sule, 65

Suru Valley, 81 101

Swayambunath Temple, 121 233; *121 231 233*

Table, 51

Tasker, Joe, x 209

Tatopani, 148 150; *152*

technological advances and conservation projects, 123 144–6 148 154 160 176 192 194 197

Teta, 51

Thami, 167 173 180 191 217 222 228

Thamserku, 180 182 214 228 230; *172 179 181 229*

thankas, 23 60; *60*

Thikse, 94 96 98

Thornicroft, John, x xii 6 116ff 233; *134 158*

Thyangboche, 167 170 178 180 188 190–2 194 197 209 218 220 222 225 227; *191 192 194 195 225 226 227*

Tickoo, Mr, 11 15 18 25 41

Time, Tsei, 187 201

Tirkhedunge, 140 141 144

Toudepani, 152

tourism defined, 130

Trashingo, 190

trekkers in general, 138 178 180 214

trekking equipment, 3 25 30 36 65 237–8

trekking permits, 134 167

Tsarap Gorge, 55, 57; *57*

Tsarap River, 55 57 65; *56 64*

Wander, Josette, 123 144 146 148

water, 3 30 120 123 140 144 148 162

Wilson, Maurice, 209–10

yaks, 185 190 194 202 210 214; *186 191 194*

yetis, 216–18

Zanskar, xii 13 40 43 45 49–50 62 63 71 72 74 76 144 180

Zanskar Valley, 5 51 235

Zoji La, 74 86 90 93 99 100 102 103 105